D0422774

MAKING A DIFFERENCE

ALSO BY CAPTAIN CHESLEY "SULLY" SULLENBERGER

Highest Duty: My Search for What Really Matters

MAKING A DIFFERENCE

Stories of Vision and Courage from America's Leaders

CAPTAIN CHESLEY "SULLY"
SULLENBERGER

WITH DOUGLAS CENTURY

WILLIAM MORROW
An Imprint of HarperCollinsPublishers

HarperCollins books may be purchased for educational, business, or sales promotional use. For information please write: Special Markets Department, HarperCollins Publishers, 10 East 53rd Street, New York, NY 10022.

FIRST EDITION

Library of Congress Cataloging-in-Publication Data has been applied for.

ISBN 978-0-06-192470-5

12 13 14 15 16 OV/RRD 10 9 8 7 6 5 4 3 2 1

To my wonderful wife, Lorrie, with love.
You are my inspiration.

CONTENTS

MAKING A DIFFERENCE

INTRODUCTION

A WEEK AFTER THE HUDSON RIVER LANDING OF U.S. AIRWAYS Flight 1549, on January 21, 2009, six people met in a government building in the nation's capital. The flight data recorder and cockpit voice recorder (CVR) had just been recovered from the Airbus 320 and rushed to the National Transportation Safety Board headquarters in Washington, D.C. There, in the NTSB's sound lab, a windowless room with metal furniture and fluorescent lights, these six people gathered to listen to the CVR for the first time.

The cockpit recording of Flight 1549 has never been released to the public. By law only the investigators and parties to the investigation may hear it. The only audio that has been released to the public is the Federal Aviation Administration's's ground recording of the radio communications.

As these six people—two NTSB officials, an FAA official, a pilots' union safety representative, and representatives from the aircraft manufacturer and the engine manufacturer—gathered in this closed room in Washington, they did not know quite what to expect. All six wore headphones, concentrating intensely, often closing their eyes to better focus on every sound, every voice, in this dramatic recorded event.

My first officer, Jeff Skiles, and I had suddenly found ourselves in a crucible, fighting not only for the lives of our passengers and crew but also for our own. For three minutes and twenty-eight seconds the six in the room heard two men working rapidly, urgently, and closely together. They heard a cacophony of automated alarms, alerts, warnings, synthetic voices, continuous repetitive chimes, ground proximity warning alerts, and traffic collision avoidance system alerts, reaching a crescendo with "TOO LOW, TERRAIN. TOO LOW, GEAR. CAUTION, TERRAIN. CAUTION, TERRAIN. TERRAIN, TERRAIN. PULL UP. PULL UP. PULL UP. PULL UP. PULL UP. PULL UP. PULL UP. PULL UP—" until the recording suddenly stopped.

The six were thunderstruck. They had never heard anything quite like this. They were overwhelmed by the suddenness, the intensity, the rapidity, and the severity of this 208-second-long event.

They sat in stunned silence until finally one of the six said, "That guy has been training for this his entire life."

He was *almost* right. In fact, I believe my preparation for the events of Flight 1549 began even before my birth. I would trace it back two more generations, to my grandparents, all four of whom were born in the nineteenth century; all four went to college, which was a remarkable thing, especially for women, at that time. My mother was a teacher, my father was a professional, and I grew up in an environment in which education was valued, in which ideas were important, and in which striving for excellence was expected.

I was born in 1951, in the heart of the postwar baby boom. My father, who'd been a naval officer in World War II, returned from his tours of duty carrying oversize reference books filled with specifications, drawings, and armaments of ships from all the navies of the world.

I devoured those military books, as well as stories about men like Churchill and Eisenhower, those larger-than-life figures, culled from the copies of *Life* and *Look* magazines that my grandparents had lovingly collected during the war years. This idea of *genuine* leadership—of intense preparation, rising to the occasion, meeting a specific challenge, setting clear objectives—was deeply internalized, burned into and ingrained in my young mind. . . .

• • •

I became a captain fairly rapidly relative to most airline pilots' careers. After eight years with the airlines—starting as second officer, then first officer—I made captain. This meant I had a lot of time—twenty-two years—leading a team, trying to inspire people every week, urging them to be vigilant and give their best efforts on every flight. I observed the way even the most routine actions and the smallest words could resonate and have an impact on the morale of a team. I saw that few interactions with my coworkers or the public went unnoticed or were completely without consequence.

Living one's life by the highest professional standards is one of the lessons I learned very early in my career. I'd come straight from the structured, disciplined environment of military aviation, specifically tactical aviation, where the margins for error are much slimmer and it is absolutely essential to strive for excellence daily. In the Air Force, when you're flying in a formation of four jet fighters, one hundred feet off the ground, at six hundred knots, covering a nautical mile every six seconds, or ten miles per minute, success and failure, life and death, can be measured in seconds and in feet.

In that kind of environment, where the highest standards are taught and enforced, even the slightest deviation is immediately corrected because it is potentially catastrophic. In the airline world, things are slightly more complicated: there are many different life experiences, motivations, and concerns. Pilots meet the same professional standards; but if there are, say, a million ways to get from Point A to Point B, eight hundred thousand of them may be right. Or, I should say, *right enough*. So there is a wide range of possible effective choices. While we face many of the same risks as in military aviation, these risks may not seem as apparent.

I can describe what worked for me in my years as a captain and team leader, but I saw many pilots doing good work, leading effective teams, with vastly different skill sets, personality types, and outlooks.

I think most would agree that personal and professional reputations ultimately are based upon our daily actions and interactions. For thirty years, I exercised vigilance and avoided complacency on each flight—because I never knew when, or even if, I might one day face some ultimate challenge. Or, put another way, I never knew upon which three and a half minutes my entire career might be judged.

What does this mean in practice? How does this translate into other domains? Perhaps it means engaging in a lifelong commitment to learning, to expanding one's mind, and to viewing each day as a cumulative process of preparation.

This dedication to continuous preparation was invaluable to me during the events of Flight 1549. I had so deeply internalized the fundamental lessons that even in this novel and unanticipated situation, one for which we'd never specifically trained, I was able to set clear priorities based on what we did know. In seconds, I managed to synthesize a lifetime of experience and training to solve a problem I'd never seen before.

Given the rapid rate of change in today's culture and the constant state of flux in our industries, in our economic system, and in this worldwide marketplace of ideas, it is essential that we try to understand what it means to be an effective leader in the modern world. For me, there is no effective way to cope with the ambiguity and complexity so prevalent today unless one has a clear set of values. But do all our leaders share this view?

I've often felt that one of the most underrated aspects of leadership is the ability to create a shared sense of responsibility for the outcome: to inspire those around you to make tomorrow better than today, to constantly strive for excellence, and to refuse to accept anything that's barely adequate.

This means giving of oneself, rising to the occasion, instilling a sense of group confidence that yes, together we can accomplish what we might never achieve as individuals. It means setting the course, charting the path, giving your team the tools, encouraging them to do their best, then stepping aside and allowing them to accomplish the goal.

But among our best and brightest leaders today, how widespread is this desire to create a sense of shared meaning?

Effective leadership is needed even in good times, but it is critically important and more difficult when one is facing seemingly insurmountable challenges. Throughout history we have seen leaders like Franklin D. Roosevelt or Sir Winston Churchill summoning the strength to rally people when the chips were down and morale at its lowest ebb.

Where do the requisite strength, skills, and direction come from? Are they to some extent innate, or must they always be learned? How important are teachers and mentors in the process of forming a leader's personality? Do some leaders emerge without any specific training, road map, or even ambition to lead?

The very idea of leadership has long fascinated me. How does one lead in a wide variety of situations? How are the experiences of leading a team during a life-and-death crisis playing out over the course of minutes or hours different from those of rallying an organization slipping into a slow, seemingly inexorable decline?

Is it always necessary to start from a moral foundation, a core set of personal beliefs, or is the ability to lead something that even deeply flawed personalities can master? No one would dispute the brilliance of General Ulysses S. Grant and General George S. Patton and their ability to lead men in battle, despite the former's well-documented drinking binges and the latter's volatility and hair-trigger temper. Clearly, it is not always necessary to be universally loved or even admired in order to lead effectively. But is it necessary to be respected or trusted?

Is it possible to be a truly great leader without leading an exemplary personal life? And even if one doesn't live one's personal life in an exemplary way, if one follows a strict professional code that is congruent with the values of the organization, is that sufficient to be an effective leader?

In the past couple of years, many people across the country have described me as a leader. It's not always been easy to comprehend this new national profile. Most of those who approach me, of course, do not know me personally. They know only the public persona. What do they think they see in me? Is it simply the narrative of Flight 1549 that has touched them, or is it the way I have conducted myself in the public eye since the winter of 2009 that has caused some to feel this way?

Being seen as a role model is not always easy. While I've been grateful for these opportunities, at other times I have had to stretch and grow to meet the new challenges as a public figure. It's something I discuss with my wife and closest friends: How do I live up to these expectations? What are the responsibilities of a leader, especially someone thrust into that role by events beyond his control?

For me, and for men like former NASA flight director Gene Kranz, the test of leadership came in a crucible event, a near catastrophic crisis. But must a leader always be confronted with some great challenge or catharsis to develop leadership skills, or can learning, observation, and long-term growth alone provide it?

Since the successful landing of Flight 1549 on the Hudson River, I have been extremely privileged. I've been granted a singular opportunity to travel the world and meet hundreds of men and women who rank as inspiring leaders and activists in their fields.

I've taken that opportunity to more closely examine the ideas, traits, and values I've been thinking about, almost constantly, since childhood. In writing this book, I have embarked on a kind of personal quest, arranging to meet with a number of distinguished Americans, young and old, famous and less well known, from fields as diverse as space exploration, business, government, education, sports, finance, medicine, and the military. They are vastly different types of individuals with varied styles of leadership, but all embody the credo of "leadership by personal example."

I looked forward to learning from this journey. I expected to sharpen my philosophy of leadership and to focus my vision on qualities that go beyond the stereotypes. Most of us have the luxury of thinking of duty, courage, responsibility, and service above self as concepts in the abstract. Yet, for leaders such as those featured in this book, these are not abstract concepts. They have real meaning, in real life, with real consequences.

I hope that these stories will stimulate you, surprise you, and inspire you. As I put their stories to the page, I thought of this collection as a contemporary version of John F. Kennedy's *Profiles in Courage*. In these dialogues, conversations, and debates, I've asked a distinguished group of trailblazers, thinkers, and leaders to consider—as I now ask you to consider—some fundamental questions: What is the essential nature of leadership? What core qualities and characteristics shape our best leaders? What is the nature of loyalty? To whom or what do we owe it? And perhaps most important, how can each of us take away lessons from these leaders that we can apply to our own daily lives?

I

ADMIRAL THAD ALLEN

For the last thirty-something years, I've told everybody that my favorite definition of leadership is the ability to reconcile opportunity and competency. It's kind of like: If not now, *when? If not* you, *who?*

Thad Allen, U.S. Coast Guard commandant, was among the millions of television viewers who watched in horror as Hurricane Katrina ravaged coastal areas of Louisiana and Mississippi as well as the city of New Orleans in September 2005. The three-star admiral saw news reports of floating bodies, flooded homes, despondent families, and lawlessness gripping the city, and his mortification turned to anger. He asked other senior Coast Guard officers, "Why isn't somebody down there being the face of the federal government, standing in front of the Superdome, talking to CNN?"

The next thing he knew, Admiral Allen was in New Orleans, serving in just that role, one for which this son of a Coast Guard chief damage controlman was very well suited.

Looking back, Allen, now retired from the Coast Guard, remembers the depressing and confused scene in Washington just prior to his deployment to New Orleans: "I was at the Pentagon, and they were talking about invoking the Insurrection Act and sending the troops in," he says. "There was this huge amount of frustration."

Finally, one week after the Category 3 hurricane with 110 mph winds hit near the Louisiana–Mississippi border, Allen was appointed deputy to Federal Emergency Management Agency (FEMA) director Michael D. Brown. That assignment put him in charge of the Hurricane Katrina search and rescue and recovery efforts in the Gulf. His orders: "Just get to New Orleans and figure out what's going on. Stabilize the situation."

A realist, the Coast Guard admiral told his wife, "'There's no guarantee this is going to be a success. In fact, there's *every* reason to believe this will be a miserable failure and nothing can be done at this point.' My wife reminded me that for the last thirty-something years, I've told everybody that my favorite definition of leadership is the ability to reconcile opportunity and competency. So it's kind of like: If not *now,* when? If not *you,* who?

"'Okay,' I said. 'I'll go.'"

LEADING IN CHAOS

While many in the federal government were castigated for the slow response to Hurricane Katrina's destruction, Thad Allen garnered almost universal praise for his leadership in response and recovery efforts along the Gulf Coast. He received similar praise for his command performance during the Deepwater Horizon oil spill in 2010.

In fact, Admiral Allen has served in leadership roles during some of the country's most recent challenging times. He also commanded the Coast Guard's Atlantic forces in response to the terrorist attacks on September 11, 2001, when every U.S. port was considered a target.

Known to his men as "the Schwarzkopf of Connecticut," Allen worked wonders inside his organization, too. He led the massive effort to update the service's antiquated command and logistics organizations, another major achievement of his thirty-nine-year Coast Guard career.

I met Admiral Allen in Pentagon City, Virginia, at the offices of the RAND Corporation, where he is a senior fellow. Allen is a large, powerfully built sixty-two-year-old with a neatly trimmed mustache flecked with gray. His ruddy cheeks and well-weathered face mark him as a man who has spent much of his adult life on the sea. Allen was casually dressed for our meeting in a striped rugby pullover over a crisp white dress shirt. The former college football star gave me a very firm handshake. Allen still carries himself with a middle linebacker's barrel-chested confidence. He speaks in a gravelly voice, and his pale gray eyes are warm and curious.

When you consider the intensity of his experiences and the success he has had in leading rescue and recovery efforts in the most extreme situations, it is no surprise that Allen exudes a high level of self-confidence, but it clearly comes from his strong values, determination, and inner strength. He is also a leader who carefully picks his team and then gives them his complete trust.

"When I said yes, I'd go to New Orleans, the next thought was 'Okay, we can do that, but *how*?'" he recalled. "On my way to the airport, I called five people that I knew, to build a cadre around me in New Orleans. And I told them all the same thing. When they answered the phone I said, 'Find me in New Orleans in twenty-four hours.' That's all I told them. And of course it was almost impossible to get to New Orleans at that point."

Allen flew to Baton Rouge later on the day of his appointment to FEMA. Arriving after dark, he was told that he couldn't get a helicopter to New Orleans until the next morning because of ongoing rescue operations. "First thing in the morning, I met with the folks from Louisiana, and it was clear that there was not a lot of understanding of what was going on or the magnitude of the situation," he said.

Allen was mortified after his initial aerial view of the devastation. "As I flew in over New Orleans, I saw it was clearly filled with black water and there were still helicopters buzzing around. This is a week after the hurricane hit. I realized that at the national level, we had gotten this wrong in terms of the problem. We thought that we were dealing with a hurricane, and had it just been a hurricane, that probably would have been okay, but then Ground Zero would have been Bay Saint Louis in Waveland, Mississippi, which is where the eye came ashore."

Admiral Allen, who currently teaches a course in leadership at George Washington University, told me that, in a moment of crisis, he often returns to the writings of Peter Senge, a scientist and lecturer at MIT's Sloan School of Management, who wrote of the importance of grasping the unique aspects of each challenge rather than relying on preconceived "mental models" based on ingrained assumptions, generalizations, or past experience.

For Allen, in those chaotic hours of September 2005, Senge's concept of viewing a situation with a fresh eye was crucial to comprehending the scope of the Hurricane Katrina catastrophe. "It allows you to create a framework to make decisions, even if it's one that you kind of make up yourself: 'I see this, and so I think this is what's going on,'" Allen told me.

The aftermath of Hurricane Katrina was much more widespread and devastating than his superiors had initially grasped, and the response was disorganized, undisciplined, and sorely lacking in resources.

"I realized as I flew into the city that I wasn't dealing with a hurricane. I was dealing with a weapon of mass effect that had been used on the City of New Orleans without criminality," he said. "And that became my mental model, my way to orient myself. It allowed me to explain a bunch of things. They had lost continuity of government in the City of New Orleans without decapitation. Usually when you lose continuity of government, you lose your leadership. They hadn't lost their leadership. They had a mayor and a governor, but forces had been flowing into that city for over a week. Those who'd come to help weren't working for anybody; they were self-deployed."

The Coast Guard would save thirty-three thousand people and earn a presidential citation for its efforts, but at that point, a week after the hurricane hit, there was no "scripted, coordinated, or controlled" response from the myriad rescue forces that had descended upon the region. Admiral Allen quickly formed a plan of attack with another much-acclaimed leader of the response, U.S. Army Lieutenant General Russel L. Honoré, "the Ragin' Cajun" who commanded Joint Task Force Katrina.

"We came up with a way to divide the city into sectors, then take his forces with rubber boats and high-water vehicles, and basically, we decided to go through the city and touch every house," Allen said. "We called it a 'Hasty Sweep.' . . . We provided the capability, capacity, and command and control the [rescue and recovery forces] didn't have, to allow them to be effective. That was the solution, ultimately, that worked in New Orleans."

Allen took command of all search and rescue operations, reporting directly to U.S. Homeland Security Secretary Michael Chertoff, who reported to President George W. Bush, because "That's about the only way you could do that and then make it happen quick enough."

By the end of the week, the White House team recognized that Allen was the man everyone looked to as the leader along the Gulf Coast, so they made it official. He was named to replace FEMA's much-criticized Mike Brown as head of the entire federal response.

Sharing the Vision, Providing Context

Once Allen had taken command, he was concerned that widespread criticism of the federal government's initial slow and disorganized response was damaging morale among those in the trenches who were scrambling to do better.

At that moment, Allen's military aide—ironically enough, named Katrina—was standing right on his shoulder and she asked, "'Okay, Admiral, what are you going to do?' I told her, 'I'm going to do the first thing that any new commander does.' And Katrina says, 'What's that?' I said, 'I want an all-hands meeting.' She says, 'Sir, there are four thousand people in this building.' I said, 'Find the biggest place you can and get as many people as you can there.' Turns out there was a big, open area down on the first floor and we got about twenty-five hundred people in it," Allen said. "I went down, and there was a sea of humanity."

He noted that one of the similarities between the hurricane and the later BP oil spill was that "the people on the ground who actually had to do the work were having their morale seriously degraded by the reporting in the press on the ineptness . . . or the public grieving that was going on. Whether it was the perception of a lack of responsiveness of the federal government or BP's role, the people who were most critical to solving the problem felt they were just getting hammered in the press every day. Whether you were a rig worker working for BP or a FEMA relief worker, all you heard was your organization getting dumped on, and that has a really, really corrosive effect on morale."

Allen described the scene that day: "I walked in that room and I looked around, and what I saw was twenty-five hundred faces that were almost dragging on the ground. I got up on a desk at the joint field office and grabbed a megaphone." After explaining that he'd taken command and that he planned on setting up a two-man leadership team for the entire Gulf Coast region, from Louisiana to

Florida, "then I said, 'I'm going to give you an order. Everybody in the room here—you need to listen to me—this is an *order*. You're to treat everybody that you come in contact with that's been impacted by this storm as if they were a member of your family—your mother, your father, your brother, your sister. That's what I want you to do. And if you do that, two things will happen: Number one, if you make a mistake, you will probably err on the side of doing too much. And number two, if anybody has a problem with what you did, their problem's with me, not you.'

"At that point there was a collective sigh that probably would have blown the doors off the place—metaphorically—and then people began to weep, because *nobody* had told them what was important, what was valued, what their roles should be, and that their boss was behind them," Allen recalled. "In a very simple and direct way, I was able to tell them that."

It was a textbook case of a leader taking charge of an organization dangerously spiraling out of control. And in a broader sense, this was a leadership moment for which Allen, like me and like so many others thrown into challenging situations, had been preparing his whole life. Thad Allen, who was born while his father was "underway" in a Coast Guard cutter, was groomed to be a man of action.

"I think I'm the only enlisted brat that ever became the commandant," he noted.

"That probably gave you a different perspective on the service," I said.

"Everybody says to me, 'You must have gone into the Coast Guard because your dad was in the Coast Guard," Allen replied. "And frankly, the reason I went to the Coast Guard Academy is, I thought I was too small to play Division I football. I walked on the varsity in my freshman year and I was a captain my senior year. As a result of all that, I ultimately became the commandant. So I tell everybody, if I'm ever going to write an autobiography, I'm going to call it *Accidental Admiral*."

Like mine, Allen's formative years had been shaped by parents who'd struggled through financial hardships and World War II, so I asked him if he felt a strong obligation to serve his country.

"Early on, I went to the academy and my goal was to spend five years, serve my commitment, and get out," he replied. "And frankly, I was a handful early on. I had a bad temper. It was exacerbated by the fact that, in my junior year at the Coast Guard Academy, my older brother died from an overdose of heroin in Tucson, which significantly impacted my dad and almost led me to leave the academy. In fact, I ultimately stayed at the academy because I thought if I left after that, it would just break my dad's heart. That's probably another reason I'm still around and ended up doing what I was doing."

Allen came to love the Coast Guard, from its history to its unique Principles of Operation, which include the *principle of on-scene initiative,* a vital part of his approach to leadership. It means "if you're there, you have the capability, you should do something," he said. "Also, we have the *principle of restraint.* We are not an overwhelming military force, we deal with our fellow citizens, and you need to treat them with respect when you go on board a boat.

"One of the things we are really good at—and this is an 'Allenism'—is being bureaucratically multilingual," he added. "We can talk military to military, we can talk incident command system to local fire chief, we partner across the federal agencies, we can work with state and local governments. We are really good at partnering and collaboration."

When individuals, departments, or organizations act in isolation without regard to their impact on others, it is known as a silo mentality. I noted that Allen seemed to be a leader who specialized in breaking down silos and organizing a united front when faced with chaos. He agreed, and then mentioned an early experience that helped form his approach to leadership under fire.

The "pivotal event" in his Coast Guard career came immediately after his graduation from the Coast Guard Academy, and ironically enough, it was a seminal aviation accident that many of us in the airline industry have used as a teaching example for years, one that eventually caused my profession to change the way we teach cockpit leadership.

Eastern Air Lines Flight 401, a wide-body jet flying from New York City, crashed into the Everglades about eighteen miles short of the Miami International Airport runway, on December 29, 1972. One hundred and one people were killed immediately. Two others died of injuries later. Seventy-five people survived, thanks to rescue efforts by airboaters who'd been nearby and the swift arrival of the Coast Guard, including twenty-three-year-old Thad Allen, who was assigned to the Coast Guard air station at Opa-Locka.

"I actually ended up getting on the first or second helicopter to arrive on the scene," said Allen. "I was in the wreckage for about twenty-four hours, hauling survivors, bodies, doing whatever needed to be done. There were about six of us who got in, and then they couldn't bring anybody else in, so we were the first ground team that was there. So, yeah, that was a pretty substantial event in my life."

Allen said the experience of being involved in a massive rescue operation under such horrific conditions—some rescuers sustained burns from jet fuel burning in the swamp—taught him the value of first responders and clearheaded crisis leadership at a very young age.

TAKING THE INITIATIVE

Flight 401 had a major impact on my life as well as on that of Thad Allen, who considers it his introduction into the sort of crisis leadership that marked his thirty-nine-year career in the Coast Guard. Nearly a year later, he was on watch at the Coast Guard Rescue Coordination Center in San Juan when a call came of an engine fire on another passenger airliner flying from San Juan to Miami. The plane had turned around, but there were concerns that it might go down before making it to San Juan. Based on what he'd seen with Flight 401, Allen went into action.

"I remembered all the things that worked and didn't work, so I immediately started doing a bunch of things that I thought I needed to do," he said. "I knew on the flight path back in they may not make it in. That's why I positioned two cutters at five-mile intervals off the beach in case they had to go in the water. I diverted a jet fighter from Roosevelt [Roads] Naval Air Station that flew escort. I recalled the public health doctors. I established a triage point at a local gym. I'd never had any formal response training like that, but as a result of the Miami incident, I did the things I needed to do."

Thankfully, that plane made it back to San Juan and landed without incident, and Allen later created a formal situation plan for handling similar crises. He was establishing himself as a leader in crisis management and emergency rescue and recovery operations, which appealed to his competitive spirit.

"Being an athlete, for me it was almost like a competition. *Nobody* was going to launch a helicopter quicker. If they were there, I was going to get to them," he said. "This ultimately spilled over into how we did search planning. You do the calculations for the wind, and sea currents, and whether or not you've got a person in the water or a boat, how long does it go downwind, so I got involved a lot in developing the search planning doctrine."

IN HARM'S WAY

In his first three years with the Coast Guard, Allen learned many of the "blocking and tackling" fundamentals of his tradecraft, but he continued to always try and learn as much as possible to make him a better leader. This commitment to continuing to invest in yourself, to constant improvement and lifelong learning, is something that I value greatly.

In the winter of 1980, Allen faced one of the most difficult choices a leader can face: whether to put his people in harm's way in order to save others in danger. A three-hundred-foot barge containing nearly three million gallons of fuel oil was grounded with two crew members aboard in a blinding blizzard and heavy surf at the entrance to the Brigantine National Wildlife Refuge in Great Bay, near Mystic Island, which is north of Atlantic City, New Jersey.

"It was certainly a life-and-death situation, and had it gone south I would have been held accountable, there's no doubt about that," said Allen, who was then stationed in Atlantic City. There were fifteen- to twenty-foot waves breaking over the barge, threatening to wash the two crew members overboard. A helicopter had been sent in to attempt the rescue, but due to the blizzard, it was forced to land before reaching the barge.

The water was too shallow for a Coast Guard cutter, but guardsmen from Long Beach Island were able to get close enough to see the barge in the blizzard. One of them, Matthew Greer, called in to Allen on the radio and said they thought they could get into the bay and rescue the crew members in a smaller rescue boat.

"We've got these Coast Guard rescue surfboats that can actually roll over, come back up. It's a forty-four-foot motor lifeboat," Allen said. "At that moment, I had to figure out whether or not I was going to intervene or say, 'Don't do it because of safety reasons.' But he was on-scene; he was in control of the boat. I didn't think it was up to me to make a surrogate call. I had to let him make the decision on-scene, and it was just killing me because I didn't think there was any possible way you could get to that barge.

"The next thing I hear on the radio is 'We're going in.' Then there was silence for thirty-five minutes. It was just torture for thirty-five minutes," he recalled. "The next thing I heard on the radio was 'We've got 'em. We're coming through the surf line.'"

Four of the five Coast Guardsmen involved in the rescue of the two barge crew members had to lash themselves to a rail of their surfboat before wading through the rough seas to reach the two men on the barge. On their return trip to the Coast Guard cutter, the rescue boat was nearly swamped and almost flipped over several times.

"I put them up for the Coast Guard Medal, which is the highest medal you can have for noncombat action. You can also ask for an additional designation of 'extraordinary heroism,' and if they get that, it's an additional ten percent on their retirement. They all got it," Allen said. "I wrote the words of those citations myself."

CRUCIBLE EVENTS

Allen's Coast Guard career had a remarkable number of these tests of leadership, these crucible events that serve as tests of your innermost core, trials by fire from which leaders like Thad Allen seem to emerge stronger, more purposeful, and more focused than ever before on their missions in life.

My first officer, Jeff Skiles, and I experienced much the same thing during Flight 1549 when we were suddenly forced to fight for our lives and those of our passengers and crew. This was a cathartic experience for us; one of those life-changing events that force change upon you in such a way that you have an entirely different perspective on everything that follows.

Sometimes, as Allen noted, these events don't change you right away, but over time their influence has an effect on how you respond and react as a leader. He recalled finding himself once again at the center of a series of challenging events in the summer of 1999, just one week after being assigned to Miami as a rear admiral in charge of the Coast Guard's southeast region.

The Coast Guard normally is held in high public esteem, but that June it was embroiled in controversy and criticism. A 1995 accord allowing immigrants from Cuba to claim legal residency if they were able to reach the U.S. shore led to wave after wave of "boat people" trying to make the dangerous voyage between their island and Florida's coast. Many were desperate and willing to turn to violence if anyone stood in their way. The U.S. Coast Guard found itself in one confrontation after another because they were supposed to turn back these illegal immigrants.

On June 29, a Coast Guard crew stopped a rowboat of six migrants off the coast of Surfside, just north of Miami Beach, by dousing them with a fire hose. Some of them continued to try and make it to shore, and they were sprayed with pepper spray. A television crew in a helicopter captured the confrontation between the Coast Guard and the "Surfside Six" on camera, igniting public outrage. Demonstrators supporting the Cuban immigrants shut down I-95, the primary transportation corridor in South Florida.

Allen promptly issued an order that pepper spray should be used only if there was a threat to the safety of officers or individuals, and that a fire hose should not be turned on anyone unless they were part of a violent crowd.

"We had fifteen hundred people protesting outside the Coast Guard base, which never happens to us," Allen said. "Then, in July of '99, we had a patrol boat collide with a Cuban boat. It flipped over and we had a woman drown."

Those events convinced Allen that the Coast Guard needed to take a less confrontational approach to the Cubans trying to reach the United States. On Thanksgiving Day 1999, his new philosophy was put to the test when his dinner was interrupted by a call from the command center. The Coast Guardsman on the phone said that one of their crews had been stopped at sea by two fishermen who had with them a five-year-old Cuban boy they'd found adrift in an inner tube.

The standard procedure in such cases was to keep the immigrants offshore and interview them to see if they had a "credible claim of persecution" in their own country. If the claim seemed legitimate, they were allowed to enter the United States. If it did not seem credible, they were returned to Cuba. That was the policy,

Allen said, but he wasn't sure it applied to a five-year-old floating alone in an inner tube in Miami Bay.

"Okay, he's five years old. Does he speak English?" Allen asked his Coast Guard crew leader.

"No."

"What's his condition?"

"He's dehydrated and he's a little hypothermic."

"So, you had to make a critical decision here, but little did you think that it would lead to an international crisis and political upheaval lasting more than a year," I said.

Allen ordered the boy to be brought in to see a doctor, and he decided not to check first with his superiors in D.C., because he didn't want to take a chance that they might send the boy back to Cuba.

The boy was Elián Gonzáles, whose mother had divorced his father and fled Cuba with her boyfriend and Elián. They'd tried to make it to the United States with a large group of immigrants on an overcrowded boat. The boat had capsized. The mother and ten others had died. Elián was initially placed with his father's relatives in Miami. His father demanded that his son be returned to Cuba.

The matter set off controversy and conflict in the Cuban-American community and inflamed anti-American sentiments in Cuba. After a federal appeals court ruled in favor of the father, federal agents had to take Elián from his Miami relatives at gunpoint and return him to Cuba in June 2000.

"That year in Miami was a tumultuous year," said Allen, practicing the art of understatement.

In this series of crucible events, Allen found himself at odds with Coast Guard policies that allowed for harsher treatment of seafaring immigrants than he believed necessary or humane. He chose to stand up for what he felt was right, even though it meant possibly incurring the wrath of his superiors.

As an airline pilot for more than thirty years, and a captain for twenty-two of those years, I know firsthand how important it is in every organization to have people with the integrity *and courage* to do what is right, and to resist what I call the "drift toward expedience," which is the tendency to cut corners due to production pressures. Airline captains know that we owe it to our passengers and crew to be the conscience of the industry.

TEAM BUILDING

The crucible events in Allen's career forged his values and principles and his very approach to leadership. They also gave him the opportunity to see how those around him responded in times of crisis. Over time, he surrounded himself with those who impressed him, making them part of his leadership team.

One of those was "a brand-new, green lieutenant straight out of graduate school" who was serving as his public affairs officer in Miami during the Cuban immigrant crises. That young man held the rank of commander in 2005 when Allen called and asked him to join his team in New Orleans after Hurricane Katrina.

"Turns out he was just pulling into the driveway of a brand-new house, after a transfer with his family and three kids, and he got right out of the car and left for New Orleans," Allen recalled. "Another one I took was a guy who ran my command center in the Atlantic area after the September 11, 2001, attacks. He had been a former flag aide, but he was a search and rescue planner like I was, and I knew he could run operations."

Allen spoke of his group of "core leaders" or "cosigners," a trusted crew he could rely upon to follow his plan, act out his orders, and make decisions that matched up with his values and principles. "Early on I called the people who went with me to New Orleans 'Dogs That Hunt,'" he said. "You know the expression 'That dog don't hunt.' If you're going to go to New Orleans with that assignment, you'd better have dogs that hunt. So I grabbed people from my past that I knew could do anything under any conditions."

With tongue in cheek, Allen called his crack crisis team the "Deployable Operations Group," or DOG. They were like destiny's children, the right people with the right skills at the right time—time after time after time. Their search and rescue efforts in New Orleans proved to be simply a prelude to even greater challenges by land—in Haiti, after a 7.0 magnitude earthquake—and by sea, on the Gulf Coast after the Deepwater Horizon drilling rig explosion.

Because the Coast Guard has cutters always patrolling off Haiti and Cuba, Allen's people were the first to arrive at Port-au-Prince after the January 2010 earthquake. Once again the veteran crisis commander stepped into the leadership role while others pondered what to do. The scale of the destruction and the inaccessibility of Haiti because of damaged harbors and airfields were mind-boggling even to many veteran responders, but for Allen it was "been there, done that."

As in New Orleans, he noted, this was a natural "weapon of mass effect" that had made it all but impossible for local governments to respond. President Obama called together his cabinet members and issued marching orders: "You guys get on this thing and you give it your full attention and you make this work," as Allen recalled.

"And we did. And it worked," he told me.

Always an innovator, Allen came up with a plan that put a senior FEMA official and a Coast Guard admiral in charge of the rescue operation with a command-and-control communications structure based on the grounds of the American embassy in Port au Prince.

The vast extent of the devastation and the fact that it was on foreign soil proved to make this mission even more complicated than New Orleans, Allen admitted. With only one airport runway open and relief supplies and teams coming in from all over the world, someone had to maintain order and control the airspace. Once again, Allen stepped up.

"You'd have the vice president of Bolivia taking off with a planeload of relief supplies, and they'd be in midair calling and saying they want clearance to land. You can't turn them around, so the question is, how are you going to equitably handle the landing slots, given that it was an international response," he said.

"We sent some Coast Guard people over, and they started managing a landing-slot vetting process on how to sequence not only who got in but also the logistics. If you send five planeloads of water and you don't have any people or trucks, you can't get the water from the airport. We had to have a way to get the supply chain flowing.

"Bottom line, while the long-term issues for Haiti are huge, our response down there was pretty damned effective," he noted. "The first twenty-four hours after the earthquake, there were about twelve or thirteen landings at the airport. And at the height of the operation, on our busiest day, we did a hundred and sixteen landings."

PREPARATION MEETS OPPORTUNITY

Great leaders learn from every experience, both failures and successes. Many of these leaders talk about how they help their people thrive and experience success. For Admiral Allen, the lessons learned during the response to the earthquake would prove to be essential in managing the Deepwater Horizon disaster in the Gulf of Mexico just a few months later.

The unprecedented oil spill that followed the April 2010 explosion on an offshore platform operated by BP (formerly British Petroleum) flowed unabated for three months, with a twenty-four-hour-a-day underwater camera feed watched by millions of horrified viewers. When BP's efforts to lead the cleanup drew heavy criticism, Admiral Allen was dispatched by the president of the United States to take command, thirty-seven days into the disaster.

"The biggest thing with the oil spill was to control the well. You can talk about oil in the water, you can talk about cleaning up the oil, but until we got that well capped," he said, "we had an indeterminate, omnidirectional threat that was releasing a major oil spill every day: huge amounts of oil coming to the surface and then going in different directions based on the wind. We didn't have a large, monolithic spill; we had hundreds of thousands of patches of oil from Port Saint Joe, Florida, to southwest Louisiana, and there was not enough equipment in the world to defend that amount of coastline.

"As I was focusing all my efforts on getting the well capped, BP went out, trying to ameliorate the economic impact, and established what they called a Vessel of Opportunity Program," Allen recalled. "They started hiring local shrimp boats to use in the response. Well, it was a nice concept. The problem is, *everybody* showed up. At one point, we had close to ten thousand vessels on retainer, and there was nobody to organize it."

ORGANIZING THE TROOPS

An avid student of history, Allen immediately drew the parallel to one of the defining moments in the birth of the United States: "I made the analogy to the guys that showed up at Concord before the Revolution," he said. "They showed up with commitment, passion, and resources, but some of them had a musket and some only had a knife. You had to form them up, teach them how to march and how to beat the British. I didn't have time to do that, and so there was a huge issue on what to do with this floating militia."

At one point, within a one-mile radius of that well site, Allen was trying to control thirty-five vessels and twenty-two remotely operated vehicles. "I have a picture of one of the offshore supply vessels, looking out the bridge, and you cannot see water. All you see is vessels. I could not convince everybody about how dangerous that was. And the fact that we didn't have a major midair or major marine casualty was extraordinary."

As if the problems at sea weren't enough, there were also looming dangers in the airspace above the Gulf. "We'd had eight near midair collisions in the first five weeks, with the helicopters going to the rigs, spotter planes for the burning and the skimming. The National Guard was flying out there because the governors wanted to know what was going on, and we had press in their planes," he recalled.

Allen called upon his experience in asserting control of the only airstrip and its airspace in Haiti and came up with a plan. Then he boldly took it right to *the Man* while flying to Pensacola with President Obama aboard Air Force One.

"The president was talking to some folks, I was sitting in a chair just outside this meeting room, thinking about what I'd seen that day, and somebody bumps into me, and I look up and it was the president," he said. "The president sits down. He's going back that night to do the address from the Oval Office, so he's feeling no small amount of pressure. He asked, 'Do you have enough resources?' I said, 'Mr. President, this is *not* a matter of resources.' . . .

"Then I said, 'Do you know what I think I need to do, Mr. President? I think I need to take control of the airspace. I need to unify all the surveillance activities—bring them to one point, integrate it, and then come up with a way to send these vessels and coordinate everything. I can't do that unless I have a true operational picture. I can't do it unless I take control of the airspace.'

"President Obama looked at me and said, 'Okay, do what you've got to do. But just remember this: There are no do-overs.'"

Allen replied that he understood.

He offered a wry smile at the memory of the conversation on Air Force One. "That was pretty direct guidance," he said.

"Sure was," I said. " 'Don't screw it up.' "

At four the next morning, Allen typed for two hours before sending out a fifteen-page e-mail. Then he called all the government and military officials involved in his takeover of the airspace over the Gulf. "We took the airspace," he said. "And from then on, everything just started getting better and better in this response."

The similarities between the challenges of the Haiti earthquake and the Gulf oil disaster were actually few and far between. One of the most striking differences was that there was a very clear-cut villain identified in the Gulf—BP—and the animosity directed toward its workers was making Allen's job more difficult because he needed them to fix the well.

"I was telling the press, because they kept asking me about Hurricane Katrina, there's *no* similarity between these events," he said. "The biggest thing about this is that we have a well that's out of control five thousand feet below the surface, where we have no human access to the site. And I told everybody, it's closer to *Apollo 13* than it is to Hurricane Katrina, so let's throw everything on the table. How are we going to fix this?

"Everybody wanted to kill BP. I've got senior officials pillorying BP publicly. I need BP to fix the well, and they need their workers to be well motivated. So I was actually going out to the rigs and talking to people on the rigs about how important their jobs were, almost the same as I did with the FEMA employees after Hurricane Katrina."

LEADERSHIP ASSESSMENT

Given Admiral Allen's incredible experiences in managing crises and finding solutions amid chaos, I had to get his assessment of the failures in leadership during the Gulf oil debacle. I asked him to talk about BP and their organizational culture, especially in terms of safety, and the kind of leadership that they exhibited. "If you'd been the CEO of BP, what would you have done differently?" I asked.

The retired admiral said he'd discussed that same question in independent conversations with former BP chief executive Tony Hayward, his replacement, Bob Dudley, and BP's chairman of the board, Carl-Henric Svanberg. Allen said he told Hayward and Dudley that they did very well as leaders of an oil and exploration company, but "when it comes to setting up a claims process for the Gulf Coast citizens, dealing with oil removal on the beaches, dealing with the media—you *suck*."

Allen said that large corporations like BP aren't set up to do "personal transactions. You don't have the competency, the capability, and the capacity inside the company to do that. When something happens, you need to acquire it. And as I've told Tony and Bob Dudley and everybody else, you can't outsource core values, empathy, and compassion to a third party. Your company is not involved in dealing with the customers and stakeholders every day at that level. So you're not going to be as well equipped to deal with it from a media—or leadership—standpoint as you might otherwise be, because you don't deal with the public every day in drilling for oil."

STAYING IN CONTROL

Like most of the other leaders I've spoken with, Allen believes it is critical to be in control of yourself and your message at all times. "When you're at the top of the organization, you can't be having mood swings and acting out like Tony Hayward did when he let his emotions get the best of him," Allen said. "If you're in a leadership situation in a very large, complex event, there's very little room for error publicly in what you say and how you act; it's a very unforgiving environment."

Allen did not find fault with Tony Hayward's saying that he

wanted his life back—a statement that drew scathing criticism—but he did fault him for stating that publicly after so many lives had been lost and so many other people were suffering hardships because of BP's mistakes.

"Frankly, when Tony Hayward said he wanted his life back, he was absolutely right. There's nothing wrong with that. He was feeling normal. I mean, there were some times when *I* wanted my life back too. But it was one of those cases where you don't have the luxury of appearing to be too 'human,' to the point where it appears to be a fragility issue with your leadership skills, and then it becomes a confidence issue with the public."

"Or lack of empathy," I noted.

"He had *no* margin for error. And Tony, who is from a working-class family, and is a geologist who worked his way up through the organization, he's actually a nice guy. I still stay in contact with him. But put in that situation, there is no margin for error," Allen repeated.

Allen also faulted Carl-Henric Svanberg, the chairman of the board of BP, with not understanding how to communicate effectively during the crisis situation. Once, when Allen met with Svanberg in the middle of the turmoil, the BP board chairman told him, "We want to do the right thing. We're trying to do the right thing. We care about the little people," Allen recalled.

"And I thought, *That is the wrong way to say that.* I understood it was a translation issue from his own language to English. And I was going to tell him, 'Do *not* say that publicly.' We got off on another topic, and I forgot about it—and sure as you're born, the next day he said that to the press."

Svanberg's "little people" remark ignited yet another media firestorm and once again made BP seem both patronizing and wholly out of touch with the human cost of its man-made environmental disaster. But Allen blamed himself for not stepping in to alert Svanberg to the dangers in his choice of words.

"That was a leadership failure on my part," Allen acknowledged. "And frankly, I told him later on that I thought that that was a leadership failure on my part. I felt terrible afterward because I knew immediately he shouldn't say it, and I just got distracted and never got back to it."

Given all that was going on, Allen can be forgiven for his failure to communicate, but the incident does highlight how important it is for leaders to express their concerns readily in such situations.

Allen found fault with BP's reliance on a "single-point-of-failure device" without a secondary containment system on its deepwater well.

"The same things have happened in other industries—mine included," I told Allen. "The way I put it is that you cannot define safety solely as the *absence* of a lot of recent accidents and incidents. I think the Gulf oil spill will be seen as a leadership failure and a safety culture failure more than a technical failure. Because they had not had a lot of blowout-preventer failures, they thought it would always save them."

The admiral noted that the "blowout preventer was not constructed with the remote sensing and redundancies you see in the aviation community, which they're going to require now. This is a no-brainer."

STRIVING FOR EXCELLENCE

My conversation with Thad Allen had touched on many crucial points, including seeing the unique aspects of each challenge, building upon experiences, learning from mistakes, leading by example, taking responsibility, articulating a vision of the mission and its goals, controlling the message, building your team, and trusting them to do the job right.

I told him that he seemed to be a leader with a firm set of values that helped him navigate each and every challenge. I've been much the same way, but the importance of strong values and knowing who you are was brought home to me by an experience I'd had just two days after the landing of Flight 1549 on the Hudson.

I'd finally returned to San Francisco, but the press was waiting at the airport. The NTSB and my employer did not want me speaking to the press at that point, so they took me down the jetway's stairs to the tarmac and into a van. One of the airline agents who was meeting the flight intercepted me in the jetway and handed me a greeting card that he and his wife had picked out. The card said "Congratulations" and "Thank You" and then it closed with this memorable line: "When your values are clear, your choices are easy."

"Yes," Allen said, nodding. "It allows you to exclude a lot and narrows the field."

Admiral Allen seemed to have a very good handle on who he is and how he works best. I'd been impressed too with his ability to learn from each situation, to devise fresh approaches, and to constantly evaluate to see what worked, what didn't work, and what he needed to do to build upon his strengths so that he could be a better leader. "Where did this striving for excellence come from?" I asked him.

"Early on, I was extremely competitive in an athletic sense. I've always been competitive in a way that I'd almost treat everything as if it's an athletic challenge. If somebody's lost at sea and we don't know where they're at, it's like somebody threw down a challenge," he said. "I wasn't the most talented athlete on the field, but I think I worked harder than everybody else. You translate that over, and I take almost everything as if it's an athletic competition, except, in these situations, if you win, somebody *lives*."

"That's a weighty definition of success," I said.

"That becomes your motivator to be as well trained and as effective as you can be," he said, noting that he often stayed up late at night reading background materials to make sure he fully understood each challenge he faced.

"During the hurricane and then during the oil spill, I needed to acquire information rapidly, digest the information, and try and understand what was going on intellectually," Allen explained. "Part of all of this, too, is being able to see through the data glut and pull out what you need. During the oil spill I was looking at three or four hundred pages of content a day that I had to wade through and somehow make sense of, and then still be able to make decisions."

Allen said that his successes have been built upon his processes for preparing himself, building his knowledge base, assessing each situation thoughtfully, and then coming up with fresh mental models and methods for achieving clear-cut goals.

"You've got to do the preparation up front, rather than just go out there and start acting," he said. "I've always tried to put one of those frameworks around everything I do in life. And I think it starts from getting ready to play the next week's opponent and all that necessary athletic preparation."

"Are you a perfectionist?" I asked.

"No," Allen said.

"Are you an optimist?"

"Yes," he said. "Colin Powell says optimism is a force multiplier. I always believe that you're in control of events. I mean, you can't control *everything,* but you have a great deal to do with what happens. People can do a lot of things to you, but they can't mess with your mental attitude. You own that and you control it. And being optimistic is part of it. Peter Senge would say, when something happens and your emotions get carried away, you go to an emotional basement. The question is: How do you bring yourself out of the basement when you need to?"

I asked Allen how he instills the same values, the same drive for excellence, and the same optimistic approach in those he leads and mentors.

"A lot of it has to do with storytelling and passing it down intergenerationally by saying, 'Listen, I wasn't much different from you at a certain point.' I think the big deal is to put yourself in situations early on where you can start practicing this stuff, where you can make mistakes and they aren't life- or profession-ending decisions if you do make a mistake. I tell everybody, 'The only way to get good at this is by *doing* it.'"

THE NATURE OF LEADERSHIP

When teaching his George Washington University course Leadership in Complex Organizations, Allen asks his students to focus on "this notion of personal mastery and how you build this body of work, looking at your life and your profession as a craft, almost like an artisan does, and how you do that over a lifetime."

Allen and I agreed that you should master your craft and then master yourself.

"I know I've had a good class when I'll get about twenty minutes into the theory and somebody raises a hand and then I don't have to say a word the rest of the class because they are all talking to each other and talking to me," he said. "As I walk out, I tell my graduate assistant, 'We had a good class tonight because *they* taught it.'"

One of Allen's basic tenets in his class on leadership is borrowed from our mutual friend Warren Bennis, who is an author and a pioneer in leadership studies as well as the founder of the Leadership Institute at the University of Southern California. Allen and I both admire Bennis's ideas on leadership, and I particularly like his saying that "When leaders treat followers with respect, followers respond with trust."

Allen and Bennis agree that failure offers some of the best lessons of leadership and that, as Bennis has written, "managers do things right and leaders do the right thing." Allen also agrees with Bennis on the question of whether leaders are born or made. The retired admiral definitely feels that all leaders are made and shaped by specific challenges and experiences. "I think when something happens and you have a great demonstration of leadership, it has to do a lot with subject matter expertise, how long you've been working the blocking and tackling," he said. "I'm not sure you could come up with an equation that says if you do this, then that happens. I do believe that everybody can be a better leader. It doesn't matter who you are or what you're doing, you can be better."

Great leaders are great learners, Allen added. "If you have insatiable curiosity, you're into lifelong learning, you keep an agile, flexible mind, you'll be resilient and you can adapt. If you have something that comes along that you're not accustomed to, you can usually do pretty well as long as you keep that portfolio growing and building as you go through life.

"You've got to build a body of personal and professional expertise that allows you to fly a plane, do the search planning, or whatever it is. Then you've got to continually refresh your knowledge. You've got to put yourself in situations where you can make decisions under conditions of uncertainty with incomplete information, have that feedback loop come back on whether you did good or bad, and then keep getting better at it by doing it."

"If our roles were reversed today," I asked, "what question have I not asked that you think would be an important one to ask?"

Allen paused—then deadpanned, "Our roles would never be reversed, because I decided that I could swim better than I could fly—and I never became a pilot."

We shared a long laugh. "I don't know, the water temperature that day was thirty-six degrees Fahrenheit, close to zero Celsius," I said.

"You don't know it, but I was in direct contact with those guys who were in the Coast Guard boats right outside, because we were there right after the ferries, and we got about fourteen of your folks. No, I was completely involved that day. I was on the line with Secretary Napolitano at the other end. . . .

"But to answer your question, throughout my entire career is this thought about being able to reconcile opportunity and competency. And it's really less about being a leader and more about being as good a person and getting as much out of life as you can. Because the more you do that, the more you're going to have a rewarding life and career. It's going to mean a hell of a lot more to you and the people around you if you do that. There's an intrinsic value to doing this without saying, 'Ultimately, I'm going to become the president of the United States, or commandant of the Coast Guard, or pilot on an airplane.' There's intrinsic value in intellectual wellness—it's almost like physical wellness—and I think that everybody should probably strive to do that. If you're going to be on the surf walking around, you'd better have as much fun while you're doing it and try and get as much done as you can."

"We were talking about your parents, members of the Greatest Generation, and their values," I said, "and you said that for a while those values were not as apparent in society. But now, because of this economic downturn the last several years, that some of those core values might be embraced once again."

"Yes," Allen said. "I think we have a tendency to question—when you have successive generations in which life is apparently easier—whether or not lessons are being lost. Two things lead me to believe that probably is not going to be the case. I do think we're going to be in for a period of financial austerity, and that's going to test everybody even further. I don't think we're going to fall back to what was the equivalent of the Great Depression, but we certainly are facing the possibility that a future generation may not be as well off financially and economically as the one that came before it. It places a significant premium on people who are in leadership to have a conversation about what that means and how you deal with that so we don't—as a society—go to the basement, if you will."

Allen said that while leading the Coast Guard, and particularly when visiting the wounded young servicemen and -women in our nation's Veterans Administration hospitals, he'd seen other signs that the current crop of young people are made up of the "right stuff."

"As commandant of the Coast Guard, I tried to get over about once a quarter and walk through the wards at either Walter Reed or Bethesda, talking with the wounded warriors who were coming back from overseas," he said. "You only do that once or twice, and you understand that there's *nothing* wrong with this generation. Their ability to sacrifice, lead, serve, and everything else—yes, we're in pretty good shape."

2

JOHN C. BOGLE

Leadership has a lot to do with not thinking about yourself as a leader. Not thinking about yourself is important. Suppress the arrogance.

ON A BRIGHT WINTER MORNING IN DECEMBER 1949, JOHN C. BOGLE, a Princeton junior studying economics, was glancing at a *Fortune* magazine in the reading room of Firestone Library. The headline "Big Money in Boston" caught his eye. The article was about an industry Bogle never knew existed—mutual funds. He was instantly intrigued.

"I had this wonderful, wonderful accident," the eighty-one-year-old founder and former chairman of the Vanguard Group recalls today.

On that morning long ago, he'd been sitting near the second-floor balcony of the library's cavernous reading room in search of a topic for his senior thesis. "This goes to the contrarian in me," he says. "I wanted to write about something that *no* thesis had ever been written on before. That was my goal. I had never *heard* of the mutual fund industry, and when the article described it as 'tiny but contentious,' I thought, *Bogle, you have found the topic for your thesis. It's just like you: tiny but contentious.*"

It's fair to say that the "wonderful accident" of his haphazard flipping through *Fortune* changed not just the course of Bogle's life but also the entire course of the investment industry in the United States. His senior thesis, "The Economic Role of the Investment Company," led to a lifelong passion for him and opened the door to stock market investing for the masses. His creation of index funds provided average investors with their most reliable means for tapping the potential of the stock market, which had traditionally been an investment tool only for the wealthiest, most money-savvy investors.

Today, more than a half century after Bogle first read the fateful article, the mutual fund industry has grown to 7,691 funds with combined assets of over $11 trillion, according to the Investment Company Institute. Jack Bogle has been called the man who revolutionized mutual funds and "arguably the greatest shareholder advocate in the history of Wall Street." In 2004 *Time* magazine named Bogle as one of the world's hundred most powerful and influential people. He served as Vanguard's chairman and chief executive officer until 1996 and as senior chairman until 2000.

In retirement, Bogle serves as the primary voice for reform in an industry plagued by greed, excess, and complacency. His admirers point to his advocacy, his clarity of vision, and his call for humanism in an arena not exactly famous for placing people over profit. Indeed, Bogle's dedication to clients' interests above all else has earned him a reputation as the "conscience of the investing industry."

I drove to the sprawling campus of the Vanguard Group in Malvern, Pennsylvania, to meet with its founder. Bogle started his fund company on May 1, 1975, with just three other employees. Today, Vanguard's team includes 12,500 people serving 18 million shareholder accounts and managing nearly $1.6 trillion in U.S.

mutual funds. The Vanguard 500 Index Fund, the first-ever index fund, is also the world's largest mutual fund. The company introduced a radically different corporate structure, one that serves mutual fund owners by allowing them to essentially own Vanguard Group, which provides all the administrative services at cost.

Bogle still keeps a prominent office in the headquarters. Now something of a charismatic éminence grise at Vanguard, he wore a navy blue crewneck sweater, khaki pants, and a pair of oxblood penny loafers that would not have seemed out of place on a Princeton undergraduate in the late 1940s. His office is decorated with paintings, artifacts, and even needlepoint pillows, most of them depicting the Battle of the Nile, from which the Vanguard Group derives its name.

"*Vanguard* was a British warship, the flagship of Lord Nelson at the Battle of the Nile, which was the most complete victory in all naval history," the history buff said. Only after naming his fund did he learn that *vanguard* also means "leader in a new trend," which applies to both the amazing company he built and to the founder's position in the mutual fund industry.

Bogle was born in Montclair, New Jersey, on May 8, 1929. Nothing in his childhood could have predicted his future success. His was not an Ivy League legacy. Bogle made it to Princeton on an academic scholarship and graduated magna cum laude. His family had once been wealthy but lost its fortune during the Depression. His father succumbed to alcoholism. Yet, Bogle said, the turn of fortune eventually worked to his advantage.

Like so many children whose families were devastated by the Great Depression, certainly like my own father, Jack Bogle grew up with an incredible work ethic born of strife. "As kids, we ol' Bogle boys were working—particularly Little Jackie—probably from the age of nine or ten, delivering papers and magazines," Bogle said. "Then later I was a waiter at Blair Academy and at Princeton. In retrospect, I only had *one* job that I thought was real work . . . when I was a pinsetter in a bowling alley. Talk about Sisyphus: down they go, up they go, down they go, up they go. So out of that came, I guess, a great determination to do better."

Bogle credits his mother's emphasis on education and hard work with fueling that determination. He noted that his own defining characteristic "is not always attractive." This business leader was often so focused that it was like living with blinders on, he admitted. Still, his ability to focus was helpful when Bogle began to experience heart problems at the age of thirty, resulting in a long series of hospitalizations leading up to his heart transplant just fifteen years ago.

SERVICE TO OTHERS

Bogle's years as a waiter serving others also appear to have had a lasting influence on his approach to leadership. During his tenure at Vanguard, he insisted that his "crew members," never "employees," should describe mutual funds as "products," and "clients" were never called "customers."

"Choice of words is a very, very important thing to me," he said. "And as I've often said to people, for a company without employees, without customers, and without products, we seem to be doing all right."

I asked Bogle if his careful use of language reflected his philosophy of focusing on building relationships rather than simply ringing up transactions.

"Exactly, Sully," he replied, noting that his goal always was "to treat those whom we serve and with whom we serve as honest-to-God, down-to-earth human beings with their own hopes and fears and financial goals."

Bogle's reputation within the mutual fund industry reminded me of something I have been saying for several years: that airline pilots, and in particular airline captains, are the conscience of the airline industry. By law, we are the final authority, directly responsible for every aspect of the safety of our flights. Airline pilots, and in particular airline captains, must help those around us to understand safety and the fundamental values of integrity and courage. They also must be dedicated to doing the right thing even when it is not at all convenient.

For airline pilots, our passengers' very *lives* depend on it. For investment leaders like Jack Bogle, this sense of duty and responsibility involves protecting the financial interests of clients and his "crew members." This idealistic vision of leadership can be a rare thing in business, especially in the financial world, so I asked Bogle where his values and sense of obligation to his clients were formed.

"I think people would say that I came from difficult circumstances, from a family that was not quite so solid," he said. "There was a lot of moving around from one place to another. And you've got to be something of a dreamer not to think this is the way your life is going to be for the rest of your days. So it was always ingrained. Particularly by my grandmother, a very determined woman of that age, who left me with the idea that everything you touch, leave it better than you found it."

LEADERS LEARN FROM MENTORS

One of Bogle's most important business mentors was an older Princetonian named Walter L. Morgan, founder of the Wellington Fund. Bogle had sent Morgan his senior thesis, and Morgan was suitably impressed. Morgan became Bogle's model of a business leader who exhibited goodness, strong values, integrity, honesty, and good humor.

Bogle had received a job offer from Philadelphia National Bank, so he had to choose between going to the bank, which unbeknownst to him would fail at a later date, and accepting a job offer from Morgan at Wellington. "Mr. Morgan kept saying to me, 'Why would you want to go to work for a bank?'" said Bogle. Realizing that Morgan was truly interested in him, Bogle opted to go where he had a mentor already in place at the very top. It proved to be a fundamental business lesson, one that Bogle tells young people constantly during speeches: "Get a mentor!"

I asked Bogle what he learned from that key mentor early in his career.

"Number one, he was—you're not going to believe this—a good human being," Bogle said. "He had good values. He had integrity. He was straightforward. He was good-humored. He was just a good person to be around, okay? Is that a credential? I think you're damned right it is. Second, he was in a lot of ways a Renaissance man. His training was as an accountant, but he was interested also in the investment side of the business. He started the Wellington Fund in 1928, when he would have been thirty years old. And so he knew the accounting side, he knew the investment side, he was pretty good on the marketing side—there was no question back in those days of having a lot of funds. He believed in the Balance Fund: that was a conservative fund. And it's still around, and doing quite nicely. It had some bad times in the sixties, but it's still pretty much run the way he ran it.

"He was also—and I always admired this but never emulated it—a much better-rounded person than I am," Bogle continued. "He liked hunting and fishing, and he'd go off to a place he had up in the Poconos. It was a different age, to be sure."

He laughed as he recalled his response to a question he'd recently been asked, after delivering a speech at Baylor University. "This young couple—graduate students—had just gotten married, and they said, 'How have you handled the work-life balance?' And I said, 'Badly.'

"Mr. Morgan was focused on business at the time he had to be focused on business. But he was not a relaxed kind of person. He was smart; he had a sense of integrity; he was a perfectionist—I probably learned a little bit about that from him. But we were very different people."

Morgan was tough on his young employee at times, "which was good," Bogle said. "But I found out later—his secretary told me—that he looked at me as the son he never had. Well, that's pretty nice. That's a mentor plus, plus, plus."

More than as a son, Morgan also looked to Bogle as a successor.

"Maybe I'm just not very sensitive to that kind of thing, but to me it wasn't particularly obvious," Bogle said. "Although in a very small company like Wellington, with quite a few clerical people, probably only fifteen people in the office were college graduates, everyone sort of knew that I would be the heir apparent. And at one point, he thought maybe I would be too young to run the company. It became apparent I was going to do that, earlier than I knew. He trusted others, another important quality. He liked the limelight okay, but didn't particularly seek it.

"He'd brought me along quite quickly, and when things started to get a little shaky in 1965, he told me to run the firm and do whatever it takes to get it fixed. And I was, at that point, a ripe old thirty-six, overconfident, terribly naive. Not with the experience or wisdom that one would really need for that kind of a job. But I always thought I could handle it. My little ego thing ticking away down there."

LEARNING FROM MISTAKES

Bogle was subsequently fired from Wellington, a form of shock therapy that he took well. He would later write of the firing with typical erudition and humor:

> At that time, the Company was lagging its peers, and he told me to "do whatever it takes" to solve our problems. Young and headstrong . . . I put together a merger with a high flying group of four "whiz kids" who had achieved an extraordinary record of investment performance over the preceding six years. (Such an

*approach—believing that past fund performance has the power
to predict future performance—is, of course, antithetical to everything I believe today. It was a great lesson!) Together, we five
whiz kids whizzed high for a few years. And then we whizzed
low. The speculative fever in the stock market during the "Go-
Go Era" of the mid-1960s "went-went." Just like the recent
"new economy" bubble, it burst, and was followed by a 50%
market decline in 1973–1974. The once happy band of partners
had a falling out, and in January 1974, I was deposed as the
head of what I had considered my company.**

To this day, Bogle considers the merger his "biggest mistake"
in business. But the "great thing about that mistake, which was
shameful and inexcusable and a reflection of immaturity and confidence beyond what the facts justified, was that I learned a lot."
Indeed, the firing from Wellington would, he maintains, prove
a blessing, as he set out to start his own company, the Vanguard
Group, taking the best of what he'd learned from Wellington and
from his mentor.

Bogle became a hero to many investors upon his launching of
the Vanguard 500 Index Fund. For the uninitiated, index funds
track segments of the market like the Standard & Poor's 500, and
thereby aim to match their performance. They are a low-cost al-
ternative to actively managed funds that seek to beat the market.

Much of the success of Vanguard is attributable to the simplicity
and common sense of indexing as an investment concept. Indexing provides investors with the means to gain exposure to a whole
market—or "index"—at minimal cost. The challenge for investors,
therefore, is to keep those costs as low as possible while being di-
versified throughout a market.

Bogle is famous for arguing, in numerous media appearances

---

* John C. Bogle, "The Vanguard Story: 'Luck, Leadership, and Strategy'" (Executive
Lecture Series, Stern School of Business, New York University, October 19, 2000).

and op-eds, for the superiority of index funds over traditional actively managed mutual funds. He believes that it is "foolish" for the average investor to attempt to pick actively managed mutual funds and expect their performance to beat a well-run index fund over a long period of time.

Perhaps surprisingly for a man who is often described as a visionary, Bogle claims he is not much of an innate leader.

"We've got a young man here [at Vanguard] going to Wharton by the name of Pat Burke," he said with a chuckle. "Called me up one day and said he's had to write a paper on leadership and he wanted to talk to me. I said, 'I don't know, Pat—but sure, I'll talk to you.' He comes into the office. I said, 'Pat, the first thing you have to understand is I am not a *natural* leader. I'm not the hail-fellow-well-met. I'm not the charismatic guy. I'm a determined, introverted kind of soul, who probably is a terrible subject for a paper on leadership. Please understand: I'm not a natural leader.'

"Out comes this paper and it's titled 'John C. Bogle—Natural Leader,'" he noted with a shake of his head.

In our conversation, Bogle said that if he is to be described as a leader, it should be as one who has been compassionate and empathetic to both his employees and his clients. "It's a human side of leadership that I'm not sure a lot of so-called leaders have, and that is an ability to identify personally, as far as it's possible, with the people who are doing all the company's hard work. The people working long hours, who are committed and believe in the mission."

He drew a distinction between the sort of CEO who dropped in, like an elite Airborne Ranger, to rescue or remold an existing corporate structure and his own experience of "building a company out of nowhere. Now, very seldom do you get the opportunity to do that. Someone comes in to run General Electric, and everything is in place there. It's a very, very different kind of job, and requires very different kinds of characteristics.

"Leadership has a lot to do with not thinking about yourself as a leader. Not thinking about yourself is important. *Suppress* the arrogance."

Bogle cited the following "wonderful quote" from Benjamin Franklin: "In reality, there is perhaps no one of our natural passions so hard to subdue as pride. Disguise it, struggle with it, stifle it, mortify it as much as you please, it is still alive, and will every now and then peep out and show itself."

It's necessary for business leaders to do "all that stomping and stamping to make sure that everybody realizes that there aren't *two* classes of people in the company," he said. "I've always been much more comfortable, to be quite honest with you, with the people who were doing all the hard work rather than the 'suits.' And here at Vanguard, they're *good* 'suits,'" he added. "It's important for people to know that somebody up there—if it's the founder of the company, so much the better—is working just as hard as you are for the same cause, and not thinking that he's a hell of a lot better than anybody else."

WALKING THE TALK

Bogle was not shy about singling out Jack Welch as the kind of corporate leader he does not hold in high regard. "I couldn't stand Jack Welch," he said. "I was speaking down at Duke a couple of years back, and Jack Welch had spoken there the week before. And I think there were probably a hundred and fifty young men and women in attendance. I said, 'Probably every businessman who comes down here says that the first requirement for a leader is integrity. And I'm going to guess actually that a hundred percent of the leaders who come and talk to you all say integrity is the most important thing. Now I have to tell you this: *Less* than a hundred percent of those leaders actually *demonstrate* integrity. I'll let you figure out how much less.'"

The veteran financial expert said that he doesn't think it's possible to lack integrity in one area of your life and have it in another. "You either have it or you don't." He added, "I'm a very demanding and a very tough critic, perhaps *too* tough a critic. I did a short interview with *Fortune* not too long ago and they said, 'Who in the financial field do you admire?'" Bogle named only former Federal Reserve chairman Paul Volcker, billionaire investor Warren Buffett, former SEC chairman William Donaldson, and John Whitehead, former chairman of the board of the Federal Reserve Bank of New York.

"That's a pretty short list," I said.

"That's a *very* short list," agreed Bogle.

CHARACTER COUNTS

We talked then about the importance of leaders setting high standards and creating a sense of mission.

"Well, I'm sure what you've found in your search is there's probably not a single pattern for leaders or CEOs," Bogle told me. "By the way, I don't like the 'CEO thing' too much. Don't quite understand why everybody has to call themselves the president *and* the CEO. It seems like a little bit of overkill.

"There are a lot of different routes to being a leader," Bogle said. He advises college graduation classes not to emulate any leader but instead to emulate characteristics that they like while remaining true to themselves. "Pick and choose, but don't try to be somebody you're not, for God's sake."

Bogle glanced around his office at the images from the Battle of the Nile, the framed editorials, and other mementos from his incredible Vanguard journey, which began almost by chance in a sun-splashed college reading room. He said that strength of character, hard work, and determination certainly played a role in his success, but there were other factors as well, including being prepared for serendipitous opportunities that arise.

"You have to have a *break*. I've known a lot of people, extremely able people, who've never gotten the break they deserve. That's so sad," he said. "And it happens a lot in life. You don't get a chance to live up to your potential. But what's far sadder—this is always my message to the young people—is the people who *do* get that rare break and aren't prepared. So be ready *all* the time, because that break, if you get it, you'd better be *ready* for it."

CONCERNED OPTIMISM

This belief that into each life come opportunities and that preparation is the key to acting upon them is certainly one I've shared. It is, I believe, one of the hallmarks of an optimist, and most great leaders I've known have been optimists to a large degree.

"Are you an optimist?" I asked Bogle.

"Yeah, I am an optimist," he said without hesitation. "Sometimes, in these days, I'm kind of pushed."

Bogle noted that as a student of history he has seen, and written about, comparisons between the Roman Empire and the United States. "It's obviously true: no empire has ever lasted forever," he said. "And so I'm worried—worried about our country. Very worried. And I see very little in the press every day that gives me very much encouragement."

Yet he does draw "staggering encouragement" from the fact that many young people coming out of college today "are so totally remarkable, more than I can remember in my generation. Of course, this is very selective and anecdotal. If somebody showed it to me in a survey, I wouldn't believe it. But at least the kids I've been associated with are pretty darned good and have much more brains than my generation of college graduates did. They have much more interest in community values than in being self-serving, infinitely more global reach. I mean, they're all over the world. And you see it in a lot of projects."

He named as a favorite example Wendy Kopp, who founded Teach For America while still a student at his alma mater. "They had our Princeton theses together in a little exhibit a couple of years ago because I think they were the only two Princeton theses that did one of two things: one, created a business; or two, were published as books," he said.

LEADERS BUILD BRIDGES

In Bogle's view, Kopp represents an impressive generation of young people with "this global grasp, this willingness to go all over the world, this concern about our society and our community, and this extraordinary energy and intelligence."

Bogle's optimism about today's young people and their future is great, but he is concerned about our nation's "absolutely appalling" and increasingly polarized political system, he said.

"If you want to get into that, I happen to be a Republican, but I voted for Obama. I'm a Teddy Roosevelt Republican; I think they're pretty much gone now. But I voted for Obama. And while there was a lot of bitching about him—I think in some cases justified—I look around and I don't see anybody else I can imagine being in the White House than Barack Obama.

"And so I have a mind that, at least for a Republican, is open. I see the bickering, the party-line-ism, the lobbying, and the power of money. And our political system . . ." Bogle shook his head sadly. "'We the People'—isn't that there in our Constitution? 'In order to form a more perfect union'?"

In recent years, Bogle has stepped forward as a business leader calling for reforms of campaign finance laws that allow corporations to make huge contributions to political campaigns. "I'm using whatever it is that I have—platform, bully pulpit, call it what you will—mainly to reform the financial system," he said. "I was really troubled when the Supreme Court came down with this idiotic decision in that Citizens United case, which allowed corporations to give, basically, all they want to political campaigns. I mean, it turns over years of precedent; it's insane, because big corporations have so much money it's a rounding error for them. They don't even know where it's going."

Bogle went so far as to write an editorial for *Bloomberg Businessweek* about his concerns over corporate campaign contributions. "I argued that this terrible problem would be mitigated by disclosure, and now, of course, we know that the disclosure has been pretty much eliminated with all these foundations that can do this and that."

He also made the recommendation that investors—particularly those large institutional investors who own 70 percent of all the stock in America and virtually control corporate America—should band together "and for all the companies in our portfolios, put in a proposal in each company's proxy resolving that 'This corporation shall make no political contributions without the approval of seventy-five percent of its shareholders.'"

Bogle's modest proposal went over like "the biggest of lead balloons," he admitted. "It was the approximate equivalent of the *Hindenburg,* which blew up when I was living at my grandparents' farm in Lakewood, New Jersey, so I remember the crash in 1937. Nobody paid any attention to [my proposal], nobody in the industry—nothing. But I haven't given up. I'm trying to figure out other ways to do it."

The biggest problem, Bogle told me, is that "there's no money in being an activist investor. You'll be alienating the corporations whose money you're running. A huge conflict of interest—always denied, but still always there. And so that's the closest I've come to activism on the political side, other than writing about it generally in my books. I have not been a very political person. I don't usually make many political contributions. I just don't like the system. And it seems to me the system has got to be fixed, but it's going to take a lot of work to fix it."

SERVING THE GREATER GOOD

In that vein, I asked this leader with a social conscience what he thinks of the relationship between the financial industry—his industry—and the regulators.

"I don't think there's that much coziness between the regulators and the financial industry. It's the elected representatives and the financial industry—that's where the relationship is too cozy. Far too cozy," he replied. "No, I think the SEC has done a pretty good job of being independent. I think the Federal Reserve has done a very good job, in spite of those Goldman Sachs–isms, of being independent. I don't think the Commodity Futures Trading Commission, CFTC—where all the derivatives, eventually, are going to go—has done a good job at all. But the new guy, [CFTC chairman] Gary Gensler, seems like he's a pretty serious regulator. No, again, I think the real problem is with the politicians."

Yet, I noted, so many people from the financial industry end up moving back and forth between their corporate jobs and the government agencies that regulate them. I asked Bogle if he thought there's too much of a revolving door between the financial industry and political appointments. "You mentioned, for example, the number of major people who were at Goldman Sachs in government now," I said.

"That's a hard question for me to answer, because these guys at Goldman are really damned smart," Bogle replied. "They are unusually smart, and of course, Goldman makes so much money they can afford to hire the smartest people in the world. That's one thing that does trouble me about our system."

The rewards of the financial world have become so much greater than in other fields that "many of our best and brightest—when they go into engineering in college in these days—instead of going into mechanical engineering or electrical engineering or aeronautical engineering or civil engineering, they are going into financial engineering," Bogle said. "And that's a tragedy for the country because financial engineering subtracts value from society, and 'real engineering' adds value to society. To have our best and brightest—so many of them going into that—that's very depressing."

The rewards are almost so disproportionate in finance that it's hard to know quite what to do about it, Bogle said. "You can't tell Wall Street not to pay them so much. What you have to do is get, finally, a much wiser investment community."

He also lamented the fact that there is far more salesmanship than stewardship in his own field, the mutual fund industry. "It's become a giant consumer products market in business. Most funds that operate that way are not going to be concerned about corporate governance. My idea is to have a federal standard statute of fiduciary duty that requires you to put the interests of your clients first—not the interests of your money managers first."

I asked him why more investment companies don't do just that.

"We institutional owners have been backed away from governance, partly because we're traders," he said. "In a rent-a-stock industry, you're not going to get the participation in governance that you'd get in an own-a-stock industry. Pretty obvious, just like a home. The renters don't care. As [former U.S. Treasury secretary] Larry Summers is reputed to have said: 'No one has ever had a rental car washed.'"

CRISIS OF LEADERSHIP

Since he has long been a respected leader in the financial world, I also asked Bogle what he thought the recent recession and financial meltdown said about the nation's business and government leaders. He smiled wryly at that question.

"I'll observe parenthetically that only in America can you appoint a congressional commission to look into the causes of the financial collapse and find out the causes and pass a law to deal with them six months *before* the commission makes its report," he said. "I don't think we have a very good law. But the commission, basically, says pretty much exactly what I've been writing: that there are *multiple* causes.

"I don't go with those who say it's all the fault of the mortgage agencies. It's not all the mortgage agencies. And it's not all the Federal Reserve, because the Federal Reserve could have and should have disciplined banks from issuing these kinds of mortgages, but they had no authority over the IndyMacs and Countrywides. If you'd taken a stroll, spent a day with one of the Countrywide salesmen trying to sell homes and seeing the kind of person they were trying to sell $300,000 and $400,000 homes to were working out in the grapevines in Southern California making $20,000 a year—if that—you could tell trouble was coming."

Bogle said that anyone paying attention to housing prices could have seen the bubble was about to burst, because homes were being priced way above their inherent value. "I was not smart enough to see it, because I didn't pay that much attention to it," he acknowledged. "And Warren Buffett says he didn't pay any attention to it either. But anyone who focused on it—and there were a lot of people who should have focused on it—should have done something about that."

The regulatory agencies did play a role in the collapse, Bogle said. "They had the authority over broker-dealers. They could have told them that thirty-to-one leverage is too much. But all these things have a genesis. You've heard the expression 'Victory has a thousand fathers, but defeat is an orphan.' But I think, in this case, defeat has a thousand fathers."

Bogle said that if he'd been in charge of the SEC, he would have "brought back the Glass-Steagall Act," which had once prevented investment bankers from gambling with their depositors' money held in banks owned or created by investment firms. "Although I have no particular evidence to prove that that would have helped," he said. "All these investment banking firms used to be *privately* held. You had your own money on the line as an investment banker, and you had unlimited liability in a partnership. Would they be leveraged at thirty-to-one over a bunch of junk in the portfolio?"

I noted that Bogle had once written a guest editorial for the *Wall Street Journal* comparing Wall Street to a giant casino in which investment bankers were making bets with other people's money.

"Absolutely!" Bogle said. "Talking about Wall Street being a casino—of course it is. We're all there, every day, trading, just trying to outtrade somebody else. This creates no economic value; it *subtracts* economic value. And it's just exactly what goes on in the casino. Our money goes back and forth: it's indifferent to us. You may win; I may win. Then I may win and you may lose, whatever might happen. But the only guy guaranteed of winning is the guy in the middle—the croupier. And I use that expression a lot."

He then gestured to a framed copy of that *Wall Street Journal* editorial on his office wall.

LEADERSHIP FAILURES IN THE FINANCIAL CRISIS

Greed and highly paid leaders who really didn't understand the financial vehicles they were profiting from were major factors in the collapse, Bogle said.

"I mean [the disgraced Countrywide CEO] Angelo Mozilo's salesmen were making a lot of money by selling these things. All along this chain that I'll describe—I use this expression somewhat bastardized from Upton Sinclair: 'It's amazing how difficult it is for a man to understand something if he's paid a small fortune *not* to understand it.' And money corrupts. I guess you'd add absolute money corrupts absolutely.

"Mozilo owns the firm and he owns a lot of stock in the firm, and the more mortgages they sell in the short run, the more his earnings go up. Then he sells these mortgages to a bank, and there's another fee there—the bank pays for that, and then the underwriters pay the bank, and then the salesman who sells these things to the public. There's a whole chain of money going on there."

"All of them had a vested interest in the status quo," I noted.

"A vested interest in moving out the merchandise, from one level to another level to another level to another level," Bogle said. "Then you've got the corruption of the rating agencies. Imagine! It just doesn't take a genius—again, if you're paid a small fortune *not* to understand it. These rating agencies are paid by the people who want to be rated. So if I go to you—you're a rating agency—and I say, 'I'm a really nice guy and I will pay you three hundred, four hundred thousand dollars if you'll rate me AAA. . . .'"

"There was a whole series of perverse incentives at play," I said.

"Yes, there are all those perverse incentives, but it's a whole chain, and the Financial Crisis Inquiry Commission did get it right. It certainly has to do with greed in the abstract," Bogle said. "I think it has to do a lot with complexity. I don't think these bankers understood the instruments, the chief executives probably did not understand. I was struck by a comment from Bob Rubin, who is paid, I believe, seven and a half million dollars a year by Citi—some huge number—for being chairman of their executive committee. And *he* had never heard the phrase 'specialized investment vehicle.'

"It's a money market sold by a bank; you think it's a money

market fund and they put the investments in it—and these are risky investments—so the bank guarantees it," Bogle explained. "But that guarantee is not on the banks; it's not visible to someone who looks at the banks. It wasn't visible to Bob Rubin, the chairman of the executive committee. He didn't know, and they had twenty billion dollars' worth of these things—every one of which they finally had to make good on. They didn't lose, I'm sure, a hundred percent of every one, but they probably lost ten or fifteen percent on every one."

BAD ACCOUNTING PRACTICES

Bogle also cited overly lenient accounting practices in corporate America as a factor in the collapse of the financial system.

"I don't like the accountants in all this," he said. "Admittedly, so-called generally accepted accounting principles—GAAP—are lenient enough to drive a truck through. But I think that the accountants have done a very bad job. And one of my favorite themes is [that] they allow corporations to manage their earnings by changing—raising—the assumptions of what they will earn on their pension plan. And corporations are now using eight percent, and the state and local governments are now using eight percent. Eight percent isn't going to happen. The government bond is yielding four percent—four and a quarter, maybe. And the ten-year bond is yielding probably a little under three and a half."

"Their assumptions are unrealistic," I observed.

"If stocks are going to sell at fifty times earnings, they're all going to get their eight percent, but they'd better be quick, because stocks can't sell at fifty times earnings for more than about twenty minutes before someone will figure it out," said Bogle.

DISCLOSURE DYSFUNCTION

Lax financial disclosure rules within corporate America were yet another factor cited by Bogle.

"The corporations used to say—think about this for a minute—'Our estimates of future returns in the pension plan are based on historical norms.' Well, wait a minute. That means the more the market goes up, the higher the past return on stocks was, which means the lower it will be in the future. 'Based on historic norms' is the wrong, unequivocally the wrong, thing to do. Why couldn't corporations figure that out?" he asked.

"The scary thing is that our nation's leadership has not stepped up. We could face another financial crisis, because nothing has changed," I said.

"Of course we could," Bogle said. "Well, *some* things have changed. One sort of vaguely redeeming hope is that people will learn from experience."

"But have we—as a nation—learned this lesson the hard way?" I asked.

"The investment banks are going to have to reduce that leverage. They're going to want to reduce that leverage. Businessmen don't want to be wiped out," Bogle said. "They made some modest changes in compensation—not nearly enough, in my opinion."

INSANE EXECUTIVE COMPENSATION MATHEMATICS

Bogle noted that the existing corporate compensation system "is another example of how we're captured by *insane* mathematics. I mean, it's so obvious. I should say, parenthetically, that I was in a public forum—at the Investment Company Institute—in a question-and-answer period, and one of the speakers, a wise guy, says, 'The only thing that poor ol' Bogle has going for him is an uncanny ability to recognize the *obvious*.' He was trying to insult me. But I take it as the greatest compliment I've ever gotten."

"Nobody else seemed to recognize the obvious in this case," I said.

"And the obvious, by definition, is something *anybody* can recognize. That makes it kind of a paradoxical thing," Bogle said. "But I loved that statement. Here's another obvious fact: You compare yourselves in corporate America with a peer group. And say there are twenty of your peers in that group. There are five CEOs in the top quartile, and five in the second, and five in the third, and five in the fourth. That's the mathematics. If you're in the third— and God forbid if you're in the fourth . . . But guess what? *Somebody* falls into the fourth quartile, right? There's no way around it. You can only have five in that second quartile, so somebody drops down there. So you get this ratcheting effect, and every year it goes up and up and up and up. And it's inevitable.

"Warren Buffett says the names of these consulting firms should be Ratchet, Ratchet & Bingo!" Bogle continued. "Warren's got a great gift for words, by the way—certainly the best in the business."

Restlessness in the Ranks

I asked Bogle what effect it has on companies and their employees when executive compensation is so out of whack with the average worker's salary compared with just twenty years ago.

"First, to state the obvious, there must be a little restlessness down there among the people sailing the great ship when the captain gets paid all that money," Bogle told me. "Rebelliousness, maybe. And it's a very unhealthy environment for a company. Long-term leaders realize that the huge income inequality in our nation is bad for our society, our corporations, and investors.

"And nobody can put cause and effect on there," Bogle added.

"I think we have to use our intuition. But it would be very, very difficult not to accept that there's a lot of restlessness in the ranks. Everything seemed to function fine when the CEOs were making twenty or twenty-five or thirty-five times as much as the average employee."

But in 2010, chief executives at some of the nation's largest companies earned an average of $11.4 million in total pay, which is 343 times the pay of the typical American worker, according to the AFL-CIO.

Somehow, the executive compensation system ran off the rails. Bogle said that data kept by Morgan Stanley showed that since the 1980s most CEOs had expected their earnings growth to be *11 percent* a year on average.

"Corporate America grows at the same rate as America grows. So if America grows in GDP at three percent a year, then throw in three percent inflation, which is about what we had in that period—that's *six* percent. How the hell is the average corporation going to get eleven? They're not! And if you look at the numbers, they in fact did get six. But they're very bad forecasters."

Bogle described this disparity as "an insidious part of the system."

"Once you give out your earnings expectations, you will move heaven and earth to meet them," he said. "And if doing it the old-fashioned way—building market share—doesn't work, you will do some things that aren't good. I mean, you fire the R & D department, for example; or you merge, and a lot of mergers you see are done just to muddy the damned numbers, and then you go pro forma."

Individual companies can grow, of course, at 11 or 12 percent a year for a while, he said. "But if they think they're going to grow like Google or Apple, at twelve percent a year forever, that's just not the way the system works. And a lot of these companies that thought they could do that are now *gone*."

CHASING BONUSES

Bogle said that while the Internet boom has been good for consumers, it has been bad for business, with too many top executives acting in their own short-term self-interest rather than leading for the long term by finding innovative ways to increase efficiency, build bonds of trust with the workforce, and grow the business over time. "Business is doing things to keep its 'bottom line' up that probably won't work very well in the long run," he said. "It must be clear that the CEO wants to get earnings up to earn his own big bonus. [Earnings] come at the cost of firing—laying off, putting on part-time—a significant portion of the workforce. And I always wondered how you could fire twenty percent of your workforce and still do business. Maybe you weren't operating very *efficiently* in the first place. But there's a direct conflict when you get rid of people to make more money yourself."

"It's a matter of focusing on the short term—the next quarter's results—to meet Wall Street analysts' expectations and targets, rather than focusing on the long-term health of the company," I said.

"Very much so," Bogle agreed. "And part of the problem is [that] you're going take some actions to do that. But another part of the problem is [that] you're going do some financial manipulation—raise your pension plan assumptions—and there are all kinds of other things you can do. And when you do a merger, you can put together what Arthur Levitt calls a 'cookie jar.' You pull together some reserves, so when you don't get your estimate, you take a little out of the ol' reserves and put them over there."

Bogle said it's much more difficult for corporate leaders to raise the intrinsic value of their company than to simply raise the price of their company's stock. Yet, in most cases, top executives are paid for raising stock prices rather than the value of their businesses.

"I built a business—or tried my best to build a business—with the help of a lot of other people. And it's *very* hard work," he said. "We don't have a stock out there—one of our great assets, great advantages in this dog-eat-dog game is that nobody even wants to compete with us. Get the stock price the hell out of there because it's too easy to manipulate. You have your quarterly earnings; and you meet them, of course, all the time."

General Electric was a classic example cited by Bogle. "Their stock was worth six hundred billion dollars at one point, and now it's worth, maybe, a hundred and sixty billion," he said. "But that was all Jack Welch's manipulation [of earnings at] GE Capital. Then it all falls apart; and they had to be rescued by Warren Buffett."

The pay of executives is based not on what competitors make, not on what peers make, but on performance. And what is performance? Bogle asked. "Well, it ain't the stock price. It's raising the intrinsic value of a corporation. Ultimately, in the long run—just to be very clear about this—the stock price always comes back to the corporation's intrinsic value. It can go up and down, but in the long run, all that matters is corporate performance."

LEADING INVESTORS ASTRAY

Too often, stockbrokers and financial advisers don't have their clients' best interests at heart. Instead, they are focused on their own welfare, Bogle said. "Most people in this business don't seem to really care. They're trying to sell you a certain fund or set of funds, and they have no idea—none—whether those funds will deliver the kind of returns that they have delivered in the past. They sell the public on the idea—and the public participates by believing past performance is prologue to the future. And it is not; it is unequivocally not. As a matter of fact, it's the reverse."

The stock market is "a giant *distraction* to the business of investing," the economist said. "It's stupid that we watch it like we do.

And it means nothing except for traders, because value is not *created,* it's *reduced,* as we now know, in the stock market." Instead, value is created by "all that corporate earning power, all those earnings, all those plants and equipment, all that investment capital, as well as all that human capital. So you build, you earn money, you reinvest some of the money in the business, and you pay out dividends. And in the long run, the data are crystal-clear on this: long-term value of corporations is the earnings yield—dividend yield—at which you buy in and the subsequent earnings growth. It's as simple as that.

"Valuation and value must be the same in the long run," he added. "Warren Buffett says that he likes Berkshire Hathaway shares to trade at around the intrinsic value of the firm. If they trade above the intrinsic value, it's good for sellers and bad for buyers. And if the shares are trading below intrinsic value, it's good for buyers and bad for sellers."

Bogle took a long pause, and grinned. "Trying to educate the world about these things is a little like beating one's head against the door," he said.

I asked if he sometimes feels like the lone voice crying in the wilderness.

"Yeah," he admitted, "but I actually like that. First of all, I have absolutely no doubt about the accuracy or validity of my ideas, because they're mathematically based. To quote Brandeis, 'The relentless rules of humble arithmetic—you can't escape them.' Brandeis was talking about some very different things in a very different area, but I like the phrase."

3

WILLIAM BRATTON

I think of myself as a transformational leader. But most importantly: a change agent. I always want to be in environments where I can create change.

AFTER NEWLY ELECTED MAYOR OF NEW YORK CITY RUDOLPH Giuliani named him the thirty-eighth commissioner of the New York Police Department in December 1993, William Bratton stepped into a maelstrom. The NYPD was by far the nation's largest, a sprawling, dysfunctional organization with a $2 billion budget and a workforce of nearly 35,000 police officers. Some experts deemed the NYPD unmanageable. There were turf wars over jurisdiction and funding; morale among the rank and file was at an all-time low. Police officers complained of being underpaid, and promotion seemed to bear little relationship to performance.

Since the 1960s, increasing violence and "quality of life" crimes had made the great city seem unlivable to many. The plague of murders and rapes and armed robberies made headlines, but it was the graffiti scrawlers, purse snatchers, subway muggers, belligerent panhandlers, and pushy "squeegee men" who made daily life a grind for many New Yorkers and visitors. Some social scientists concluded that after three decades of increasing crime, the NYPD had lost the battle for control of the city.

Bratton, a Boston native who rose to commissioner of its police department, also had served as chief of the NYPD's transit police. He did not lack for bravado. "We will fight for every house in this city," Bratton declared at the mayor's press conference announcing his appointment. "We will fight for every street. We will fight for every borough. And we will *win*."

It was, as Bratton later recalled, a cocksure proclamation, not unlike Babe Ruth pointing his bat at the bleachers indicating where his next home run would land. Crises, confrontations, and controversy would ensue. Yet, New York City would undergo a phenomenal turnaround during Bratton's brief tenure.

Bratton and his team transformed New York into one of the safest large cities in the nation. Felony crime fell 39 percent, murders, 50 percent, and theft, 35 percent between 1994 and 1996, according to a study in the *Harvard Business Review*. Gallup polls reported that public confidence in the NYPD jumped from 37 percent to 73 percent, even as internal surveys showed job satisfaction in the police department reaching an all-time high.* In a rare honor for a city police commissioner, Bratton was featured on the cover of *Time* in 1996 with the headline "Finally, We're Winning the War Against Crime."

The reduction in crime rates in New York City was sustained even after Bratton stepped down as commissioner because of a falling-out with Mayor Giuliani. While some more recent studies suggest that the effect of innovative policing strategies on crime reduction may have been overstated, experts said that the systemic changes Bratton enacted caused a fundamental shift in the department's culture and its strategic approach to fighting crime. How did he achieve so much reform in so little time?

---

* W. Chan Kim and Renee Mauborgne, "Tipping Point Leadership," *Harvard Business Review* 81 (April 2003).

As the NYPD's leader, he oversaw the development and deployment of CompStat, a system now employed in police departments worldwide. CompStat revolutionized policing by employing accurate, real-time intelligence, rapid deployment of resources, and relentless follow-up. Most police departments in large cities get trapped into being reactive, simply responding to crimes instead of preventing them. Bratton's was a more proactive approach that focused on stopping crimes before they happened.

Bratton, who later headed the Los Angeles Police Department, led fundamental changes in the way policing was conducted in two of the largest cities in the United States that are widely credited with reductions in crime, while simultaneously improving police relations with minority communities and minimizing police corruption and abuse.

A CHANGE AGENT

I met Bratton in New York City, where he is now working in the private sector as chairman of Kroll, the world's largest risk management, security, and private investigation company. Bratton was casually but smartly dressed in a blue button-down shirt with gray slacks. Though he's spent many years living in New York and Los Angeles, he still speaks with a distinctive Dorchester brogue from the working-class Boston neighborhood where he grew up. Neither his self-confidence nor his commanding presence appeared diminished since his police chief days.

Bratton told me that he regards himself as a *transformational* leader. "But most importantly: a change agent. I always want to be in environments where I can create change. I just don't want to be in a maintenance situation."

Bratton is of my generation, and like me, he grew up with parents determined to build better lives than they'd experienced during the Depression. His father worked two jobs, as a postal worker and in a chrome-plating shop, to support his family, while his mother stayed home to watch over Bratton and his sister, Pat. As Bratton talked about his parents, I felt an even stronger affinity for a man I'd long admired from a distance.

Massachusetts and Texas may be worlds apart, but our families had experienced similar deprivation. When I was in my thirties, my father let me read part of his diary from his high school years in the depths of the Depression. While still in school, my dad had morning and afternoon paper routes and was an usher in the movie theater. His father had a job but struggled to make ends meet, sometimes borrowing money from his son to make it through the week.

My father learned to eat on twenty-five cents a day while in college. He would go to the local diner, order a bowl of chili, and keep adding saltine crackers and ketchup to make it more of a meal. Our parents' stories from the Depression era illustrated for me and for Bill Bratton that nothing in life should be taken for granted, and that there is no substitute for the willingness to work hard.

Bratton was drawn to police work in part because of the television shows, movies, and books he read as a boy. Most were about law enforcement. He enjoyed *Dragnet* and *Naked City* on television, and his favorite books were a 1950s children's picture book titled *New York Police* and the novel *The Commissioner,* which was made into a movie called *Madigan,* with Henry Fonda playing the commissioner and Richard Widmark playing a first-grade detective.

These books and television dramas, Bratton stressed, were instrumental in shaping his desire to go into law enforcement. "The very idea of being a police officer was the excitement of it, and the ability to do good," he said. "At that time, you could make a pretty good blue-collar living. When I went on the Boston Police Department in 1970, I was making a hundred and fifty-seven dollars a week, whereas when I left my job at the phone company, I was making a hundred and forty dollars a week. That seventeen-dollar-a-week raise added to the excitement of becoming a police officer. Seventeen bucks back in those days was basically a tank of gas for the week and a night out. . . ."

NATURAL-BORN LEADER

Unlike many of those I interviewed for this book, Bratton made no bones about his ambitions to be a leader or about seeing himself in a leadership role for most of his life. "I would describe myself as a natural-born leader, if there is such a thing," he said. "Instinctively, I was always comfortable in the leadership role. As a Boy Scout, I was junior assistant senior patrol leader—how's that for a title?" he said, smiling broadly. "Throughout my youth and growing up, I was always exhibiting leadership traits, some of which I took from my father."

Others seemed to recognize those qualities in him. His sister nicknamed Bratton "Captain Billy Bones" because "I was skinny as a stick and I was always in charge."

Though Bratton didn't always apply himself academically, he says that even his grade school teachers singled him out as a potential leader. "I can remember in sixth grade, there was a parents' assembly with kids showing off different traits and skits and acts. And I was chosen to be the master of ceremonies. I was there in my Boy Scout uniform, and even at that age I remember being very comfortable onstage," he said.

Bratton had a natural ease with taking charge and being at the forefront in public gatherings. He compared press conferences and other public forums to "being in a batting cage with five batting balls being thrown at you. I like that challenge of *boom-boom-boom-boom*. That was kind of a turn-on for me, the idea of in the spontaneity of a press conference you never know where the questions were coming from. I liked honing that ability to dance with the questions."

Bratton's first law enforcement job was as a military policeman in the U.S. Army during the Vietnam War years. But his assignment was not an especially demanding or dangerous one. He was a military-police dog handler guarding an ammunition dump at a nuclear missile site in the Florida Everglades. He volunteered for military service specifically to get military-police training because he thought it would help him land a law enforcement job when his service was completed at the age of twenty-one, "but that wasn't the sort of police work I had in mind."

Shortly after his discharge from the military, Bratton took the police academy entrance exam in Boston, and one of the training sergeants quickly marked him for a leader, saying, "That kid's going to be a police commissioner someday." Bratton had yet to complete his first week with the police department.

Still, Bratton quickly learned that the realities of law enforcement included "inefficiencies, corruption, brutality, and incompetency." He'd been assigned to one of the worst divisions, so he considered leaving the Boston Police Department and taking a job on a suburban police force. Before he could make a move, though, a reformer was named police commissioner. The new top cop, Robert DiGrazia, became a role model for Bratton.

"Six-foot-three, handsome Italian guy with an Afro, very full of himself. And they hated him in the Boston Police Department because he was a change agent," Bratton said. DiGrazia had a profound impact on the young Bratton. "When he came in, I saw how one person can make such a difference in such a short period of time. I was there during that period and took advantage of the opportunities he provided. They were creating rules and regulations and they were setting up all these committees where they were asking officers to participate, and the union was discouraging people from participating. Anyway, I went on ahead and joined the rules and regulations committee."

A Passion for Justice

Bratton told me that the corruption, brutality, and incompetence he'd seen offended his sense of what was right, and he welcomed the reforms brought by the new commissioner. "I had great pride in the profession, what it could be and what it meant to me in terms of when I put that badge on," he said. "I still have my first police patrolman's badge. I still have the memory of the first time I put that badge on. When I put the badges on all of the cops in Boston and New York, I told them, 'Never casually put that badge on. When you take it out, take a look at it and remind yourself of what that badge means to you before you put it on your chest.'"

Bratton is obviously a passionate leader whose heart is in his work. His motto in the 1990s became Cops Count, Police Matter. The message was meant to remind both his police officers and the public that the work done by law enforcement personnel is important. But he always let his police officers know that "we matter only if we do it constitutionally, compassionately, and consistently."

Bratton's attitude about his profession is similar to my attitude about the piloting profession. We also must take our great responsibilities seriously. The profession is important and deserves respect because what we do and how well we do it matters.

"In a democracy, the first obligation of government is public safety," Bratton said. "It's in the Constitution, in the Declaration of Independence. And in a democracy, police are empowered to control the behavior of others. That's agreed to by common consensus through our legislation. If you think of it, what a powerful role that is, and it should not be treated casually. And the opportunities I've been presented to lead that change, to participate in that change, to be mentored in creating that change, it's really shaped me in terms of what I think I've become."

BOLD MOVES

Bratton was inspired by Commissioner DiGrazia's bold methods for dealing with long-standing corruption within the Boston Police Department. "One Saturday morning, he transferred every detective sergeant in the city, which broke the back of corruption, because they were basically the bagmen for the captains and everybody else. He also understood that part of what he needed to do was create new leadership in the department. He was never going to be able to do it in a department where the average age of a police sergeant was fifty-five, and the average age of a patrolman, I think, was forty-three."

DiGrazia also brought in more educated outsiders, civilians, and the so-called whiz kids, while trying to modernize the department's communications, the markings on the cars, and the police academy training. "I was on the street with a gun and a badge after six weeks of training," Bratton recalled. "Incredible, when I think back on it now, that in 1970, within six weeks you've got twenty-three-year-old Billy Bratton out there, basically, protecting you. God help you! DiGrazia understood the importance of six months of training and also continuous training."

Bratton's role model also changed the way sergeants were selected. He pushed through new legislation that greatly minimized the role of seniority in advancement within the department, and he also built civil rights training into the process. In the sergeants' examination, Bratton again excelled, scoring number one overall.

He was twenty-seven, the youngest sergeant ever in the history of the Boston Police Department. The eight members in his group of new sergeants were enrolled in a special program at Boston University that had been prepared by Harvard's Mark H. Moore and other leading academic lights creating new approaches to law enforcement and public service. The class included instruction in policing but also in criminal law, human rights, and race relations, Bratton said.

Education was one of the tools used to bring change to the Boston Police Department, but there was also a major effort to "break the back of some of the old school," he said. That included transferring those old-school sergeants, but Bratton still had to deal with many others who outranked him and had been on the force much longer. He remembers that in his first roll call, it struck him that every officer there "had been on the Boston Police Department longer than I had been alive."

Bratton understood, as any leader must, that their respect had to be earned, and he didn't waste any time doing that. "I had the good fortune to be involved in a bank robbery hostage situation two weeks before I graduated from a hostage-negotiation training program," he explained. "I rescued the hostage and got the name Captain Billy Balls—you know, the guy that had balls of steel. Or 'cannonballs,' they also called it."

Then, on a Father's Day Sunday morning, Bratton found himself standing next to the reform-minded police commissioner as they faced off against thousands of antibusing demonstrators, including tough longshoremen, postal workers, and off-duty cops. "It ended up in a major riot in which I found myself standing in the front entrance to South Boston High School beside the police commissioner, basically fending off rocks and bottles that were being thrown at us by literally thousands of the men of South Boston," he said. "About a hundred Boston police officers were surrounded in this high school yard.

"As we're dodging the rocks and the bottles, DiGrazia said to me, 'I'm thinking about bringing some of you new young sergeants up to work in the police commissioner's office so you get a sense of what it's like up on the sixth floor. Would you be interested?' I said, 'Sure, Commissioner! I'd love that!'"

The activist police commissioner obviously had seen the potential in Bratton, but before he could become a mentor for the young officer, DiGrazia had to step down because of turmoil in his personal life. Fortunately for Bratton, DiGrazia's successor, Joseph

Jordan, adopted many of his predecessor's "whiz kids," including Bratton, who was assigned to work for the civilians who served as chief of administration and chief of operations.

"The chief of operations in the Boston Police Department was a fellow named Bob Wasserman," Bratton said. "He's probably one of the smartest and most influential people in American policing who nobody's ever heard of. He's always been behind the scenes. And so many of my ideas of policing were instilled in me by Bob Wasserman, by the things he exposed me to."

At the first meeting with Wasserman, Bratton recalls, "he sits me down in his office. He's direct and gruff and he hands me a book, *Policing a Free Society,* by Herman Goldstein, who was one of the early-on thinkers and writers about American policing. So my education exposure to what policing could be was continuing."

Bratton began to see himself as a candidate for leadership, though even he didn't dream how high he would climb. He'd thought of maybe becoming chief of bureau field services one day, so he took the lieutenant's exam and finished second in his group. Wasserman then assigned him to create a neighborhood policing program, "which basically was the forerunner of community policing twenty years later." That assignment brought community exposure and even national media attention to Bratton, who discovered that not only was he comfortable being in the limelight but he enjoyed it.

TAKING RISKS

Bratton's dogged efforts and ambition didn't go unnoticed. After a major departmental reorganization, Bratton was named number two in rank within the police department. He still marvels at the speed of his ascent. "Within ten years of joining the department, I'm now the executive superintendent."

He was thirty-two years old, at least twenty years younger than the other nine superintendents. Bratton now allowed himself to dream of being police commissioner one day, if not in Boston, maybe in Los Angeles or New York City.

"I'd get knocked on my ass once in a while, but I'd use that as a learning experience and bounce back up again," he said. "And it's kind of like those little inflated dolls you'd punch and they'd bounce back. They'd always bounce up. I think that was me. I was always striving to get ahead. I really believed that I could make a difference in policing."

It wasn't long before the "Boston boy wonder" was recruited for a leadership role in the nation's largest police department. In 1990 he took a job leading New York City's Transit Police Department. He didn't like leaving his native Boston but wisely figured that if he made a name for himself as leader of the transit police, he might have a shot at becoming the NYPD's police commissioner. This was not a move without considerable risk. Until that time, the NYPD had always drawn on New Yorkers for its police commissioners.

"That's the other aspect about me: I've always been a risk taker," Bratton said. "I think it's a key element of leadership, that you have to be willing to take risk. The risk here was, I was on a pretty good career track in the Boston area, very well known. And I gave that up to go to New York with the idea of getting known in that city, but in a transit police, a very specialized police department. But who knows? I might have a chance in this off-Broadway production to get on Broadway as the police commissioner."

Bratton remained with the New York City Transit Police Department for a little less than two years, in part because his wife had remained in Boston and they were maintaining two homes. He returned to the BPD as superintendent in chief in 1991 and was appointed Boston police commissioner in 1993. Six months later, he returned to New York City when Mayor Giuliani recruited him for the job Bratton had long coveted, police commissioner of the NYPD.

Unlike many of the other leaders I interviewed for this book, the ambitious Bratton had carefully and astutely taken the long view early in life and set his sights on rising to the top in his field. "Here's this fulfillment of something that had begun in the fifties, in the book *The Commissioner* and the movie *Madigan,* and now here I am. What I felt very good about was that I had engineered it," he said. "And if you look at my career, so much of my life had been the idea of looking ahead, looking at the various avenues to get to a destination, all of them entailing risk, all of them requiring a certain degree of confidence, and in almost every instance, achieving it.

"So in '94, the NYPD gives me the opportunity to, in a sense, take all of these experiences and combine them in one place. It was like getting to the Super Bowl—that's how I describe it."

CRISIS MANAGEMENT

Bratton noted that, like me, he had trained his whole life to master his field of expertise, and a big part of his focus was on preparing himself for the worst that could happen so that if it did, he would instinctively know exactly what to do.

"Isn't that what you do, Sully?" he asked, aptly comparing a police commissioner's challenges to those my crew and I faced with Flight 1549. "You flew planes for twenty years, and whatever crises you might have had in those twenty years, you and few others knew about them. But then, basically, what are you trained for? It's when the shit hits the fan—excuse the expression—when a crisis arises."

"During my forty-two years of flying, I never knew on which two hundred eight seconds my entire career might be judged," I replied.

Bratton offered that the test of a leader is how a person in that role responds not when times are easy but in times of crisis. "When a crisis arises, you want somebody that's cool, level-headed, that basically does the right thing," he told me. "And you had that opportunity with great exposure [in landing on the Hudson River].

I've had that opportunity . . . to 'fly' into crises. But then . . . the nature of policing is you never quite know where the next crisis is coming from."

Though Bratton acknowledged that he was known and sometimes feared for his quick temper and for his ability to unnerve subordinates with "The Look," he prided himself on remaining calm, cool, and collected in times of crisis. "Al O'Leary, who was my director of communications at transit police, my press guy, he always liked to tell the story that you could tell how serious a crisis was by watching me after I'd received the news," Bratton said. "I'd get up and walk out to the coffee machine, which is in the outer office, and get a cup of coffee and come back in. And then I'd say, 'Okay, this is what we're going to do.' And Al O'Leary used to say that you could tell how serious a situation was by how long it took me to get the cup of coffee. More time to think about it, come back, and figure out a way to tackle it."

FINDING OPPORTUNITIES IN CRISES

One of Bratton's leadership tenets I've found to be true in my own experience is that within every crisis there lies opportunity, so every leader should welcome challenges as catalysts for positive change.

"I want to go into organizations in crisis because I'm a strong believer that crisis creates opportunity and also accelerates the pace of change," he said. "In the case of the NYPD, the two years I was here it seems to me that we had a crisis a day, if not multiple crises every day. It was, again, that batting cage analogy."

Bratton cited as a "perfect example" a crisis that unfolded on the night before he became NYPD police commissioner. As he stepped off the plane from Boston, he was informed that eight NYPD officers responding to a disturbance call at a mosque had been beaten and thrown out. The situation was all the more volatile because decades earlier an NYPD officer had been killed in a mosque under similar circumstances, and the racial and religious controversy that resulted had never been resolved.

In this case, the mosque attacks on police officers occurred just after a white mayor had been elected to replace a black mayor, so "you've got a very disenchanted African-American community," which included Black Muslims, "a group of people who really feel set upon by white society and cops in general," Bratton said. "And you have the media, you have the police department, you have the public in general, you have the black population watching the handling of this situation."

Where many might have seen impending chaos, Bratton saw multiple opportunities in this explosive situation. "I've got the opportunity to convince the new boss he made the right decision, the opportunity to convince the new organization that this guy's got a lot on the ball, the opportunity to show the media that this new person is going to be able to handle himself, the opportunity in a moment of crisis with a very hostile community to find ways to defuse the situation and to create a platform for rebuilding," he explained.

A key to seizing opportunities in times of crisis is being in control of the message, Bratton said, noting that while he's been accused of being a grandstander who never met a camera he didn't like, the truth is that he always tried to use the media to his advantage. "It's not so much the idea that I like to see myself on the evening news, but that's how in a public agency you get the word out to your rank and file, who watch the same newscast as the public," he said. "And you get editorial support. You get political fear, or political support, because they fear how strong you are."

I mentioned that after Flight 1549, even though I'd never been interviewed before, I had to very quickly rise to the occasion to be able to fulfill my new responsibilities as a public figure. This attention gave me a greater voice about important issues that I had cared about my entire professional life, especially aviation safety and the state of the piloting profession. While the media frenzy was overwhelming at first, it became the source of many opportunities to use it for good.

Bratton agreed, noting that being comfortable with the media became more and more important to him, especially as he came to abandon the traditional leadership philosophy of being guarded and secretive for a more open approach. "In addition to being a risk taker, I'm also very inclusive in a profession that's been known for its exclusivity, for its parochialism: 'We're the police. Leave us alone, we'll take care of it.' Or 'Top secret investigation, can't share any information,'" Bratton said. "I have increasingly become an advocate for inclusiveness. The more people in the tent, the better—the more ideas to share. It's only going to speed up the process that I'm most interested in—the process of change."

SITUATIONAL LEADERSHIP

Since I had been one of a group of pilots who had led culture change at our airline, I was curious to know how Bratton had brought about change in his career. He and I both agreed that there is nothing new under the sun. There are very few completely original ideas. Many innovations are the result of building on the work and ideas of others.

I'd read that CompStat was the brainchild of Jack Maple, that colorful derby-and-spats-wearing NYPD transit chief under Bratton. He agreed that Maple was one of the keys, along with chief of patrol Louis Anemone and himself.

The more proactive approach to law enforcement that he used opened up lines of communication and resulted in greater sharing of information and responsibilities between top police administrators and their local precinct commanders. It also used crime reporting and statistical tools to decrease response time and to implement follow-up that shifted the emphasis from crime reaction to crime prevention.

Bratton explained that in the 1980s, robberies comprised the majority of violent crime in the city's subways. Maple tracked the robberies by pinpointing them on several hundred maps on his wall. Maple referred to the maps as the "charts of the future." He used them to discern crime patterns and dispatched police officers accordingly. Maple noticed that when officers were placed at these locations, the robberies were being displaced to other areas of the subway. He dispatched officers in what he called a "rapid response," and robberies in the subway were greatly reduced.

CompStat allowed Bratton to bring all the precinct commanders together to discuss what was working and not working, creating more of a shared mission culture than one based on a quasi-military command-and-control environment. "Crime doesn't restrict itself to our geographic precinct boundaries. It ebbs and flows," Bratton explained. "The idea was to break down the silos and have all these seamless bridges. So you ended up having a seamless organization instead of one that was defined by its silos. That's top-heavy bureaucracy."

Bratton told me that CompStat can be used as a multifaceted tool "for leading organizational change. I'm a great believer in decentralization, in pushing power down to an appropriate level in an organization. And in that empowerment, encouraging others to take risks and to step up and to have opportunity. I'm very much into accountability: the idea that I'm going to give you some of my power, but I'm going to hold you accountable for how you use it."

Bratton said that different circumstances, different challenges, and different opportunities create the need for "situational leadership." He then outlined the core components of what he calls "The Christmas Tree Effect" or "The Christmas Tree of Leadership."

Leadership requires having well-defined core beliefs, but it is also very different from management, he said. "Leadership is much more about the idea of vision and the idea of getting others to embrace the vision, to expand upon it, to participate, to be included in its creation so they have ownership and then develop the goals.

This is the Christmas tree I talk about. You start with the most beautiful ornament at the top—the idea. And then you get a few others around you that basically share it. And then you move down the tree, and now you have goals. Okay, where do we want to go? How do we want to get there? Why do we want to get there?"

Next, you look at strategies, Bratton said, "and the strategy is where you start getting down into the middle management. In the case of the NYPD, for example, back in '94, Giuliani had a vision that I shared: the idea that cops can do something about crime, and by doing something about crime you can deal with fear, you can deal with disorder, and you can begin to make the city safe. If you make the city safe, then the things that Giuliani's certainly concerned with—more business, more tourists, more taxes—will result from that."

The mayor and his police commissioner outlined their approach, and then they recruited talented leaders to help them implement it. Bratton and I agreed that this is also the approach recommended by author and leadership expert Jim Collins, who wrote *Good to Great*. "Collins articulates this wonderful thing in the book that I use all the time," Bratton said. "When you're taking over an organization, you've got to get the right people on the bus, get the wrong people off the bus, and then get the right people into the right seats."

SHARING THE VISION, TRUSTING YOUR TEAM

Bratton said that when he became police commissioner of the NYPD he already had a vision of what he wanted to do to improve the city's law enforcement. "I knew where I wanted to go: I needed double-digit crime declines. I needed people who understood the importance of going after broken windows, the importance of dealing with the corruption issues in the NYPD, the importance of dealing with the exclusionary culture of the organization. And

I had like-minded people that I had gathered around me over the years—my consultants, if you will—the team. But I also needed insiders."

Following Collins's strategy of getting the right people on the bus, Bratton had his transition team assess every leader within the department by asking each of them what they would do if they were running the NYPD. Their responses provided Bratton with "a sense of the organization before I even got into it. That's also an important aspect of leadership. You don't need to have intimacy about all aspects of the entity that you're being asked to lead, but you have to have an understanding of it. The intimacies can reside with others that you surround yourself with, who can help to inform your decision making. But you really need to have a sense of the place."

Bratton's transition team identified six of the eight top administrators as people who needed to be taken off the bus because they did not share his vision for the future of the department. "Then we needed to replace them with new people and believers," he said. Once those team players were on board, Bratton invited them to identify others who shared their vision. "I'm a great believer in empowering," he said. "I am not a very autocratic leader. My style was to pick the right people, trust that they had the vision, they understood the goals, they had developed the strategies, then go to it. You pick the people to get the job done. There's a degree of trust involved there."

Bratton said that he tends to trust those around him until they prove themselves unworthy of trust, and he doesn't mind sharing power with those who remain trustworthy. "I'm very trusting in the people I select, and if you prove me wrong, I'll deal with you very effectively," he said. "But I'm very comfortable giving away power and letting people feel the joy of being able to make decisions."

Bratton recalled that when the Boston police commissioner entrusted him as a young sergeant to totally re-create a police district in Boston, "it really gave me my head start. I loved the idea that as a sergeant I could go and convince my deputy superintendent and my captain that this was the right thing to do. I am nothing if not the product of learned experiences and environments."

Delegating Authority

A leader who insists upon complete control and uniformity within every aspect of his organization might be challenged in a massive police department like the NYPD, which has seventy-five precincts in seventy-five neighborhoods that are themselves made up of diverse smaller neighborhoods, Bratton said.

"My mind is just not that good," he said, laughing. "I cannot, basically, manage all of that. But a lot of leaders are going to try to be monolithic and do the same thing everywhere. I don't think that works. Of course you have to have certain rules and regulations. You have to have certain standards. You can't tolerate corruption, for example. But you let the captains, to a degree, decide how they're going to do things."

Bratton's leadership style at the NYPD was to outline his goals, vision, and strategy and then to set priorities so that his captains knew what was expected of them. "Here's the eight things in New York City we want to focus on: guns, youth crime, drugs, auto theft, quality-of-life broken windows, police corruption, traffic, domestic violence," he said. "These are the eight things that, individually and collectively, are destroying the quality of life in New York. If, in your precinct, you have those eight things, here are developed strategies you can draw upon, but you're free to craft your own ideas to deal with it."

Bratton sought to empower his captains at the precinct level so that they felt free to be creative within their areas of responsibility. He was, in effect, leading them in a way that prepared them to be managers as well as leaders. "I think I'm a successful leader most of the time," he said. "But I think I'm also a very good manager.

And I think I'm a better leader because of my management skills. I'm also a better manager because of my leadership skills. The best combination you could possibly have is a person that's good at leadership and a person that's good at management. Then you've got the ideal world."

Leadership manifests itself in many ways, he added. "Once again, it's wholly situational. But you're not going to find anything new. What is new is how you effectively teach people to take all these prescriptions and, depending on their own personalities, try to apply leadership to their particular situation."

INTERNAL AFFAIRS

Since Bratton had been reflecting on his strengths and successes, I asked him to also talk about his more troubled moments: "What would you consider to have been your biggest failure?" I asked.

"You know, as early as 1980, I thought my career was over, and yet the best was still to come thirty more years after that. The Giuliani situation was certainly one where I thought, once again, the career was completely over. It was a circumstance of not managing up to the mayor, not managing my own staff, because my own staff was battling it out with his staff. There was a lot going on that I should have controlled better."

Bratton noted that he had rightfully earned the nickname "The Great Delegator," but some in the mayor's office mistakenly took that as a sign that they could assert themselves in police matters. "And because we're all very strong-willed people, very strong managers, there was a real resentment with their constantly compressing us," he said. "So, yes, there was pushback at all levels. And it resulted in my early departure. It also resulted in the early departure of a lot of other people. It took them years to recover professionally. We had a great thing going in the NYPD. We were a great team. We were accomplishing great things. But then the internal battles with the mayor and his people started, and we all ended up the losers, if you will, in that we were out of power, out of an environment that we loved, and one in which we were becoming very successful."

I asked Bratton if there was any point in his career when he was asked to do something that was just absolutely not in accordance with his values. Something that he felt was wrong or something that called for a difficult decision because of a conflict with his beliefs and values.

Bratton paused. Then he described a major battle with the mayor's staff over the size of the NYPD's public relations team, which numbered fifty people and was larger than the mayor's own. The primary target was the department's chief spokesman, deputy police commissioner John Miller, a former correspondent and anchor for ABC News, who pulled off a rare interview with Osama bin Laden in Afghanistan in 1998. He was an award-winning expert on international and domestic terrorism and organized crime, but he had drawn the wrath of some on the mayor's staff who felt he was working against their interests. "But they also wanted to decimate our public relations staff," Bratton recalled. "They immediately wanted to cut twenty-five or thirty people out of there, some of whom were symbolic, so our staff would be smaller than theirs."

Bratton saw this as an assault on his carefully formed team. "There were twenty-five innocent people who were going to be transferred out of functions where they were doing a good job, had worked hard to get into, and were now going to be sent off to less desirous assignments. And that was wrong," he said. "It was just plain wrong. And we came very close to resigning en masse around that situation."

Miller defused the situation by resigning. He later worked for the FBI and then for the federal Office of the Director of National Intelligence. "He sacrificed himself because he really did believe that if all of us left, that all the gains, the momentum, would all fall apart," Bratton said. "And it would have, because we were only a year into the process. A lot of the institutionalization, the changes we were making, occurred in the second year. So if we had all left at that time on a point of principle, the significant good that accrued to the city by our staying for that extra year would have been lost."

"So John Miller, effectively, fell on his sword to allow the rest of you to continue," I said. "If he had not resigned would you all have turned in your resignations instead?"

"We would have," Bratton said. "It was the issue of principle, and we'd all had enough. There'd been the death by the thousand cuts. But we all lived to fight for another year."

Bratton said that he regretted that early turmoil and tried to learn from his mistakes. "We were doing extraordinarily well on crime and motivation of personnel. But I did not feel that we were hitting on all twelve cylinders. And the two cylinders I was not hitting on ultimately ended up causing the car to break down and get us ejected."

The Core Values of an Effective Leader

The ability to self-assess and self-correct is essential for great leadership. I asked Bill Bratton what other values he had identified as important.

"Oftentimes you hear things about integrity and—well, if that's the case, where the hell did Hitler come from?" he said. "Values, I think, are important. But, once again, if you look at leaders, there are good leaders in the sense of good people and there are bad leaders in the sense that they may attract followers and be in command, but they're bad people."

Bratton said that those who lead positive change most likely have a combination of several values, including inquisitiveness.

"Do you mean that to be a leader you need to keep growing

and expanding your knowledge throughout your life?" I asked.

"I'm constantly seeking to learn," he agreed. "I'm on a journey. I think most leaders are always on a journey in which they never get to where they want to be. In my profession, I've had phenomenal success and opportunities, but do I think it's over? I hope not. I'm never where I want to be. But going back to your question about what makes a leader . . . they come in all shapes and sizes, don't they? And has anybody ever come up with the perfect definition of a *leader*?"

I pressed Bratton on this point, asking him to come up with a few attributes shared by the best leaders he's known. He paused to consider this, and for a moment all we could hear was the hum of midtown Manhattan traffic in the streets below his high-rise office.

"The qualities they have, I think, are creativity, situational capabilities—being able to lead in a wide variety of situations—and inspiration. For better or for worse, leaders are all about inspiration. You must excel in getting others to follow you."

One of Bratton's leadership role models is Ulysses S. Grant, the Civil War general who became president of the United States. Bratton admires him because of Grant's ability to deal with crises and handle adversity. "He was very misunderstood during his time," he said. "He wasn't fully appreciated until a hundred years later."

I recalled the famous words of the Civil War historian Shelby Foote, who said that Grant had what they called "four o'clock in the morning" courage: "You could wake him up at four o'clock in the morning and tell him they had just turned his right flank and he would be as cool as a cucumber," Foote said of Grant.

Bratton also found leadership qualities to admire in Mahatma Gandhi and the Reverend Martin Luther King Jr., who both led movements that changed the world. "As a leader, I often think of Gandhi's expression—I'm paraphrasing—to create change you must *become* the change," Bratton said. "If people believe that you really believe in what you're talking about, they'll be more responsive to you. And when you look at Gandhi or Martin Luther King, the movements they created [succeeded] because they believed in their cause."

Constant vigilance is another leadership trait Bratton cited. "There's another great aphorism: You can *expect* what you *inspect*. That's a Jack Maple saying—and that's what CompStat was all about," he noted. "It might take longer sometimes—might take shorter—but eventually, the idea is that it requires constant vigilance."

I added that in my experience, you consistently get only what you measure and reward in any organization.

Bratton then offered one leadership idea "that I really think encompasses it all. I attribute it to Admiral Bill Halsey," he said. "And I'm not sure if he's the actual creator of it or it's just used to reference him. There was a movie starring James Cagney where he played Bill Halsey during the Battle of Guadalcanal . . ."

"Sure," I said. "*The Gallant Hours.*"

Bratton chuckled. "*The Gallant Hours*. I've watched that movie a hundred times. I know exactly where I saw it for the first time, with my dad. And Robert Montgomery does the voice-over: 'There are no great men, only great challenges that ordinary men are forced by circumstances to meet.' I've used that line in every place I've ever been.

"In some respects, it's true: There are no great leaders. There are ordinary men who, in response to great challenges, end up exerting leadership. And sometimes, yes, that leadership is great."

4

LIEUTENANT COLONEL
TAMMY DUCKWORTH

The theme for me as a leader is that it's easy to make the big decisions—attack that hill, fight your way out of an ambush. The tough decisions are the day-to-day things that involve discipline, the things that are not popular, when no one's watching, when there's no glory involved.

WHEN LIEUTENANT COLONEL TAMMY DUCKWORTH WAS A YOUNG officer in the Illinois National Guard, her first command was of a helicopter unit in Chicago, where the winters are very cold. She wanted her pilots and crews to have something warm in the morning before they flew, but she worried that the caffeine in coffee would be a problem.

"I didn't want them to get the jitters, especially when we were doing very tight formation flying and executing precision maneuvers," she told me. "So I would always have hot cocoa out for them instead."

Her pilots and crews may have appreciated the warming drinks, but Duckworth, who was the only woman platoon leader in her unit, took flak from her male counterparts. "They started calling me the 'Mommy Platoon Leader.' I took that phrase in exactly the way that they meant it—as an insult. It was meant to be derogatory," she said. "So I stopped putting hot cocoa out there."

The teasing stopped, but Duckworth's decision left her platoon cold. "The readiness of my unit went down. My guys took longer to get warm. They weren't performing as well," she said. "I realized that I'd let my own ego get in the way of what was basically a commonsense decision. Just because I had a personal hang-up: I didn't want to be called the 'Mommy Platoon Leader.'"

Tammy Duckworth isn't the type of woman to back down from a fight. She was raised in a family with a proud military tradition. Her father served in World War II, Korea, and Vietnam, and his ancestors fought in every major American conflict since the Revolutionary War. She'd chosen to attend flight school because it offered one of the very few opportunities for women to engage in combat. It was no surprise, then, that Tammy decided to hell with what her critics among the other company commanders said. She went back to serving her pilots and crews hot chocolate because she cared about them.

Our lives are determined by the small decisions we make day in and day out, Duckworth said. They form the foundation for the person we become, how we feel about ourselves, and how others feel about us. "It's easy to say, 'Attack the enemy.' It's a lot harder for your ego to say, 'I don't care what people say about me. I'm going to make sure that I do this to take care of my guys so that we can execute the mission.'"

Back then, her platoon consisted of veteran helicopter pilots, nearly half of whom had flown in the Vietnam War, "which was very interesting to be a young, twenty-one- or twenty-two-year-old leading a bunch of combat veterans and trying to tell them what to do," she said.

I can identify with Duckworth's feelings of respect for those veterans. I trained as a military pilot under seasoned veteran combat pilots whose stories then and even today often give me pause to wonder how I would have responded in the situations they describe. Fortunately, I never saw combat during my military service, but I sometimes ask myself how I would have performed under such intense, life-and-death conditions.

A LIFE OF SERVICE

Duckworth was born in Bangkok, Thailand, to an American serviceman and his wife, who is of Chinese ancestry. Duckworth, who grew up speaking Thai and Indonesian, was raised in Hawaii, graduated from the University of Hawaii with a bachelor's in political science, and later picked up a master's degree in international affairs from George Washington University.

Even with her strong education, Duckworth said, she learned a great deal from the veterans she commanded in her youth. "Some of my first mentors were those Vietnam veterans, in how they conducted themselves. I learned the concept of 'walking the walk' and 'walking your talk,' and doing some of the tough things—the things that are maybe not fun to do but need to happen."

She also learned that it was possible to be a leader who put the needs of her troops ahead of her own ambitions and even her own instincts for self-preservation. "I learned that from the minute I took command of that platoon, and throughout my time in the military—to stand up for what I believe in even if it was at a personal expense, even if it meant sacrificing your own ego," Duckworth said. "I think a lot of times leaders fail when they let their egos get in the way."

Her early training for leadership in the military prepared her for high-level civilian positions later. "There are definitely born leaders," she said, "but I think that you can make a leader too. I don't know that I was a born leader, but I do know that if I had some leadership tendencies in me, they have certainly been enhanced and improved." She added that the military is not the only place where you can get leadership training, "but it's certainly a place where very young people get a lot of it, very early in their lives, and it molds them for the rest of their lives."

One of the many beneficial results of Duckworth's style of leadership is that the men and women under her command returned her care and concern in a big way. That became obvious to the world eight years after she'd taken her first command in Chicago.

While studying for her Ph.D. at Northern Illinois University in 2003, Duckworth was mobilized in Operation Iraqi Freedom. She went to Iraq as a captain in the Illinois National Guard's First Battalion, 106th Assault Helicopter Battalion. On November 12, 2004, she was copiloting a UH-60 Black Hawk helicopter with Chief Warrant Officer Dan Milberg and two others: crew chief Christopher Fierce and gunner Kurt Hanneman. They were flying in formation with another Black Hawk manned by Chief Warrant Officer Patrick Muenks and his crew.

The two military helicopters were about twenty minutes from their home base in Balad on a mission to move troops and equipment. After six hours of work they were headed for their last stop in Baghdad, flying fast and low around 4:30 P.M. As they passed over a dense date palm grove near the Tigris River, the two helicopters took small arms fire from a group of insurgents hiding in the grove. Then they saw a rocket-propelled grenade launched at them. It hit Duckworth's Black Hawk, creating a huge orange fireball.

"I'd flown the whole day," she recalled. "I was getting ready to take my pilot-in-command check ride. We had just done a hot refuel and we were taking off, and Dan said, 'Give me the controls, you stick pig, and let's get us home.' He was teasing me a little bit for hogging all the stick time. He wanted a turn to fly. And thank God for that, because when the blast hit we were ten feet above the trees, flying at a hundred and twenty knots."

Duckworth said that if she had been on the controls when the explosion blew her body forward, it would have pushed the helicopter down into the trees. "Dan pulled back and was able to keep us from going into the trees, and then I got on the controls to try to help, because I didn't know that Dan was okay." The cockpit was filled with smoke. Their number two engine—on Duckworth's side of the helicopter—was damaged, which made them fear a hydraulic failure. She did not realize at first that she'd been injured. "I did everything I could to help fly the aircraft," she said. "It was like every instructor pilot I'd ever had was with me for that one or two minutes that it took to get the aircraft on the ground."

Muenks and his crew in the other Black Hawk saw that Duckworth's helicopter had been hit and was in distress. There was a large hole in one side. The insurgents' rounds had knocked out her aircraft's electrical systems, so the two Black Hawks could not communicate, but Muenks realized that Duckworth and Milberg were landing, so he followed them down to initiate rescue and recovery.

Within seconds, the damaged helicopter had landed safely, but when Milberg checked on Duckworth, she did not respond. Her face was pressed against the instrument panel and covered in black soot and grime. Both legs were shredded beyond recognition, and one arm was barely attached.

Oil or hydraulic fluid was pouring into the helicopter cabin as Milberg shut down the engine. He then helped injured crew chief Christopher Fierce, whose leg was bleeding badly, out of the helicopter and dragged him to safety. While some of the crew stood guard in fear that the insurgents would come after them on the ground, the second Black Hawk landed and assisted those who were wounded in getting out of the damaged chopper and into theirs.

Milberg, who would earn the Distinguished Flying Cross for his actions on that day, next went for Duckworth, unbuckled her, and pulled her out of the burning Black Hawk, placing her next to Fierce in a field of tall vegetation. Duckworth was still unresponsive and covered in blood. They assumed she was dead. Fierce had a tourniquet on his injured leg, which had stopped the bleeding from a gaping wound just below his knee. The injured crew chief also had assumed Duckworth was dead, but then he noticed blood pooling on the ground around them. Since it wasn't his blood, he realized it must be Duckworth's.

"He was the first guy to realize that I may be alive even though they thought they had recovered a body, because somebody's heart was still pumping out blood, and it wasn't him because he had a tourniquet," Duckworth told me.

When the crew from the second Black Hawk came to carry Fierce to their helicopter, he told them, "You need to take care of *her.*" They then started first aid on Duckworth, probably saving her life, and continued it on a fast flight to an airstrip where a medical evacuation helicopter met them and flew the wounded to a military hospital in Baghdad.

Duckworth had regained consciousness by the time they carried her through the doors of the emergency room. "I was propped up on one arm. My legs were gone. My right arm was essentially severed, and so I had the one good limb, my left arm. I was talking to the medics and the doctors and the nurses, demanding a status update of my crew. They couldn't get me to respond to anything because all I kept saying was 'How're my men? How's my crew? How's my crew?'"

Meanwhile, her crew had similar concerns about her. "My door gunner, Kurt Hanneman, who had been shot, was refusing treatment until he knew I was taken care of, and all he kept saying was 'How's Captain Duckworth?' And 'Don't touch me, you've gotta take care of her.' And my crew chief was doing the same thing," Duckworth recalled.

Some of her crew had been with her just ten months, she told me, "but our commitment to each other, that commitment to making sure that the rest of your crew was okay, and that freedom, the relief I felt when I found out I had done my job as a pilot was critical to me. That unity of effort, I think, is what humbles me every day. It was the turning point for me," said Duckworth, who'd lost both legs and half the blood in her body.

"I could've lost both arms along with both legs and I would have been okay, knowing that I did my job," she said. "Even as I thought I was dying, I was thinking about my guys. And they were doing the same thing for me."

LIVING IN GRATITUDE

I interviewed many great leaders of all types for this book and I've known scores more over the years, but Lieutenant Colonel Duckworth stands out for her incredible dedication to serving others. Her selflessness is beyond inspiring, and it is easy to see why those she served with in Iraq were so dedicated to her.

She told me that her first few hours in the military hospital in Baghdad were "the depth of my despair" but not because she realized that she'd lost both legs, the use of one arm, and nearly her life. Instead, she was despondent because she thought she had crashed the damaged helicopter in her attempt to make an emergency landing. "I felt like I had failed as a leader, I had failed as a pilot, because there were guys in the back who'd needed me to be the pilot," she said. "My crew chief almost lost his leg. I felt that I had failed my men as a soldier, as a leader, as a crew member."

Only later did Duckworth learn that she had helped Milberg land the helicopter safely and that she'd passed out trying to shut down the engine. "That was incredibly important to me," she said. "Because, for me, I would have been okay dying knowing that I did my job and did what I had to do until my last breath."

Once her initial concerns about the safety of her crew were allayed, Duckworth had to focus on learning to live without legs and with a severely damaged arm. She might easily have become caught up in her own pain and frustration over her disabilities. Her loss might have made her angry and bitter. She could have given up or retired on disability, figuring she owed her country nothing more.

That was never an option, Duckworth assured me. This is a woman for whom gratitude and giving back are simply a way of life.

"I will tell you that since my injury, I spend my life trying to live up to what my crew did the day they saved me," she said. "Yep, I have to be worthy of this forever. For the rest of my life I have to be worthy of my pilot in command, Dan Milberg, and what he did to save me.

"There's not a morning that I don't get up and say a word of thanks for my guys for saving me when they could have left me behind," she added. "They thought I was dead, and yet they recovered my body. Not a day goes by where I don't set the standard of 'I'm never going to do anything that would dishonor their actions on that day.'"

Since the emergency landing on the Hudson, I have had to grapple with the *hero* word, and some have asked me who my heroes are, whom do I admire and respect. My answer has often been our nation's Medal of Honor recipients. I recently had the amazing opportunity to meet twenty-six of the living recipients of our nation's highest military honor for valor. As a student of history I knew some of their stories and some of their names, but meeting them exceeded even my expectations. To a man, they are the most humble, down-to-earth people you will ever meet. They will be the first to tell you that others have done more and greater things than they, but the others' actions either were not noticed or there were no surviving witnesses. They will also tell you that the easier part was the action that earned them the medal; the harder part, it turns out, has been trying every day since then to live up to what the medal represents.

WALKING THE TALK

Thanks to amazing advances in prosthetic limbs and to her own determination, Tammy is fully mobile today, but with or without artificial limbs, she is a woman who has always walked the walk and walked the talk. Less than two years after she lost her legs in service to her country, she was recruited by Illinois Democratic congressmen Dick Durbin and Rahm Emanuel to run for the U.S. House of Representatives from the sixth congressional district of Illinois.

Duckworth had become a well-known figure because of her outspoken criticism of the invasion of Iraq once she'd left active military service. She had used her platform to criticize decisions on military spending that left those in the armed forces poorly equipped and without adequate protection. She also became a strong advocate for greater benefits and better health care for veterans.

She lost her first political campaign by a mere 2 percent of the total vote. Still, her first run for public office attracted even more admiring attention from the Democratic Party in Illinois and the support of one of its leading young stars, Barack Obama, who first met Duckworth in a VA hospital visit during her recuperation.

When Obama decided to run for president of the United States, Duckworth worked for his election. She was invited to deliver an address to the 2008 Democratic National Convention in support of his nomination. After Obama entered the White House and Emanuel became his chief of staff, Duckworth was appointed assistant secretary of public and intergovernmental affairs for the U.S. Department of Veterans Affairs in 2009.

She resigned from that position in June 2011 and announced plans to run in 2012 for the redrawn eighth congressional district in Illinois. She continues to serve as a major in the Illinois Army National Guard, as does her husband and fellow Iraq veteran, Major Bryan W. Bowlsbey.

I asked Lieutenant Colonel Duckworth if her continuing public service is just part of who she is, given her family's history of military and government service. Her father was a member of the Greatest Generation, who served in World War II and believed in giving back to their country and their communities. They were quiet and humble men who led by example.

"My dad was a classic World War Two guy," she said. "He never spoke about his military service, ever. Only toward the end of his life would he talk to my husband, because my husband is also a military officer—and Dad talked to him about it only during football games. But he never talked to the family about it, and he certainly never said anything to me. When I joined ROTC, all my father ever said to me was 'So you think you can make it?' And then he showed up on my commissioning day with gold-plated second lieutenant's bars."

VALUES HANDED DOWN

Duckworth's father inspired her to always work hard and to be a leader in whatever she did, because she always wanted him to be proud of her. She doesn't recall him ever saying he was proud of her until he made a point of it just before he died. He also taught her that there were no barriers she could not overcome.

"Once I overheard him telling someone that 'Tammy is not the super-bright, straight-A student, but she does four to five hours of homework every night, and she's going to do great because she's willing to do the work,'" she noted. "He said that with pride. I was probably in the seventh grade at the time. And I always remember that. From him, I learned the importance of the work, the discipline, sticking with something even if it's not a lot of fun, and making it happen. Those are the values of that generation that just rolled up their sleeves and built this country."

They felt a sense of civic duty, of service above self, and a willingness to make sacrifices. I agreed with Duckworth on that. Our parents taught us so much about leadership, hard work, and serving our country just by their examples. I asked Duckworth if, like those in our parents' generation, she felt an obligation to serve.

"Definitely I felt an obligation to serve," she said. "From very early on, I knew I was going to be in public service in some way. I thought I was going to join the State Department and become a foreign service officer. But from a very early age, my dad taught us that it was our obligation as Americans to give something back."

Duckworth's father also gave his daughter a greater perspective on her life and the world around her by taking her on his trips around the world. "My dad, for a short time, worked for a United Nations refugee relief program. His job was to be an official bribe maker," she said. "He would accompany convoys of relief supplies from Bangkok all the way up to the refugee camps on the Thai-Lao border to all those Vietnamese refugee camps. His job along the way, through all of those different countries and at all these border crossings, was to pay out as little as possible in terms of the relief supplies and to get as much of that convoy up there as possible."

Duckworth was struck that so many of the children in the refugee camps "had faces just like mine, and they had nothing. They were selling themselves on the street just to survive, if that's what they had to do. I remember thinking how lucky I was that my status as an American was assured, and that I needed to do something in repayment for that. I don't think the majority of people who grow up in this nation and don't travel overseas have any idea of the privileges we have here and the importance it is for each and every one of us to do a little something."

That doesn't necessarily mean serving in the military, she said. "But everyone needs to do something; volunteer at the PTA, go cook in a soup kitchen once a month, whatever it is. Give something back."

STANDING UP

Despite her loyalty to the United States and its military, Lieutenant Colonel Duckworth quietly opposed the decision to invade Iraq after the September 11, 2001, terrorist attacks. She believed, as did many who opposed that war, that the terrorist groups that had attacked her country were not in Iraq but in Afghanistan and other areas of the world.

I asked Duckworth if her willingness later on to take a stand on that war and other issues, including veterans' rights, was related to her early experiences seeing other cultures and how they lived compared to those in the United States.

"I definitely think it's where it started," she said. "I also think that having been wounded has made me so much more fearless. I would never have gone into politics prior to being wounded. As a matter of fact, despite my personal opinion on the war in Iraq being wrong, I was proud as a military officer to maintain my neutrality and not speak up, and not provide a partisan viewpoint."

Yet being wounded made her feel fearless in speaking out for what she believes is truly important, she said. "I joke about this, but it's true: At the end of the day now, nobody's shooting at me. At the end of the day, I'm still here, and I have an obligation to try to make things better."

BUILDING A REPUTATION DAY BY DAY

I told Lieutenant Colonel Duckworth that I've come to believe that our reputations are built one interaction, one person, one day at a time, and at the end of our lives, we may look back and ask, "Did I make a difference?"

I recently returned to my alma mater, the U.S. Air Force Academy, where I received the Jabara Award for Airmanship. While there I was given a tour of the campus. Since the military places such an emphasis on protocol, I was accompanied by a group of high-ranking officers, generals and colonels. As this entourage surrounding me began to enter one of the academic buildings, a female officer, a major—which is one grade above the rank of captain that I attained in my six years of service—quickly stood aside to make room for the large group to pass. She stood with her back firmly against the wall as we walked by. As we passed her, I looked at her, nodded, and said, "Major." No one else in the group seemed to notice her or the interaction.

The next day I received a ride in a glider piloted by a cadet—something I had done forty years before. When we landed, one of the people who greeted us was the major from the day before. This time she was dressed in a military flight suit. She walked up to me as I was still strapped into the glider and said, "I'm the one you passed in the hallway yesterday."

"Yes, I remember," I said.

She then said, "I have witnessed four-star generals and secretaries of defense visit the academy, and what you did yesterday was one of the best personal examples of leadership I've ever seen."

I was surprised and somewhat saddened by her reaction, but I understood it. I said to her, "Thank you. In every encounter there is an opportunity. Pass it on."

In that brief moment, when I took the time and effort to do something no one else did, it made a difference, and all I had done was acknowledge her *existence*. It's also true, I believe, that no matter how hard we work over thousands of days to build a good reputation and do a good job and be a good leader, all it takes is one or two examples where we don't "walk the talk" to undo all of our good work.

Duckworth doesn't seem to have a problem in that area.

"The theme for me as a leader is that it's easy to make the big decisions—attack that hill, fight your way out of an ambush. The tough decisions are the day-to-day things that involve discipline, the things that are not popular, when no one's watching, when there's no glory involved," she said.

Her parents instilled in Duckworth a sense of responsibility that was reinforced in her early days as a platoon leader, she said.

"The earliest lessons I learned were in my helicopter units, even as a young platoon leader, when my guys were getting ready to go fly a mission," she said. "I had to sign off on the risk assessment. Their lives were my responsibility. That is where I learned the importance, the responsibility of leadership, because it's not abstract in aviation." If Duckworth didn't train her platoon well, if she didn't make certain each of them spent enough time in the simulator, or practicing emergency procedures, or staying sharp on their skills, "somebody could die on every single mission," she said.

Just as I learned a great deal of valuable information studying aviation accidents and their causes, Duckworth learned about the responsibilities of military leadership in analyzing what had gone wrong when soldiers under her command were injured or killed. "There is a tradition of doing after-action reports and seeing what was done wrong," Duckworth said. "You have your safety brief so that you learn from that incident—no matter how hard it is, because that was your buddy who was hurt. But you have to go through it. You have to have that discipline."

PROTECTING YOUR PEOPLE

Guarding the safety of those under her command has sometimes put Duckworth at odds with her superiors. She was an assistant operations officer in Iraq when an infantry unit asked her to send her helicopters to Abu Ghraib to pick up a prisoner who had been seized during a raid a few weeks earlier. The prisoner was to be released. Duckworth's soldiers were supposed to take him to the release point.

When she looked at the location, a bridge outside a village, she didn't like what she saw. "They were going to tell the villagers when the army Black Hawk helicopters were going to land on this bridge outside their village," she said. "I asked if they realized they were setting us up for an ambush."

When Duckworth, who was then a captain, asked the lieutenant colonel with the infantry unit if his soldiers had secured the area, she didn't like his answer. "Oh no, it's fine. They're a friendly village. And I don't have the forces to spare," he replied, according to Duckworth.

She told him her helicopters would not be flying into his "friendly" zone. He didn't like her answer either. "So then I've got our lieutenant colonel yelling at me, saying, 'You will do this!'"

"No, I am not going to do it," she replied. "And you're insane if you think that I'm going to do this."

Duckworth's commanding officer backed her, but they both lost to higher authority. She took some heat for defying a superior officer, but in the end she won, because more support was provided to prevent an ambush. "They beat up on me for a while, but we were able to make sure that there was a company of infantry that had to secure the area for a certain number of hours," she said. "We did the mission, and it was secure."

This was neither the first nor the last time Duckworth demonstrated that she was willing to take on her superiors if she thought her soldiers were being put in harm's way unnecessarily. "First, you do everything you can to mitigate the risk to your people," she said. "There was more than once that I've had to say no to a higher-ranking officer because he wanted me to fly in bad weather conditions. I've just had to say, 'Ah, sir, no.' I will fly if there is an American bleeding to death. I will personally fly that mission to go in there, and I will—if I have to—taxi my bird down roads in bad weather to get to an American who needs help. But I won't waste my guys' lives on something that could be better prepared. That's just stupid."

"How many times in your career has making the right choice, doing the right thing, come at a personal cost to you?" I asked Duckworth.

"I've never been punished for making a right choice. I've had things threatened that were never carried through in the end," she noted. "I probably gained in the long run because I developed a reputation as someone who would stand up for my guys. While I may not have been popular with some of the folks trying to get us to do things that were dumb, I'd gain a lot of respect and trust from the men that I commanded. They knew that I would take care of them. It's very paradoxical: because they trusted in me, I gained their willingness to do things that they probably wouldn't have done for anyone else."

THE TWO-WAY STREET

You can be a leader only if someone is willing to follow you. Loyalty and trust work both ways, and they are built over long periods. Duckworth, like most leaders, had to walk the talk every day to earn the respect of her soldiers. She pointed out that some leaders make the mistake of commanding respect instead of earning it. "I believe very strongly that loyalty goes both ways. Sometimes young leaders, or inexperienced leaders, try to command respect and loyalty. And people forget that you have to treat your subordinates well. It's that old saw: rank has its privileges, but rank also has its responsibilities."

The disabled veteran said that her loyalties are mission, country, and her soldiers. "You have to take care of your guys. Even in my job with the Veterans Administration, I told my staff all the time that they can expect me to be loyal to them. They can expect me to provide them with cover if they have to make a tough decision. That I will be there."

Stepping Up

Leaders who develop strong bonds of loyalty to their followers also feel the weight of responsibility that comes with their position. That sense of responsibility can lead to life-changing decisions, as Duckworth well knows. When she saw that soldiers were put in harm's way in Iraq because of bad political decisions, Duckworth was compelled to take a step she'd never dreamed of taking.

"One of the most difficult personal decisions I ever made was deciding to run for political office, because it ran counter to anything I'd ever wanted to do," she said. "I made that decision partially because I was mad. It was a buildup of things from me being the captain in Iraq and having to tell my guys who were driving five-thousand-gallon tankers of aviation fuel, 'Hey, go get in those tankers and drive down the road in Iraq, but I don't have any armor for you. I can't up-armor your vehicle.'

"I just got mad," she told me. "I got mad when I looked at how we were being sent into combat without all the equipment that we needed, and money was being wasted. I got mad when I was at Walter Reed because there were some politicians coming through and having their pictures taken with us. It was so bad that we patients at Walter Reed called it the 'amputee petting zoo.' You know, 'Come through and have your picture taken with us.'"

I felt as though she was saying that the wounded veterans would rather that the politicians not visit them and instead make sure our military had more and better protection in combat.

Still, other politicians challenged her to be the catalyst for the changes she sought. Illinois senator Dick Durbin, who had also opposed the invasion of Iraq, befriended Duckworth as she recuperated at Walter Reed and since then has served as her political mentor. He was among those who first urged Duckworth to run for elected office, by challenging her to use her anger and frustration to make a difference.

"So when Senator Durbin called, he said, 'Look, if you want to make a change, then you've got to ante up,'" she recalled. "'You need to run for office or do something, because there's not very many veterans—especially of your generation—who are serving in Congress right now. Frankly, the Congress needs the voice.'"

Duckworth and her husband still had to think long and hard about stepping onto the political stage in such partisan times, when many of her friends and supporters in the military were Republican. She drew fire especially for taking a stand against the invasion of Iraq, but today many of those critics congratulate her for taking a courageous stand. "Now, five years later, a lot of those same guys have come up to me and said, 'You know, you were right. We didn't belong in Iraq,'" she said. "But it took them a while to come to that. It was hard, leaving my comfort zone. I lost some friends I was really surprised to lose. But I just felt that it was important, because I was still going back to Walter Reed, and I was still seeing guys and gals who were hurt. It's war. You're going to get hurt. And I was okay with being hurt. But we were not adequately prepared."

I asked her what provided the tipping point, compelling her to run for Congress. "Was there one particular event, or was it an accumulation of things that finally pushed you over the top?" I asked.

"It was an accumulation of things. I found out that at the time there were no members of Congress who were Iraq and/or Afghanistan veterans."

I noted that relatively few high-level government officials have family members in the military. And it is the same for members of both political parties.

A MISSION TO SERVE

When Duckworth realized how few of the decision makers actually had a personal connection to those in the armed services who were dying and sacrificing, it pushed her over the edge, she said. From my point of view, you also have to admire a young woman who has lost both legs and the full use of an arm but says she reached her decision to run for national office after assessing the situation and deciding, "I am in the best shape of anybody among my peers to do this, and I have an opportunity, and I have an obligation to run."

Duckworth said she was not trying to be noble, "But there's definitely a part of me that was like, 'All right, somebody's got to do it. I guess it's you.'"

I found it interesting that Duckworth said she often uses her combat experience as a source of strength and clarification in making critical decisions like the one that led her to run for public office. "Do you feel like you got a second chance?" I asked her.

"Oh, yeah, every single day," she said. "Every single day I get up and think about the fact that I should have been dead in that field in Iraq."

Many of those who were on Flight 1549 have told me that it was a life-changing event for them. They too feel like they were given a second chance. Some have made important life changes and gone off in new directions. Others talk about trying to live more fully and to follow their own paths rather than meeting the expectations of others.

People who have survived major injuries, life-threatening illnesses, near-death experiences, or other major challenges often learn to look back and tap them as sources of strength and clarification for the rest of their lives. They find solace and courage in thinking, *I've gone through much worse and survived. This is nothing compared to what I've already been through.*

Duckworth said she has done much the same thing, using her survival of the insurgent attack on her Black Hawk as a reference point in making decisions and as a sort of driving force to keep her focused and moving forward on her "mission."

"It does let me take that big-picture approach to things," Duckworth said. "When I get to a point where I'm not sure of a decision that needs to be made, it very easily is a guidepost by which I can relate and I can make those decisions. Especially if there is some sort of—I don't want to say ethical decision—but a *tough* decision that I have to make, I can step back and say, 'Okay, people's lives are not on the line here. What is the right decision that needs to be made? What do we need to do to move forward?' It allows me a clearheadedness that I think I wouldn't have if I were constantly not seeing the forest for the trees."

Duckworth feels that she owes her life to the crew members who came to her aid after the helicopter was hit, and she has taken her gratitude and extended it to all who serve. "I think it's the mission that I have now—veterans. It's this mission to serve all the guys like my crew members," she said. "I go back to Walter Reed and I do peer visits as much as I can. Every time I go back, there are more guys and gals who are hurting, and I know there's more work to be done. In my job, I see it all the time, and that renews the commitment. I'm blessed to have the career that I have right now, and to be surrounded by folks who remind me all the time about the importance of what I'm allowed to do here."

WORKING ON THE INSIDE

Tammy Duckworth advocated change while working outside government, and then she moved inside, where she found that it was not as easy as she'd hoped to enact change. Once she became a top administrator in the Department of Veterans Affairs she had to adapt to being within the bureaucracy. So I asked her how successful she was in leading change while working within the federal government.

"It was tough because it is such a large bureaucracy," she admitted. But one of the fruits of her labors was the creation of an Office of Tribal Government Relations within the department. "The VA didn't have a formal relationship with the tribal governments, and yet Native Americans have the highest per capita population among veterans," she said. "Working on the homelessness issue was very rewarding too. I'm seeing those things happen, but it's taking probably twelve months longer than I thought it was going to take, or had hoped for. There's always more work to do." She noted that there are as many as seventy-five thousand homeless veterans living on the streets and in shelters across the United States.

I asked how she thought our country could do a better job of making sure all veterans get the medical and social care they've earned.

Duckworth said there were no quick solutions to such a deep social problem. "Frankly, if we wanted to, we have enough build-ings in the Veterans Administration that we could throw a bunch of beds in them and get seventy-five thousand people off the street," she said. "But that's not what it's about. It's about stopping that downward spiral, that lack of access to health care, so they can get the mental health counseling. It's about that lack of access to ad-equate jobs so that they can pay their rent and their mortgages. It's about the lack of access to the right type of education so they can get those right jobs."

The way to solve the crisis of homelessness among veterans is "to build up the capacity in the community, either within the VA or with the community partners, so that there is no wrong door," Duckworth said. "So that when a veteran comes for help, he or she is going to get it, and we stop that downward spiral."

LEADING THROUGH PERSUASION

Her powers of persuasion appear to be among Duckworth's many leadership skills, I told her. Then I asked, "When you've run up against budget issues, which are terribly difficult right now, how do you convince people to do things that might not be in their best short-term interest, whether it's in Congress or within a govern-ment agency or department?"

The art of compromise is critical, she said. "It's about trying to figure out what that other entity needs, and then how can you give them what they need or some component of what they need so that they will agree to the compromise. It can't be a zero-sum game. I find a lot of my time is spent not just relationship building but trying to figure out what the person that I'm trying to work with needs and what can I do to get that to them so that we can come to an agreement to take the next step."

BRIDGING THE GAP

Duckworth's sense of responsibility to her fellow soldiers and veterans and her obligation to serving a greater good strike me not only as highly commendable but also as increasingly rare. I told her that I'd attended a major international dinner while in Davos, Switzerland, to make two presentations at the World Economic Forum. While I was seated at a table with about two dozen people, the subject of duty and obligation to society came up. I took an informal poll, and out of all those at the table of influential people, I was the only one who had served in the military.

Many in previous generations served in World War II, Korea, or Vietnam, but today a very small fraction of the population has direct involvement with the military. For the vast majority of Americans, the wars in Iraq and Afghanistan seem like faraway events that don't affect their lives. This is unlike World War II, where everybody was affected in some important way, whether it was having loved ones in the military or working in a factory producing war supplies or just living with rationing at home. So I asked Duckworth how we could bridge that gap of relevance and connect more Americans with those in active military service who are doing all the heavy lifting in Afghanistan, Iraq, and around the world. "How do we ensure that we fulfill our obligation as citizens to honor, support, and care for those who serve?" I asked.

Duckworth is hopeful and optimistic that the current generation of veterans will step up as leaders and make sure that future generations are well served. "I do have a great optimism that this generation of veterans, with all the leadership training that they've had and that they've shown in combat, I think as they come home, they'll follow the path of that World War Two generation. They will go to school on the GI Bill and get jobs and become the future leaders of this country.

"Hopefully they will take those values and that military training with them, that idea of being part of something greater than themselves. It would be great if we could promote that ethical leadership and that training for these folks so that when they go into business, they will always carry that with them for the rest of their lives," she said. "In that way, they will touch other people in American society who may have no experience with the military."

She noted that a sense of duty could be applied "even in business, when your sole goal is to make a profit because you have an obligation to your stockholders. I believe that duty and honor and ethics can all be part of that. And that those things can also be learned and experienced. If you take it seriously and you teach it and you demonstrate it, a sense of duty will make your organization stronger. There is a sense of a mission greater than yourself."

STAYING HOPEFUL

Since she mentioned being optimistic and hopeful for the future, I asked Duckworth if she's always had what I call "realistic optimism," which I've come to believe is one of a leader's most effective tools, especially in providing hope. She offered an interesting perspective, that of someone who became more optimistic after nearly losing her life and experiencing great trauma and pain.

"I would not have said I was an optimist before I was wounded," she said. "I do now, but it's not that I'm optimistic that the sun's always going to shine and things can always be better. But I'm optimistic that you can always find a solution, that there is a way forward, that this is not my darkest day and this is not my darkest hour. Because I've had that darkest day and that darkest hour, and this is not it."

"Is part of that optimism occasionally taking a long-term view and not just getting mired down in the short-term details of things?" I asked.

"Yes, it is," said Duckworth, who then related a compelling story from her "darkest hour."

"I had an experience in the hospital ten days after I was injured. I went through a five-day period when I had a bad reaction to some of the pain meds. I basically lived five days without painkillers because nothing was working," she said. Without drugs to dull the pain, Duckworth tapped internal sources of will and strength that she might not have known existed otherwise. She reached a point where she wasn't sure she could live another day, so she was inspired to live minute to minute. "Not knowing if I would live that day, I decided, 'I think I can survive a minute,' so I counted to sixty seconds, over and over for five days."

If there were any doubts about the strength of this woman, that powerful story should dispel them, I thought. Marathon runners often talk of breaking down a long-distance run over many miles, saying it's not about running twenty-six miles, it's about running one mile twenty-six times. Tammy Duckworth found a way to deal with the pain of her injuries by breaking down five days into one-minute victories, and she emerged a survivor.

GIVING THANKS

The date of our landing on the Hudson River, January 15, will always be a special day for me and my family and for all of those most intimately involved in the landing and rescue operations, so

I can very much understand Tammy Duckworth's annual celebration with her former helicopter crew on the anniversary of their life-changing combat experience. I am most impressed, though, with the fact that, whenever possible, they all come together on November 12 to express their gratitude for each other and their blessings on what they call their "Alive Day."

"Instead of it being a day where I sit around and feel sorry for myself because I lost my legs, it's a day that I get to celebrate being alive and to remember the heroism of my crew," she said. "I get to look each one of them in the eyes and say, 'Thank you.' It's also the one time of year that Chief Warrant Officer Dan Milberg, who was the pilot in command of my aircraft, allows me to thank him for saving my life. He also makes me buy him a beer every year. I once asked him, 'Am I gonna be buying you a beer for the rest of my life?'" Then she answered her own question: "Apparently, yes, I am."

Their celebration of Alive Day also helps Duckworth remember what really matters most, she said. She lost her first congressional race on November 4 a few years ago, but just eight days later, she found it no longer possible to feel bad about simply losing an election.

"You know, I always have that to put me into perspective," Duckworth said. "At the end of the day, I'm going to get together with my crew and celebrate being alive. We made it, we're together, and nothing is ever as important as that."

5

JENNIFER GRANHOLM

My favorite line to citizens in Michigan was from a Chinese proverb: "Sometimes leadership is planting trees under whose shade you will never sit." To me, that is the way we should be looking at things, but it's difficult in the environment that we're in, which demands instant gratification.

MICHIGAN'S FIRST FEMALE GOVERNOR, JENNIFER GRANHOLM, TOOK office on January 1, 2003, during a national recession that had hit her Rust Belt state particularly hard. A meltdown in the automotive and industrial sectors had cost Michigan thousands of jobs and had driven up the need for services just as the state's financial resources were drying up. Yet, three years after the Democrat had become the top elected official in a state with a Republican-controlled legislature, she was reelected to a second term with the largest number of votes ever cast for governor in Michigan.

Just when everything else in Michigan had been going so wrong, Jennifer Granholm obviously had done something right. A Harvard Law School graduate who had also been Michigan's first female attorney general, she had worked relentlessly to diversify Michigan's economy, strengthen its auto industry, preserve the manufacturing sector, and add new sectors, especially clean energy, to the state's business portfolio.

"The circumstances in this environment were beyond the control of any governor in terms of the lost manufacturing jobs, because of globalization and the bankruptcies of our biggest employers, General Motors and Chrysler," she said. "It wasn't something a governor could prevent, although citizens believe that because you are the governor, you should be able to fix the problem."

Granholm compared her state's economic crisis and the general attitude of its residents to the education documentary *Waiting for "Superman."* "They expect that some great superhero is going to come in and save the day, and yet that's not possible in light of the circumstances," she said. "It was an enormous challenge to try to give people a vision and to let them know, 'We're going to be all right, but it's going to require that all of us move. All of us.'"

LEADING A STATE IN CRISIS

I interviewed former governor Granholm over breakfast at the Claremont Hotel in Berkeley, California. She and her family were in the process of relocating to the Bay Area, where both she and her husband, Daniel Mulhern, an author and leadership expert who is also a Harvard Law graduate, had taken teaching jobs at the University of California, Berkeley.

I thought this dynamic woman would be a good person to talk to because she had steered her troubled state through a series of major crises. The crises she handled included a state budget shortfall requiring her to propose $1.7 billion in cuts, the implosion of the state's biggest inner-city medical center, racial rioting in the Benton Harbor area that required her to send in the state police, and a massive blackout that left five million residents without power.

Actually, Granholm noted, she almost welcomed the blackout because it was the sort of crisis in which all hands lined up on her side, pulled together, and helped restore power within a couple of days. "When I'm in charge and I get to tell people what to do, and they do it and no one questions it—I *love* that kind of crisis!" she said.

Unfortunately, very few of the challenges this governor faced were so easily resolved. The challenges of leading an entire state are probably second only to those of being president of the United States. On top of all the diverse constituencies, competing interests, and myriad of economic and social problems, governors who hope to be reelected have to deal with the political ramifications of every move. Michigan's problems ran deep, and often they were rooted in national and even global factors.

Between 2000 and 2010, this state of ten million people lost 850,000 jobs, resulting in the highest unemployment rate in the nation. Her state has long been viewed as a bellwether for the economic health of the nation, Granholm noted. "It's always, 'When the nation catches a cold, Michigan catches pneumonia; or as goes General Motors, so goes Michigan,'" she said.

When this governor first took office in 2003, economists were predicting that the entire nation would be rebounding from the two-year recession in the third quarter. But that didn't happen in Michigan. Much to her dismay, the state continued to hemorrhage jobs, and its economy continued to contract.

"The economy wasn't doing what I ordered it to do," Granholm said ruefully.

FINDING SOLUTIONS FOR A TOWN IN CRISIS

The depth of the state's problems was reflected in yet another crisis that struck early, and Granholm's response to that challenge, a microcosm of Michigan's malaise, offers insight into her approach to leadership and governing. In December 2003, Granholm was informed that Greenville, located thirty-four miles from Grand Rapids, was facing an economic catastrophe. Known as "the refrigerator capital of the world," Greenville was a one-factory, one-industry town and it was in danger of losing that one business, which employed twenty-seven hundred people, out of a population of eight thousand. "It's owned by Electrolux, and they're threatening to move to Mexico, where they can pay a buck fifty-seven an hour," a state economic development official informed her.

Governor Granholm was at first typically optimistic and self-assured. "I said, 'Well, we'll just *fix* this one too! Let's go to Greenville. We'll bring our SWOT Team—our economic developers, etcetera—we'll call a meeting. We'll put incentives on the table, and we'll make them an offer they can't refuse.'

"We go to Greenville, and we empty out our pockets, put all of our chips on the table. The mayor's there, and the city manager is there. The UAW, which represents the workers, is there. The community college, which is going to train all the people, is there," she said.

Granholm's team put "this huge stack of incentives together and slid 'em across the table to the management of Electrolux. They looked at our offer, and they left the room. They were out for, I think, eighteen minutes," she recalled. "And they came back in and they said, 'This is the most generous offer we have ever been given. We couldn't have imagined that you guys could have pulled this together. But there's nothing you can do to compensate for the fact that we can pay a buck fifty-seven an hour in Mexico. So we're going.'"

The rejection felt as though "a nuclear bomb went off in this little town," she said.

GLOBAL THINKING

One of the marks of great leaders is that they think long-term and globally. They have the vision to see, as Granholm did in Greenville, that local problems are often a symptom or reflection of far more widespread challenges on the national and global level. To the residents of Greenville, this was a hometown catastrophe, but their governor quickly recognized that this one small town was one of many in their state and nation feeling the effects of global competition on a new scale.

"We regrouped and we said, 'Oh, my God. . . .' Because this was *one* town, but we had hundreds of towns across Michigan where the same story was playing out, place after place, businesses small and large," she said. "When there's nothing you can do in light of globalization and this movement of capital and jobs to low-wage countries, we've got to have a different plan."

Realizing that a fresh approach was needed, Granholm called together a blue-chip panel—economists, forecasters, and financial experts—to do a strategic evaluation of strengths, weaknesses, opportunities, and threats, known as a SWOT analysis. They approached the problem as if the state were a private corporation in peril. They looked at how they could build upon the state's remaining assets and resources, and they looked at every possible threat to its economic and social base so that they could identify challenges and prepare for them proactively.

Good leaders try not to be simply reactive. They strive to look ahead and prepare themselves and their organizations for the days, months, and years ahead. They try to take the long view rather than having only a short-term focus. When leaders or organizations look only or primarily at the short term, whether it is the next quarter's financial results and stock price or something else, we become myopic and blind ourselves to our futures.

"We've got to look at those threats because, sometimes, you have to steer right into them and acknowledge them," said Granholm.

"Sometimes you have to become the thing that you have most feared in order to be successful."

In light of the Electrolux rejection of her offer, the governor realized that "we just didn't have enough money to bribe companies to stay." She also accepted that Michigan would "not be able to keep the repetitive-motion kind of manufacturing jobs," she said.

The SWOT analysis did turn up some potential areas of strength where Michigan might be more competitive, such as advanced manufacturing for defense and homeland security contractors and their research and development arms. Michigan has a wealth of skilled manufacturing workers who could easily make the transition from the automotive or appliance industries into defense and security. Defense and homeland security contractors working with the federal and state governments are generally required to operate within the United States, and they offer jobs that require a higher level of skill and sophistication than that of those manufacturers who can easily move operations to less developed nations.

Granholm's team also saw potential opportunities in the pharmaceutical and biotech industries, which are less vulnerable to economic swings. "We had this great university corridor, and we already had a life sciences corridor," she told me. "We had Pfizer, and we had Pharmacia, and we had Upjohn before that. Especially near Kalamazoo, we had this great pharmaceutical industry that was nascent and growing, and spin-offs from the university that were creating companies out of great patents."

Yet another and perhaps the most promising opportunity lay in the field of renewable green jobs, according to Michigan's SWOT study. "The fourth sector was in clean energy," Granholm said. "We knew that if people can bend steel to make vehicles, they could bend steel to make wind turbines. We knew that, for example, wind turbines had gear pads, gears, brake pads, drive trains, that are really big. We knew that we had that expertise."

In Michigan's Saginaw Valley, there was "this great anchor company" called Hemlock Semiconductor, Granholm said. "It is the world's largest producer of the purest man-made substance, polycrystalline silicon, which is like gold for the solar panel industry. We knew that we had this anchor company and that we could create a cluster of jobs around the solar industry."

FINDING OPPORTUNITY IN CRISIS

I often describe innovation as "changing before you are forced to," whether by circumstances, competition, or regulation. The faster you can enact change to meet challenges, the more competitive and farther ahead your team or your business will be. Granholm's actions as governor illustrate my sense that adversity creates environments ripe with opportunities. *If* you are ready and able to meet the challenges and seize the opportunities, you will ultimately benefit from them.

Granholm's response to the SWOT analysis for her state serves as example of a leader finding opportunity in a crisis. The classic example of this was President John F. Kennedy's response after the Soviet Union became the first nation to put a man in space, in April 1961. Six weeks later, Kennedy announced his goal of sending an American safely to the Moon within nine years. The young leader mobilized the nation and its scientists to win the "space race," using concern over the USSR's success to motivate and unite Congress behind the American space program, which created thousands of jobs and resulted in many advances in a wide array of important industries including aviation and defense.

Facing the loss of industries and jobs, Granholm seized the opportunity to form alliances, including an unlikely one with a nation that had been widely regarded as a competitor to Michigan's primary industries. "We knew that instead of being victimized by the global competition, we had to, as I say, steer into the wind," she explained. "We had to court them. Part of what I did, which was very controversial at the beginning, was to go overseas and court international companies to come to Michigan, particularly Japan."

I noted the irony of that bold move, since the Japanese had learned mass production techniques from Ford and others, but after World War II their markets were too small for large-scale mass production, so they greatly increased quality and efficiency, which helped their nation rise to supremacy in automobile manufacturing in the decades that followed.

In a move that critics said was akin to inviting the fox into the henhouse, the governor and her team went to Toyota's headquarters in Japan and invited the giant auto manufacturer to expand its small research and development facility in Ann Arbor. "We wanted them to do significant expansion of it because we knew that would stimulate [hiring] also. And there was this new theme that was emerging, which is called *coopetition,* where you had cooperation and competition together, sort of this hybrid, this cluster of competing companies that fed off of one another."

The governor told me she spent enormous amounts of energy looking for investment opportunities abroad. "I took eleven international trips to try to recruit companies in those sectors," she said.

PRACTICING EMPATHY

While Granholm trekked the globe trying to drum up business, the situation back home continued to deteriorate. Elected leaders can't afford to lose touch with their constituents even when they are working on their behalf night and day. But Granholm's resolve to find solutions for her state was strengthened in the summer of 2006 when she returned to Greenville.

The last refrigerator was boxed up and shipped out from the small town's only factory early in 2006. That summer, she attended a gathering that the Electrolux employees held at the Klackle Orchards Pavilion in their small town. They dubbed it "The Last Supper," and the mood was grim.

"As we entered this large pavilion, there was a band playing on the stage and families were sitting around these little tables eating box lunches," she recalled. "There was just this gloom, this complete and total heaviness in the air. And as I went in, a man came up to me with his two daughters. He's got a ponytail. He's got tattoos. He says, 'Governor, I'm forty-eight years old. I've worked in this factory for thirty years. I went from high school to the factory. My father worked at this factory. My grandfather worked at this factory. These are my two daughters. Now I want you to tell me, Governor, who is going to hire *me*? This is all I know. Who is going to hire me?'"

Granholm told me that as the former factory worker shared his story, a line of his former coworkers formed behind him, running through the pavilion. All of them wanted to talk to their governor, sharing their grief and concerns for the future. "There was a real human crisis," Governor Granholm continued, her voice now a half whisper. "It was almost an identity crisis the state of Michigan was facing, both on the individual level as well as on the state level. Who were we going to be if we were not the automotive capital of the world?" People in her state were fearful about the future, and beyond that "you have an angry citizenry," she said. "I mean, people are *angry* in Michigan."

As she recalled this experience, the former governor paused, and her gaze turned downward in sadness and frustration. "I can't even tell this story without getting emotional, because it's just so . . ." Her voice trailed off.

"It's heartbreaking," I said after a moment. "It's a cry for help."

"And it's the cry of Michigan," she said.

PLAYING DEFENSE AND OFFENSE

The predicament of Michigan's jobless blue-collar workers, like those in Greenville, convinced Granholm that finding more jobs wasn't the sole answer to her state's economic crisis. The workforce had to be better trained and better educated if the state hoped to compete for more sophisticated manufacturing jobs.

"Michigan had one of the lowest percentages of adults with college degrees," she told me. "For a hundred years we had this fabulous manufacturing history. People could go from high school to factory and have a great middle-class way of life."

Granholm said that the only way to restore the state's middle class was to play defense as well as offense. "When you have declining resources because the economy's cratering, you have to call upon these citizens to diversify themselves, to diversify their own skills as we diversify the economy," she said.

The governor faced a considerable challenge in asking the state's blue-collar workers to go back to school after so many decades on the assembly line, I noted.

"Yes," she said. "And so many people in Michigan had not gone to college because they hadn't needed to. Imagine being that forty-eight-year-old guy or fifty-year-old guy, who has years of good work still ahead of him. Imagine his thoughts of going to college and sitting next to a twenty-year-old who just came out of high school. You know, that was a huge barrier for people to do that."

In response to the need for a retrained workforce in her state, Governor Granholm's team launched a bold program in which the state basically offered paid tuition for all displaced adult workers. The No Worker Left Behind program gave unemployed and underemployed residents the opportunity to attend community colleges and technical schools to receive training for jobs in new industries. "We had to completely revamp our adult education system to respond to those folks," she told me. "Through No Worker Left Behind we ended up turning workforce training on its head."

Her program offered ten thousand dollars in retraining to the first one hundred thousand displaced adult workers who applied. This example of creating opportunity in a crisis required some rewriting of the rule book. "We had to go to the federal government and ask for permission to do that while people were collecting unemployment, because nobody had any resources, right?" she said.

Granholm said that No Worker Left Behind was "wildly successful" because the state's community colleges reconfigured their classes to serve the needs of those displaced workers willing to do whatever it took to find jobs. Classes were even offered in union halls and on site at new businesses. "They wanted to completely take away the stigma, mystique, or the terror associated with going to college for people who hadn't been in school in thirty years and who might have tested in at third-grade math level because they just hadn't used those skills in so many years. We wouldn't pay for them to get a degree in French political science—because we don't need that—but we would pay for them to get a degree in nursing, or to get a degree in something that was necessary in renewable energy."

At the end of her tenure, No Worker Left Behind had enrolled more than 147,000 adults. "We had seventy-five percent of [unemployed workers] who either got promoted or got a job, and eighty-two percent were in the areas that they studied. That's four times the national rate, which was fabulous. But then, after the recession hit and because of continuing budget deficits, my successor in office had to, unfortunately, close enrollment this year."

The former governor said that the mood in her state has improved, but unemployment is still running high. A Gallup poll said that last year Michigan had the the most improved economy of any state in the country. But in the fall of 2011, the state's unemployment rate was 9.8 percent while the national average was 8.7.

Granholm also feels that she fell short of her goal to double the number of college graduates in her state. When she became governor, a poll found that only 27 percent of the parents in Michigan thought it was essential for their children to have a college education. By the time she left office eight years later, that percentage had grown to only 37 percent of parents.

"So we moved the needle by ten, but we should have moved it by thirty," she said. "I said it everywhere we went that our goal—our big, hairy, audacious goal—was to double the number of college graduates. You have to get your child to go to college. Everywhere I went, I had the same message. Yet it was so difficult to penetrate, perhaps because people didn't want to hear it. It's a hard message to sink in."

Granholm said she felt privileged to serve as leader of the state government, but she had hoped to do more for the people of Michigan. "You can't declare victory, because it's just not there yet," she said. Yet the former governor acknowledged that one of her biggest mistakes was doing just that in an important speech. "One of the most public mistakes I made was to overreach in a State of the State speech. I was attempting to convey optimism about where the economy was headed. And in that speech, I said, 'In five years, you're going to be blown away by the strength of our economy.'"

This was in 2006, the year Granholm ran for reelection, and her opponents were delighted to use her optimistic words as a weapon against her when the economy tanked and Michigan's automotive giants plunged into bankruptcy.

"It was such a dumb thing to say because of my overenthusiasm about where things were going," she said, noting that her advisers had cautioned her against being so optimistic about the economy.

PREPARATION MEETS OPPORTUNITY

As I listened to Governor Granholm speak about her years in office during an unprecedented economic crisis, I thought about how often leaders are thrust into situations that they'd never imagined having to cope with but for which their cumulative life's experiences had almost unconsciously prepared them. "I would imagine that when you took office, you had *no* idea that that was ahead of you," I said.

"No, I had no idea," Granholm said. "In fact, all of the advisers and all the economists were all saying, 'This is great. You come in during the trough, but you get to take credit for all of the growth in the economy that's going to happen just by the nature of the cycle.' But this was not a cycle. This was a structural change in the economy of Michigan, and the foundations on which our economy rested had completely crumbled. So we had to create a whole new platform for an economy. And of course that's a work in progress. You can't do that overnight."

"Or even in eight years," I said.

"Or even in eight years—no. It's an ongoing commitment to diversifying this economy that must continue," she said. "But, you know, it's difficult to convince people that we're going to be okay when we're *not* okay at the moment."

Granholm has received widespread praise for her efforts to help her state in a time of crisis. Her leadership skills were certainly honed under fire, but a look at her background shows that she was preparing for that role early in life. In fact, Granholm grew up with a very personal understanding of what can happen to those struggling to find work and pay the bills.

She was born in Vancouver, British Columbia, into a family of immigrants. Her grandfather, who came to Canada from Sweden, committed suicide when her father was three years old because of financial stress. "This was during the Great Depression and he had no money, and at that point Canada provided a widow's pension if a husband died," Granholm said. "He killed himself so that she could have a widow's pension for my father and his two brothers."

Despite that pension, in the depths of the Great Depression the family was nearly destitute, but her father, who never went to college, rose from an entry-level job as a bank teller to become a bank president. "It was just by pure work ethic and the fact that people totally trusted him," she said. "He never overpromised, he was completely honest, and he used to tell me as we were growing up, 'You should live your life as though everything you do is going to be written on the front page of the *New York Times*.' That example that he provided for me—and he really walked that talk—was absolutely fundamental to me knowing that I had a foundation upon which to lead."

Her description of her father touched a chord in me; my father too was an honest and hardworking man.

"What about your mother?" I asked.

She offered a soft smile. "My mother is a very mercurial Irish woman. She was born in Newfoundland, and she is a very strong soul." Though her mother did not go to college or have a career, she urged Granholm to "put on wings and fly."

"Go! Do it!" her mother would tell her. "You can be anything!"

"What do you think fueled that intense passion in her?" I asked. "Was it regret? Was it anger at what she was unable to do for herself? Was she, in a sense, hoping to live at least a portion of her life vicariously through you?"

"I think so—all of that," she said. "I think that she regretted that she wasn't really able to live, because of the circumstances."

Granholm was very focused on being the good child in her school days because she had an older brother who was "a big troublemaker and caused [her] parents all sorts of grief," though he grew up to be a minister. "I watched him very carefully and I was determined not to cause my parents that kind of grief. I was the very good student. I wasn't going to ruffle them."

"You were the rule follower," I said.

"I was totally the rule follower—absolutely."

Except that after high school, she moved to Los Angeles to become an actress, entered a beauty pageant, and became "Miss San Carlos." That brief sash-and-tiara chapter of her life seemed to slightly embarrass her, perhaps somehow diminishing her gravitas as a political figure, though she brushed off the reminder of her beauty queen title with good humor.

"Yeah, whatever, we can pass that by," she said with a laugh.

"But I did do that and hated it, hated every moment of it. And I recognized that unless I got a degree and credentialed myself, that no one was ever going to take me seriously."

A TAKE-CHARGE PERSONALITY

Granholm set a course to first attend Berkeley and then Harvard Law School, working "like a dog to do both." She takes special pride in being a trailblazer in public service because she was passionate about politics and policy and "changing the world in some way."

Her life's course changed while she was doing her legal studies at Harvard. Before completing her law degree, she met her future husband, Daniel Mulhern. "He's from Michigan, so I *married* Michigan," she said of her husband, who also aspired to make a difference. "He went to Yale to major in theology because he was going to become a priest. Daniel worked in New Orleans in this inner-city youth center. He taught at a Jesuit high school in Tampa, Florida. Then he came to Harvard, where we met, so he didn't become a priest. But Daniel did become a saint for marrying me."

Granholm, who moved from her parents' Republican Party to considering herself an Independent in college and then a Democrat in law school, told me that her leadership heroes, heroines, and role models ran the gamut on the political spectrum. "I've admired a lot of people, from Margaret Thatcher to Dr. King," she said. "But I would say my bookshelf is largely filled with Robert F. Kennedy and JFK and Dr. King and Mother Teresa."

"Now are those people whom you aspired to be like—or who inspired you?" I said.

"They definitely inspired me."

"What did you see in them?"

"Selflessness, selflessness," she replied. "Particularly with respect to Mother Teresa or Dr. King, in the sense that this was about something greater than them."

"And Margaret Thatcher?"

"And Margaret Thatcher. I loved that she was a great female role model. She was not going to be defined by her gender." Once she was elected to office, Granholm said, she was even more impressed by Prime Minister Thatcher's ability, resolve, and effectiveness in governance. "Yes, I liked Margaret Thatcher's style for that," she said. "I'm not a bull in a China shop, but I think she had a little bit of that. She was no-nonsense, and she was going to get stuff done. I appreciated that strength."

Granholm once took the Myers-Briggs Type Indicator, which is a questionnaire that measures how people view the world and make decisions. She was categorized as what she called a "field general" personality type, which came as no surprise. "I love to be able to go in and take charge and make sure that the vision is set, that we are ticking off the steps for that vision, that people are held accountable, that we are achieving those results, and we're moving the ball," she said.

DEMANDING ACCOUNTABILITY

As governor, Granholm held her team accountable by setting the vision in her State of the State address each year, and then demanding measurable results. "Every one of the cabinet officials were to stand up at every cabinet meeting and say publicly where they were with respect to the goals, so that there was some accountability, and everybody felt compelled to make progress," she said. "I really enjoy getting stuff done. That's my bent in life."

I noted that because of her organized and disciplined approach, which is similar to mine, Granholm must have experienced frustration when things didn't go according to her plan, just as I do when my plans go awry.

"Yeah, for sure!" she agreed. "I always feel like I'm a problem solver, so there has to be a solution. And if I don't know what that solution is, we're all going to muddle through this."

Her efforts to find a solution to the crisis in Greenville triggered that frustration when things didn't progress as quickly as she wanted, Granholm said. "In that year, we had three separate off-site strategy sessions with the experts and the cabinet," she recalled. "And we really hashed it out, went very deep, and made sure that we had the agenda and had it right. That was 2004–2005; we were continuing to work it. But you would think, you would hope, that by 2010 you'd have fixed the problem."

"They hadn't read your script," I said.

"What's the matter with those people out there having not read the script?" she said with a laugh.

LONG-TERM LEADERSHIP

When I asked if Granholm considered herself an optimistic leader, she said she has always tried to stay focused on solutions and remain confident that things will work out for the best over the long term. "You have to work at it, but if you have the right strategy, absolutely," she said. "I always told the people in Michigan, 'We are going to be all right. We really are. We have great bones as a state and we have set in motion this platform to change the state's economy. It's not going to happen tomorrow; we're not going to be fully normal tomorrow. But if we continue on this path to diversification, we're going to be magnificent.'"

Given the term limits that many officeholders face and the current debate over business leaders focused only on short-term results to satisfy Wall Street, I asked Granholm if she thought many of our nation's problems were the result of leaders not taking a longer view.

"This is a great question," she said. "This generation has a lot of need for instant gratification. I think the stock market has a need for instant gratification too. Therefore, it forces the companies to look more at the short term rather than the long term. However, they will say that their investment decisions are based upon a long-term forecast. So if they know that they are going to be investing a hundred million dollars in a plant, they want to know what the long-term ramifications are so that there's not something that causes them to lose money and have to rue that decision. But the gist of your question is absolutely correct—that this is a short-term environment that we are in, and it is fomented by the need of investors to see instant results."

I noted that many Japanese companies work with twenty-, thirty-, fifty-year plans.

"Which we all should be doing," she said. "Part of the problem with term limits, too, is that it forces an instant, short-term view. My favorite line to citizens in Michigan was from a Chinese proverb: 'Sometimes leadership is planting trees under whose shade you will never sit.' To me, that is the way we should be looking at things, but it's difficult in the environment that we're in, which demands instant gratification."

We agreed that the current generation of leaders in business and politics seems to have forgotten the lessons of the past, as well as some of the fundamental values of previous generations.

"I think that there used to be an understanding of sacrifice and of deferred pleasure," she said. "Deferment—I think that's really an important quality. And I say this as a parent; I'm not judging everybody in the next generation, but I know with my own kids how they want it now. And they have a sense of entitlement that others in previous generations did not have. Previous generations had to work for it. I can hear myself sounding like my own parents, but it is true."

Granholm noted that her daughter benefited greatly from taking a year off between high school and college and working as a volunteer in a New Orleans inner-city school, where she saw just how difficult the lives of others can be. "She understands now what kids who have nothing go through," Granholm said. "She's completely passionate about becoming a teacher now in an urban district, because she just feels like there were things that were so badly done, she wants to change it. But mostly, she has such a heart for these kids."

WALKING THE TALK

We agreed that it's important for young people to see beyond their own insulated lives, to understand how others live, to have empathy for those who struggle because of their circumstances. We also agreed that one of the great failures in leadership in modern times is the lack of integrity, empathy, and honesty exhibited by so many in positions of responsibility in government and business.

"Integrity has to be demonstrated," Granholm said. "Leaders go first. Leaders have to lead by example." She offered an example of when this did not happen in the Michigan legislature during her tenure as governor. State legislators had received a sizable pay raise, but at the same time they were cutting the budget.

"We had to seek concessions from state employees, but I asked the legislature to cut their own pay at the same rate that we were asking for the concessions from the state employees. Otherwise, it's so hypocritical. And they refused to do it," she said. She cut her own pay by 10 percent, "But it was frustrating that I didn't have partners in leading."

I shared with Granholm my own frustration with airline executives who cut employees' pay while granting themselves large bonuses and stock options, even as their companies performed poorly. "What do you think of executive pay that's many multiples of the average worker's pay?" I asked her.

"I think it's totally counterproductive," she said, because executives who earn so much more than their workers and insist on compensation increases while cutting wages or firing people are sending the message that they are more valuable than their employees and not part of the same team. She noted that the pay disparities are far less in Japanese companies, which are known for their loyal employees. "It's really obscene to see this huge gap in pay differential," she added.

"CEOs and other top executives are often able to insulate themselves from the outcomes, whether or not their companies succeed," I said. "They separate themselves from their failures."

"You use the words 'separate themselves,'" Granholm said. "They separate themselves from the bad consequences by having golden parachutes. And they literally are separated from the workers and the work. But the minute you start separating yourselves from the work that's being done, you completely become an ineffective leader."

I noted that this is also true in government, where leaders in Washington, D.C., are inside this bubble. They've cut themselves off from the people who elected them and instead exist in the "echo chamber" inside the Beltway in Washington.

"Most Americans right now are looking to their leaders to create jobs, but the debate in Washington seems to be all about cutting government services," I said.

Granholm said the motivation in Washington is simply to do whatever it takes to get reelected, but even there the thinking is awry. "The way they think they're going to get reelected is just by cutting, cutting, cutting, cutting as opposed to stimulating economic growth and creating jobs for the people who elected them," she said. "I don't think there's one other situation or one other subject that's more important to people than jobs out there in the real world. But they're disconnected from that conversation."

"One of the marks of a great leader is the ability to create a sense of shared purpose with followers or employees, but so many leaders in business and politics today seem to have a 'me first' attitude instead of one that we are all in this together," I said.

"Right, right, right," she agreed. "We're all in it together, but Joe CEO? He's going to be just fine. So why would we bust our asses for him if that separation exists? We all should be in it together."

PROMOTING LOYALTY

I asked Granholm how leaders should promote loyalty, and she responded that "if you are going to ask for sacrifices, the leaders should go first." She noted that the show *Undercover Bosses* is beneficial because it shows how the people in charge need to stay in touch with those who work for them. She also finds magazine articles on "best places to work" to be instructive because the organizations that are ranked high are always those that "really value the people who are carrying out the work of the organization, and they elevate them, and they make sure that there is not a huge separation between the leadership and the folks who are carrying it out.

"I think that in the United States, people who watch corporations have to just recognize [that the corporations are] not about being loyal to any particular place," she said. "They're about making a profit. They're for-profit entities, so we've got to get that in our head. They're going to do what's in their best interest, so the question is, how do we create the container for their best interests and for them to be competitive here? So what do we have to do to make sure that they are competitive here?

"I don't blame the CEOs for the decisions to maximize profit where they can in a global economy. I blame the U.S. for not going to bat to keep those jobs here and make it competitive for them to be here. I would say we've got to go to bat for these CEOs, these companies that say, 'I go to China and they steal my intellectual property, and they require me to locate there.' Well, we should be going to bat for them so that we don't have that uneven playing field. And we shouldn't be negotiating trade agreements where we are giving away the store, which we have in the past.

"So we should be saying to our trading partners, 'If you don't have the same rules or if you don't have the same environmental standards that we have, well, we're not going to trade with you. You've got to raise the game—your game.' So that we're not just allowing . . . companies to locate there where they can pollute at will and they're able to save all that money."

The United States needs "to get our act together as a nation with respect to making it competitive for businesses to locate here," she said, offering the examples of the defense and energy industries, which should be based in our own country so that we are not dependent on other nations. "If we're worried about being beholden to the Middle East during this time, and we want to create our own energy independence, well, then we'd better decide as a nation that we want to create that industry here. And that might mean that yes, we have to offer low-interest loans to those who need to get the equipment in the ground, just like China is doing to woo them over there. We've got to compete on it."

"So," I asked, "do you think there is a legitimate role for government in setting the economic agenda?"

"Absolutely, absolutely I do," she said. "I completely disagree with those who continue to say that we should have hands-off— the laissez-faire, trickle-down, free market economists—which may have worked in the last century." Granholm said that a new approach is needed in light of globalization and what our economic competitors are doing to throw sand into the engine of the free market—with subsidies and incentives and a free hand to lure businesses away from the United States.

"We've got to be in this game, and in it to win it," she said. "So we've got to fight, and right now those who are saying we should not be putting any money into creating an energy economy in the United States are basically just giving it all away to China. So, you know, they can decide to do that, but it makes us a weak nation.

If we don't have a manufacturing infrastructure, we are a weak nation, and we need to decide as a country, are we going to intervene to keep that manufacturing sector here? And I'm not talking about putting barriers up over here. I'm talking about taking barriers down over there and making us competitive."

THICK-SKINNED LEADERSHIP

In Granholm's view, those who take leadership roles need to have the courage to act and do the right thing for the greater good without worrying about what critics will say. "You have to have skin as thick as a rhinoceros hide," she said. "And you have to recognize going in that you will be criticized. In Michigan, I can't even tell you how much criticism I've gotten, but it's because of the circumstances, right? And you just have to keep your nose down and plow forward and recognize that that criticism will come."

Having a supportive spouse helped her through the worst of times when critics were piling it on, Granholm said. "I'm not saying that it's easy, but fortunately I've got a great mooring point in my husband, who was able to remind me that this is about the work, and that I had the right plan, and we were doing the right thing, and we had a great team. But it's painful for me to hear that great, qualified people see the criticism leaders take and decide they don't want to put themselves through that."

Granholm worries that many qualified women don't go into politics "because they don't think it's worth the grief and the agony of it. But what I keep saying to women who are running is that 'It's not about you. It's about the things you want to achieve, and just keep that goal in mind. You just have to know that going in, and be able to plow on and be satisfied when you get to the results you want to achieve.'"

"What do you say to those who contend that our system has reached a point where very few people are willing to put themselves and their families through the grinder of the political process?" I asked.

"I worry that is a big problem," she said. "I mean, you have to have people who have such big egos that they're able to withstand all those slings and arrows, but you want your leaders to be humble, right? You want your leaders to be people who are able to relate to the citizens. It's not something that there's an answer for, so I hate raising issues that don't have answers. In this environment, there's not an easy fix for that except to encourage great young people to say that it's worth it."

Granholm may have been the "most criticized" governor in the country during her tenure in Michigan because of the state's economic crisis, she said. "But would I look back and not do it again? I would absolutely do it again, one hundred percent, because your decisions in a time of crisis have more impact than at any other time. We never cut anybody off of health care, for example, in Michigan during this incredible contraction." There was a 70 percent increase in Medicaid demand during her tenure, which meant soaring costs during a fiscal crisis, "but we decided that we would not cut people off of health care. I don't know that somebody else would have made those decisions in my chair, and so I know we made a difference, and that's what's important."

FISCAL AND SOCIAL RESPONSIBILITY

"Is it possible for a leader to be fiscally and socially responsible simultaneously?" I asked.

"Yes," she said, offering another example from her tenure as governor. "In Michigan, I cut more out of state government as a percentage than any governor in the nation in my eight years. We saw a thirty-two percent drop in revenue. The size of our general fund was the same size as in 1972, with fifteen thousand fewer state employees. I cut out twenty-five percent of state departments. I shut down thirteen prisons. We got concessions from state employees far and above what Governor Scott Walker was trying to do in Wisconsin and way more than Governor Chris Christie's gotten out of New Jersey, and we did it by negotiating at the bargaining table.

"We did it in negotiation, but it's not that I want to see the wages and the benefits of people drop. I do believe that we are careening into this dangerous realm where wages are dropping and we all find that satisfactory. I don't think that's the case. But I do think in a tough time, in light of what the private sector unions have done, it was appropriate to ask for sacrifices on the part of the public sector unions too."

Because of the intense budget battles during her tenure, state government was shut down twice, Granholm said. "But we were fiscally responsible and we stuck with the basics. We had three priorities: diversify the economy, educate our citizens, and protect citizens as we transition from an old economy to a new one. And that 'protect' category was making sure that we weren't cutting people off of health care during this very, very difficult time." That meant halting spending on some popular items like the arts and the state fair, "but we protected people, and that's how you can be both fiscally responsible and socially responsible," she said.

NEGOTIATION AND COMPROMISE ARE HALLMARKS OF LEADERSHIP

Granholm was critical of the situation in Wisconsin in which the governor battled with state employees and the legislature about the right of state employees to bargain collectively over their compensation and working conditions. The former Michigan governor said that her state employees gave up $750 million in concessions at the bargaining table. She also went to the legislature to get changes in the public school teachers' pensions and their contribution to both health care and pensions. "The combined public employee bipartisan contributions were over three billion dollars to the state of Michigan," she said.

"Do state employees have the right to organize and collectively bargain over every part of their compensation and conditions at work?" I asked.

"They do," Granholm said. As a result of negotiating and respecting the state employees and asking for them to come forward with their ideas, she said, they "saved us an enormous amount of money. They identified no-bid contracts that we eliminated and they identified existing contracts that had waste, fraud, and abuse in them, which we eliminated." The state employee unions identified $1.1 billion worth of savings because they're the ones on the ground doing the work, she said. "They were channeling what was happening on the ground to the folks at the bargaining table and saying, 'You can save a lot of money here.' So it's working with the people you employ to achieve the continuous improvement that you need."

Granholm, a Democrat, described the Republican governor in Wisconsin and his threat to lay off fifteen hundred state workers as "an incredibly terrible example of leadership." She believes that failure to compromise is a failure of leadership. "Those who say, 'It's my way or the highway,' are the ones who cause breakdowns in the system. And that, to me, is a failure of leadership," she said. "I'm somebody who firmly believes in half a loaf. If you can get a half a loaf, take the half a loaf. Maybe you can get the other half in the next go-round. But don't say it's all the loaf or nothing, and I'm going to throw a bomb into the works to try to achieve my ends. I think that's terrible leadership."

"So, you would disagree with those who say that there are certain ideologies on which there can be no compromise. Instead, we should be pragmatic, not dogmatic?" I asked.

"Yes, I think we should be pragmatic," she replied. "Like, for example, one of the principles that I really, strongly believed is that we weren't going to cut senior citizens or people with disabilities off of health care. That was a principle, and, you know, I came to the bargaining table and I said, 'Look, I'll negotiate on a lot of stuff, but on that one I won't.' And they were fine with that, as long as there were other places to give."

LEAVING A LEGACY

I asked Granholm what she created in her eight years as governor that will outlast her tenure.

"We laid the foundation for a new Michigan economy," she said. "Manufacturing is no longer the largest sector in Michigan; that obviously happened as a result of our globalization. But we added these sectors that are now bearing fruit."

She noted that Michigan passed an energy bill during her tenure that created a foundation for the growth of an energy market in the state. The federal Recovery Act then allowed Michigan to "pancake state incentives onto the federal to make it irresistible" for companies like those that make lithium ion batteries for electric vehicles to locate there. "In the two years between 2008 and 2010, we had forty-seven companies in renewable energy, clean energy companies, come to Michigan," said Granholm, who projected that those companies would create ninety-two thousand jobs over the next ten years. "Now that's one slice of trying to replace those lost manufacturing jobs, but I know that those will continue to bear fruit into the future."

Granholm said that her team also helped raise the bar in education by requiring every child to take college preparatory classes. "Now we are seeing the increases in the state testing. We are seeing increases in the graduation rates," she said. "We saw a thirty-five percent increase in community college enrollment. So I know that these things will bear fruit."

BREAKING DOWN BUREAUCRATIC
BARRIERS

I observed that Granholm seemed to have encouraged a holistic approach to leadership in which multiple agencies could break out of silos and in a collaborative fashion address global issues in terms of government services, community colleges and education, companies, and local governments. "Do you think that's a model not only for the state but also for the federal government?" I asked.

"Oh, for sure," she replied. "I think the federal government is so siloed and bureaucratized, and when you've got bits and pieces in all of these different agencies and you don't have a coordinated approach, then it's a waste. It's not efficient. It's not streamlined."

Granholm overcame bureaucratic barriers by identifying issues that needed to be addressed and then forming teams of individuals from various departments and across disciplines. "We had an economy team. We had an education team, and some cabinet members were on several teams," she noted.

She also merged a number of state departments into the Department of Technology, Management, and Budget to take greater advantage of technologies and the Internet to make the bureaucracy more efficient and open online access to state residents. "Michigan is forty-eighth in terms of the size of government per capita in the country," Granholm said. "But we're number one in the country in terms of leveraging technology in order to serve. The merger enabled these departments to work together, and it enabled us to put our plans online and to update them for . . . the citizens as well as internally."

One of her goals was to use the Internet and related technologies to "create sort of a do-it-yourself—DIY—citizenry, to put every permit, every process, every business process, everything online to make it super easy," she said. "By leveraging technology, I think the federal government can do a lot more of that."

The former governor also took pride in streamlining the

state's system for environmental permitting, which had become so time-consuming that it took eighteen months to get an air quality permit. "We asked the private sector to come in and help us do what is known as 'value stream mapping,' which essentially is what the auto companies do and the manufacturers do—a continuous improvement," she said. "And so we removed all of these steps in the process so that we could collapse permitting time. So it went from eighteen months to thirty to sixty days."

BUILDING THE FUTURE

I asked Granholm if our government had become so complex and its bureaucracy so bloated that it was no longer possible to have coherent policies or to accomplish major undertakings such as those accomplished by previous generations—grand achievements like the interstate highway system and putting men on the Moon that benefited every segment of our society.

"Has that period come to an end?" I asked. "Have we somehow lost our vision, lost our way? Are we still capable of doing great things? Or is the short-term bottom line so all-important now—and is the ideological climate such that people want to limit the role of government so much—that unless it's immediately profitable for private companies to do it, it won't get done, whether it's infrastructure or something else?"

"I think that the only way that we will be able to change the trajectory of the public toward reinvesting in our nation for the greatness of America is by exposing those who are holding on to twentieth-century economic theory to what other countries are doing. To let them know that in a competitive and global world, that if we don't invest, instead of being a great America we will be a weak America," she said. "And if that's okay with you, then you can go on and hold on to those theories. But if you really love our country and you want us to be great, then we have to invest in America in the same way other countries are investing in their strength."

Granholm said that those who only want to cut government and do not want to invest in high-speed rail systems or other infrastructure improvements need to think more about what it will take to keep the United States competitive in a global economy. "You've got the business community out there saying, 'You've got to invest in infrastructure. You've got to invest in infrastructure.' But they're not identifying ways to pay for it," she said. "We have to decide it's worth mutual sacrifice to make America strong again."

Many of those who make cutting their number one priority perhaps are not aware of what's happening in China or in other countries where their governments are investing and intervening in their economies to make them strong, Granholm said: "I want to take a bunch of them to China so that they could see what's going on and what we're up against, and what the policies that they're advocating will do to weaken America." She acknowledged that the United States needs to find ways to cut its debt to China while also investing for the future in our own country.

"So in our educational system and our business schools, are we not teaching our future leaders the right skills?" I asked. "Are we making them only financial experts and not leaders?"

"Yeah," she said. "I worry that a lot of people who teach in the business schools haven't run a business, number one. But number two, I would say that a lot of people teaching leadership haven't led. I think it's real important to have that experience in order to know what works and what doesn't work."

"[Attending] business school is a self-selecting process," I noted.

"It is a self-selecting process," she agreed. "And that person might be inclined to be more interested in profit maximization through what they might consider to be the easier way, which is to cut costs and make decisions to just move offshore instead of trying to figure out the harder, more lasting solutions and working with your employees and finding new business models, etcetera."

MAKING DIFFICULT CHOICES

"What was your most difficult decision, and how did you make it?" I asked.

"One was the decision to raise taxes, which ultimately led to a shutdown in government," Granholm said. "Those were very difficult decisions, but the reason why I made them is because I wasn't going to cut people off of health care. And there just wasn't any money to do any more."

The state's Republican leaders refused to go along initially. "They decided, for their own interest, to shut government down to demonstrate to the citizens that they didn't want to [raise taxes]," Granholm said. "And then four hours later—it was only a four-hour shutdown—they voted in favor of it and we got what we were asking for." Raising taxes was a difficult decision that resulted in controversy, "but it was the right decision in light of what we were attempting to do."

"How did you come to that conclusion?" I asked. "Did you agonize over it, or was it a simple choice to make, based upon your values?"

"The decision itself was obvious. This was in my second term, we had cut for five straight years, and there just was nothing else to do without really hurting people. And so I knew we had to go there," she said. "But it made the year hell because we knew there was this inexorable movement toward a shutdown, and citizens were just furious, not with the tax request, but with the fact that government wasn't getting along and doing anything. So all of the stories were about process, and the fact that Democrats and Republicans were battling like this, and there seemed to be no give. . . . So that year was the worst year of my governance."

"How does a leader align goals and persuade people to make difficult choices and take the more difficult but ultimately better path?" I asked. "How does one articulate a vision and then convince people that it's necessary to go there and it's possible to get there?"

"I would say you have to overcommunicate by a factor of ten," Granholm said. "You have to go out to the people."

She noted, for example, that her first year as governor ended with a $2 billion deficit, "the largest deficit in one year that anybody had had to deal with in anybody's memory." Granholm didn't try to run from the deficit. Instead, she ran with it, conducting town hall meetings about it all over her state.

"I did a budget tour where I went to every small hamlet and media market and partnered with the media and said, 'You pick the audience and we'll broadcast this, and I'll put up some choices out there. And I'll let the people in the audience, with their clickers, choose where they would place their first dollar and where they would make their first cut. And we'll have the audience at home do it as well, and they can e-mail in their recommendations. We'll tally them in real time and show the results back to the citizens."

Granholm asked state residents how they would deal with the deficit: whether they would cut mental health services or prisons, elementary schools or scholarships to private universities. "I just said, 'In the grand scheme of things, funding for the arts versus funding for libraries—what's more important?'" she explained.

Granholm acknowledged that the questions she put to voters were "guided" and that she knew what their suggestions would be, but in conducting the town hall meetings and soliciting opinions from voters, she was engaging them in the decision-making process and "getting their buy-in of where the cuts were going to be, so that when they ultimately happened, I could hold up their results and say, 'This is what your choices were.' When you get people to buy in and you ask for their opinion, then sometimes it's easier to lead them where they otherwise would not want to go."

THE QUALITIES OF A LEADER

"We've talked about some important qualities for a leader, such as integrity, leadership by example, and communication skills, but what other essential qualities must a leader have? What other lessons have you learned?" I asked Granholm.

"Energy is critical," she said. "And I say that because I think that when the energy goes out of a room, you've got to have a leader who is energized and can be energetic even in the most challenging of times, because somebody has to generate that energy. A leader has to have the strength to generate that energy for the team sometimes when the team is totally deflated."

Granholm also suggested a quality that might shock those from the "command and control" school of leadership. "I would say that a leader must be strong enough to give his or her power away, because you have to enlist others," she said. "If the challenge is too great—and often they are too great for one person—you have to recognize that ultimately you will be more successful if you give your power away."

It's not just about delegating responsibilities, she noted. "It is really about empowering others to pick up an oar and row in a very difficult time. And there are a lot of people I know who have refused to let go of leadership in their organizations. They hang on to every detail, and ultimately it is completely self-defeating, because you have to trust your team. You have to be able to give it away. If you have good people you trust on your team, then allow them to put on their wings and fly."

REMEMBERING TO CELEBRATE THE VICTORIES

"If you were to go back in time and give yourself some advice at some important age, what would it be in retrospect?" I asked.

"It's easier to say than it is to do, but I would have celebrated more with my team the positive steps," she said. "I would have given them small bites to keep them motivated and moving. I tried to do that with the public, but less so with my own team because of my impatience to get to the next step. So I think it's important for leaders to really acknowledge, and thank, and celebrate the work of the team."

6

GENE KRANZ

*Ego is a leader's enemy. . . . Virtually everything worthwhile
that's to be done these days is done as a team. As a leader—as
an individual—you have to learn to check your ego at the door
every day when you come to work.*

LIKE MILLIONS OF AMERICANS, I REMEMBER SEEING GENE KRANZ,
the heroic NASA leader and Presidential Medal of Honor hon-
oree, on television during the late sixties in the heady days leading to the *Apollo 11* lunar landing. I was home with my family in
Texas, huddled around a black-and-white Philips television set, as
I watched Kranz leading his team as flight director at Houston's
Mission Control Center.

Even as a teenager, I was deeply impressed by his cool demeanor
and command of the situation while seated behind the main console wearing his distinctive white vest. The craggy chief of Mission
Control appeared to be a sharp, no-nonsense leader, a tough guy,
to be sure, but there was no doubt that he had a big heart and cared
deeply for the welfare of his people.

I met Kranz some forty-one years later, as part of my own mission to explore the nature of great leadership. We had arranged to get together on a cool gray Friday morning at his home in Houston. I arrived a bit early. The retired NASA legend had told me on the phone that he and Marta, his wife of more than fifty years, wouldn't be available until after morning Mass at their Catholic church. So I waited in my vehicle, parked in front of their simple two-story house on a quiet, palm-tree-shaded street not far from the Johnson Space Center, where Kranz spent most of his working life.

Kranz waved when he and Marta drove up in his polished red Ford F-150 pickup. There was a U.S. Air Force decal on the back window, but even without the sticker there would have been little doubt that the rugged driver with the closely shorn hair came from a military background.

Gene and Marta led me into their orderly home, past a small upright piano in the front hall. The living room is replete with symbols of their Catholic faith. Crucifixes, statuettes, and images of saints adorn shelves and walls.

Dressed in a green plaid flannel shirt and black pants, the fit Kranz retains a youthful vigor at seventy-seven years of age, though his trademark blond flattop had turned to a distinguished shade of silver. From the start of our conversation, he made it clear that he's never considered himself either a hero or a leader. Still, he offered his thoughtful analysis of "this thing called leadership" with the precision of an engineer and the passion of a man who loved both his work and his coworkers.

EARLY INFLUENCES

Eugene Francis Kranz was a child of the Great Depression, born August 17, 1933, into an American family of German descent in Toledo, Ohio. When Gene was just seven years old, his father died of a bleeding ulcer, leaving a widow with three young children, no insurance, and no Social Security.

Kranz said he could not remember a time when he and his two older sisters did not have jobs to help their mother. "We were poor. We were *poor*. We had no cars. Bicycles were it. Every member of the family worked."

To support her family and keep an eye on her children, Kranz's "loving, nurturing, and tough" mother transformed their home into a boardinghouse and ran it "like a drill sergeant" for the duration of World War II. Most of those who lived with them were military men. Toledo was a transit hub for the Great Lakes naval training facility near Chicago, so most were headed there.

Kranz considers his mother to be his role model for determination, integrity, and sense of responsibility. "The characteristic of leadership is responsibility, it's acceptance of risk, and it is a strong set of values," Kranz said. "If you want to put the frosting on the cake, it's the ability to understand and seize the situation and make a value judgment that basically says, 'This is the right way to go.' The responsibility came when I was a kid. After my father died, I was responsible for the support of the family, contributing to the support of my mother. Now, I believe that leaders learn from other leaders, but they are not *made* by other leaders."

Not surprisingly, the fatherless boy was influenced and inspired also by the servicemen who shared his home. "First of all, by their dedication, patriotism, and love of country, right on down the line," he said. "But also for the intense focus that they had upon their objective. They understood risk. And they were fully willing to accept whatever risks were necessary to accomplish their objective."

His dreams of becoming a fighter pilot were born early. "We had probably more naval pilots, engineers, and officers come through the house than anybody else," Kranz told me. Some of the naval men who'd been boarders and then gone off to war would mail Gene balsa-wood boxes—a rare commodity, considered a "strategic material" during those years. A naturally talented draftsman and model maker, Gene would fashion balsa-and-paper aircraft and send them back to these soldiers and sailors serving in the war.

His involvement in the war went deeper. For a time, young Gene even volunteered as an airplane spotter. "And I saw one of the Mitsubishi Type One 'Bettys' flying overhead there," he said, still excited at the memory. "I called it in—but nobody believed me!"

Gene shared my youthful passion for flying. By his teenage years, he'd become single-minded in his determination to be a military pilot. "That was the entire focus: becoming a naval aviator. But then I flunked the physical to get into Annapolis." His blood sugar levels tested above the limit for qualification—twice. This was mostly because "I was working at AP warehouses and my diet was brownies and chocolate milk," he said.

Kranz was despondent at first. Annapolis had been the focus of everything he'd done up to that point. He'd received recommendations from his local congressman. The American Legion and veterans' groups had supported his bid. He felt he'd failed himself and all of those who'd encouraged him.

"I was devastated. In fact, I wondered if I'd even go to college," he said. "But I had a high school teacher, Sister Mary Mark. She was very important when I lost the opportunity to go to Annapolis. She picked me up, brushed me off, and told me, 'Look, you *never* surrender. You want to fly, then find another way.' She picked me up when I was down and basically propelled me forward. She taught me: Once you define your objective, you never give it up. You may find different paths to get there, but basically your objective is always there."

As it turned out, Kranz's dreams of flying weren't thwarted. He gained admission to Parks College of Saint Louis University, where he studied aeronautical engineering and joined the U.S. Air Force Reserve. There, Kranz learned to fly planes before he obtained a driver's license. He also showed early hints of what a great leader he would become.

DOING THE RIGHT THING

"For a long time, leadership never dawned on me," he explained. "Like I say, I just wanted to fly. Leadership was not something that I really came to grips with until later in college. We had a fraternity on campus, an aviation brotherly guild, and somehow or other I was elected president. The first real challenge was one where we had a black man who applied for membership. At this time it was unheard of that you'd have a black man in a fraternity, especially in the Saint Louis area. Your organization wouldn't have any place to go and meet [because of racial segregation]. That was probably the first of my real decisions that I was faced with. I convinced the membership that that's where we're going to go, and we'll put up with any impediment."

"Was that a difficult choice?" I asked.

"Yes, it was. I didn't understand anything about prejudice at that time. When I was growing up, Toledo was a very ethnic city. The Polish were here, the Irish were here, the Germans were here, and the blacks were here. We all seemed to get along. But I became intensely aware of discrimination when we moved into the Saint Louis area. The buses, the restrooms, everything else was segregated."

Kranz felt the need to do the right thing when the black student applied for membership in his fraternity, he said. "This was something where I understood very personally the implications of this decision. But it was a decision that had to be made. You must stand for something and your feelings must be strong and you must be willing to challenge yourself, to go through any obstacles or difficulties in order to achieve your objective. And this was the right thing to do. Therefore, we would elect him into the fraternity."

Kranz graduated from college as a commissioned second lieutenant in the Air Force Reserve. He was itching to get over to the conflict in Korea and prove his mettle in air combat. "At that time, in 1950, the Korean War was just beginning. I was getting ready to graduate, and all I wanted to do was get in there and *fly;* get over to Korea and become an ace."

PASSION AND PURPOSE

I shared Kranz's passion and sense of duty to serve our country at the same age. I knew what drove me, but wondered why he also felt such a deep-seated desire to serve.

Kranz paused, squinting off into the mid-distance. "Father served during the First World War. He was the oldest of the sons. He worked in the medical corps." He shrugged. "You know, I can't think of one member of the Kranz family who didn't serve. So service is a generational thing passed down from one generation to the next to the next."

Before receiving the call to active duty just after his college graduation, Kranz went to work at the McDonnell Aircraft Corporation, where he met Harry Carroll, the first in a series of professional mentors who served as guides and inspiration for him. Carroll helped shape him for the challenges he would face at NASA.

"Next to my mother, he was probably the most influential person in my life," Kranz said. "In today's vernacular you'd call him a Renaissance man." A bomber pilot with eighty-six combat missions to his credit, Carroll had flown in North Africa, England, and Tokyo, all three theaters of war. He was a graduate of Washington University, an inventor with many patents related to data reduction and aviation safety, as well as a poet, Eagle Scout leader, and dinner theater performer. "This guy did everything, and he had a passion for everything he did," Kranz said. "He communicated that passion to every person who worked for him or with him or around him. His passion was contagious. And for this young group of engineers that was coming out of college, it was probably the best thing we ever had."

When Kranz went into flight-test data reduction, which involves the analysis of recorded data from each test flight, Harry Carroll was in charge of that area for McDonnell Aircraft. Carroll considered data reduction the most interesting job in the entire aircraft industry because the data recorded during the testing of a flight was the only exact record of what had happened. Harry was fascinated by that data, Kranz said, "Because locked inside this roll of paper, and extremely difficult to read, is exactly what happened in the test of that aircraft. The flight test engineer didn't know what happened; the pilot didn't know what happened. It's all in the data."

Beyond his infectious love of all things related to flying, Carroll had a contagious curiosity about life in general, which fed Kranz's own inquisitive nature. The future NASA Mission Control chief would become a lifelong learner as a result. Carroll's mentoring also gave Kranz a deep appreciation of those who invest in and encourage others as teachers, coaches, and mentors.

Another of those who played this role in Kranz's life was his primary flight instructor, Jack Coleman. "As you know, teaching a person to fly is pretty easy, but giving him the *confidence* is what's critical," Kranz noted. "And it was interesting to watch that guy coach you through this process. Because it's uncomfortable, getting up there the first time. . . . As long as he's in the backseat, okay, you're comfortable. But all of a sudden, you've got to go up and do it yourself. So it was this question of building this confidence and this ability until finally he gets out of the backseat and you're on your own, and guess what? You do feel very comfortable. And you say to yourself, *how* did he do this?"

Kranz gives much of the credit for his success to those who guided and encouraged him along the way and to life experiences. "I don't believe leaders are born," he said. "I believe leaders are made."

HONING A COMPETITIVE EDGE

His early military training instilled Kranz also with competitive instincts he'd never known he had. "You had to get on track and compete for the best flying slot. You had to compete from a technical standpoint. You had to compete from an airmanship standpoint," Kranz explained. "As I went down through jet training, I saw the flying slots and opportunities to fly the best were very limited. So basically I found myself in this head-on competition. I'd never really competed against someone for anything in my life—never had time for sports, just work—until then.

"My best friend was a navigator bombardier who'd been to Korea, so he was one of the flying sergeants. And he turned out to be real key, because he taught me the ropes for finding ways to use the military establishment to further your objective. He was older, he was more experienced, and he had the time. Noncommissioned officers ran the Air Force then. They still do. He and I competed head-on for the flying slots to go to Nellis [Air Force Base]. We were the only two that got it. So it was really super. Then we went to Nellis and we got assigned to the same base down in Myrtle Beach, where we were again in competition."

Those competitive instincts, testing the limits of his inner resolve, kicked in even stronger when Kranz was deployed to fly patrol operations around the Korean demilitarized zone. He fulfilled his childhood dream by getting his own plane, an F-86F, the hottest jet fighter of that time, which he named *My Darling Marta*. He found himself aspiring to be more of a leader as he gained experience, eventually heading a team that directed air strikes to support the frontline troops.

When Kranz returned to the States, he was hired as a test pilot by McDonnell Aircraft, where he soon found himself under the wing of yet "another incredible boss," Ralph Saylor, who taught him that a true leader trains his people thoroughly and then lets them take off.

Kranz recalled that representatives from all the major Air Force contractors were in attendance along with top brass when he flew an important test flight of the B-52 bomber. This plane was one of the few equipped with flight test instrumentation, so he was expecting his boss to be shadowing his every move. "I'm fully expecting Ralph Saylor to look over my shoulder, make sure I'm doing all the right stuff," he said. "We get halfway down the ramp and he stops and says, 'Look, three things I want you to remember today: You're responsible for the lives of the crew members on board the aircraft. You're responsible for one of the few instrumented B-52s in the entire Air Force flight inventory. And you're responsible for the future of our company.'"

With that, Saylor turned around and walked away.

"This is another important attribute of a leader," Kranz said. "There's some point where a person has to let go and trust. First, he has to build the team. But then he has to let the team do their job. And this really became key in later years. Because I had exactly the same thing happen to me when I was working at NASA with Chris Kraft."

DESTINED TO LEAD

Most Americans became engrossed in the space race after the Soviet Union's launch of Sputnik in 1957, which triggered President Kennedy's bold promise in 1961 that the United States would put a man on the Moon within the decade. But it's fair to say that in this regard Gene Kranz was decades ahead of his time. His entire life experience had been preparation for a leadership role in space exploration. As a teenager and into the war years, he'd read about the possibility of travel in space, following newspaper accounts of Germany's pioneer rocket scientist Wernher von Braun and his early ballistic missiles, the V-2 rockets, which were bombarding England

and France. In high school Kranz also devoured the writings of Dr. Robert Goddard, the inventor of the first liquid fuel rocket.

That youthful enthusiasm ignited early and never faded. In the midst of our conversation, Kranz abruptly rose, darted up to his second-floor office, and brought back the original copy of his high school thesis, written in his junior year. Titled "The Design and Possibilities of the Interplanetary Rocket," the paper included im-maculate drafted images of V-2-style rockets. The seventeen-year-old Kranz predicted in this high school thesis that "An examination of the current technical and industrial development demonstrates the high probability that the Moon will shortly be conquered by man."

While showing it to me, Kranz flipped to the cover page to display his grade, a 98, accompanied by the teacher's handwritten note: "Very good!"

In the early years of the U.S. space program, Kranz would prove to be "very good" indeed. In 1960 he responded to an ad in *Aviation Week* announcing that the NASA Space Task Group was "looking for qualified engineers seeking to work in the space program in the newly formed Project Mercury program Langley Field, Virginia, and Cape Canaveral, Florida." He arrived at Lang-ley and came under the tutelage of yet another influential mentor, Christopher Columbus Kraft Jr., NASA's first flight director. Kranz became one of a select group of engineers, most of them former fighter pilots, chosen for command positions in the newly created NASA Space Task Group. Most were in their midtwenties. Few were older than thirty-five. Kranz was all of twenty-seven.

It was a new world for everyone involved, but few had been preparing for it as long as Kranz. "We went from aircraft moving five miles a minute to spacecraft moving five miles a second," he marveled.

Kraft and his young protégés, including Kranz, began creat-ing new rules, new techniques, and new strategies on the fly.

There was no road map for space exploration at that point. "Chris Kraft was right in the middle of developing these new concepts. If you go back into the early flight tests, basically the guy on board the aircraft was in charge," Kranz said. But by the time Kranz joined NASA, the technology had advanced so rapidly that the guy on board the spacecraft didn't even know where he was. He had no idea if he had the proper altitude or if he was flying fast enough. He needed Mission Control to tell him that and other vital information.

Chris Kraft, Kranz, and their other team members were Mission Control. They had thirteen tracking stations around the world, thirteen mini–control centers, all with independent teams, but they had no effective way to communicate with these tracking stations. Communications was a sixty-word-per-minute Teletype. "Somehow or other I ended up in charge of all these remote site teams. And the job was to tie them into the control center," Kranz explained. "So I said, 'The real key to our success in the mission is to make sure that Kraft has every bit of useful information so he can make whatever decisions on the ground.' Basically I became the scribe putting together the communications component of this operation."

Within that first year, Kraft groomed Kranz to follow in his footsteps. "He adopted me as his assistant flight director for Project Mercury [the first human spaceflight program]. You can learn an awful lot by watching other people do their job. I came to the realization that all of these experiences I'd had were preparing me for the role I was about to undertake."

Kranz moved into more of a leadership role when Kraft named him flight director of Project Gemini, the second human spaceflight program, which conducted ten manned flights in 1965–1966. Those flights developed advanced space travel techniques, paving the way to put astronauts on the Moon. It was a role that required willingness to accept even greater risk than he'd known as a pilot, Kranz said. "Leadership involves accepting personal risk, physical risk, mental risk. It's saying, 'I'm willing to step off into an area that

I may not fully understand, but I can see the objective out there, and somehow or other I have to find a way to achieve that objective. Yet if I don't, and if I fail, I'm willing to accept responsibility for that failure.'

"In the early years, with our teams, we lost probably one-third of the young people," he recalled. "Because they were unwilling to accept that kind of responsibility. Willingness to accept the risk that goes with responsibility."

"Does that level of risk require courage or confidence?" I asked.

"I don't know if I could separate the two. Confidence comes about as a result of the training and experience you've had growing up. But it also requires courage, because you have to accept the fact that you are going into this arena, which is going to be very complex. It requires both. The confidence comes from the training and the team that you're with. The courage comes about where you reach into your soul and say, 'Yes, I know the risks, but I think I'm fully capable. I accept responsibility, and I think we'll go do it.'"

LEADING OTHERS TO SUCCESS

Kranz believes that he thrived in part because his Mission Control mentor, Chris Kraft, gave his people room to grow. He guided them but allowed them to create their own unique paths according to their own personalities and styles. "We used to call Chris 'The Teacher.' That was the moniker he carried. And he *was* a teacher. He was charting this path for the rest of us, but he allowed us to carve our own. He set this broad set of guidelines; as long as we worked within them, he would support us."

The early Mission Control team was "a team with character" and a team of characters, according to Kranz. "We were extremely fortunate in the fifties and sixties and even into the early seventies—because personalities flourished. And it was this ability to accept the idiosyncrasies of these very nonstandard people who came in here, their ebullience and the buoyancy they brought to the job, it really helped in building this team.

"We had young pups in there fresh out of college. We had Korean War veterans. We had Jimmy Anson, who was a bomber pilot and had flown over the Ruhr. Peter Armitage was another very interesting young man. When they were developing ejection seats, up in Canada, he was a live test subject out of one of the CF-100s. We had this marvelous array of people, everyone vastly different. You put it into this melting pot and stirred it, and somehow or other you created this chemistry where the total was greater than the sum of the parts. It was marvelous to live and grow in that environment. Each day was a joy. That's another thing: A leader has to make his work *joyful*. Because if you don't, you're not going to get the best out of the people."

There was certainly no joy in the ranks of the Space Task Group on Friday, January 27, 1967, when a tragic event marked a turning point in the life of Kranz and the entire NASA program. To this day, no one can fully explain the precise cause of the devastating fire aboard *Apollo 1,* which was scheduled to be the first manned Apollo mission. All on board were killed: astronauts Gus Grissom, Ed White, and Roger Chaffee. They were the first Americans to die in a spacecraft.

"The *Apollo 1* fire was really difficult to accept," said a somber Kranz. The fact that the horrific deaths had occurred not two hundred thousand miles out in deep space but while the spacecraft was still on the launch pad, just 318 feet off the ground, gave rise to intense inquiry within the space program. On the Monday following the fire, Kranz gathered the entire Flight Control Division in the Mission Control Center's auditorium and delivered an impassioned, extemporaneous, and memorable address that's become known as the "Kranz Dictum":

Spaceflight will never tolerate carelessness, incapacity, and neglect. Somewhere, somehow, we screwed up. It could have been in design, build, or test. Whatever it was, we should have caught it. We were too gung ho about the schedule and we locked out all of the problems we saw each day in our work. Every element of the program was in trouble and so were we. . . . From this day forward, Flight Control will be known by two words: tough and competent. *Tough* means we are forever accountable for what we do or what we fail to do. We will never again compromise our responsibilities. Every time we walk into Mission Control we will know what we stand for. *Competent* means we will never take anything for granted. We will never be found short in our knowledge and in our skills. Mission Control will be perfect.

In the quiet of his Houston home, as the midmorning sun brightened the living room, Kranz was visibly moved by his memory of the *Apollo 1* disaster. "After the fire, that's when we wrote this set of statements, 'Foundations of Mission Control.' And there we added, 'To always be aware that suddenly and unexpectedly you may find yourselves in a role where your performance has ultimate consequences.' And this was to address this question that somewhere along the line, someone that day should have said, 'Stop. Halt. Kill this test. Let's pull the crew out of the spacecraft and figure out what's wrong.'"

LEARNING FROM FAILURE, BUILDING ON SUCCESS

Kranz admitted to being "probably the most emotional of the flight directors." He was a passionate leader, and he let that passion flow when he felt the need to reach into the hearts of his people. "I tended to express my feelings. . . . If I was mad, I was mad and they knew it," he said. "If I was happy, they knew it too. This was a time when you didn't feel like you had to hold anything back.

"I always felt like this: Success is the team's. Failure is mine. When things are going right, that was because of these guys here. If things didn't go right, it's because I missed something. And this concept was carried down all the way to the bottom of the organization."

Sometimes younger people coming into NASA felt it wasn't their place to take responsibility or to speak up. Kranz set them straight. "We were saying, 'Look, as a young guy you're *expected* to stand up and speak out, and we'll listen to you.' This became part of the culture that, fortunately, carried us through many difficult times."

Dark days at NASA would give way to historic and scientific triumphs. As flight director of all odd-numbered Apollo missions, Kranz would lead the team to the greatest achievement in the annals of NASA—landing a man on the Moon. "But by the time we got to the Apollo program, we were Super Bowl champs," Kranz recalled. "This team had fully matured. I'd say the culture had spread out and done its wonderful thing within the organization.

"Did I think about becoming a leader before that time? I don't know, I just sort of *emerged* into this thing called leadership." He'd watched, and absorbed, the best traits of Harry Carroll, Colonel Gabby Gabreski, Ralph Saylor, and Chris Kraft. "Then, as time goes on," he said, "you add your own twists."

Besides his distinctive flattop haircut and his heartfelt talks, Kranz's most stylish flourish was a dapper white vest, instantly recognizable to those watching him on TV. "The white vest was my wife's idea. Leaders use symbols. Patton had his pearl-handled pistols and his silver helmet. My boss Ralph Saylor wore an Aussie hat. Symbols are important.

"When I was flying, Marta used to make fancy scarves for me. Pretty soon she started to make fancy scarves for all the pilots. She understood the importance of the unit insignia. She understood this mystique of a fighter pilot's scarf. So when it came time for my first launch she said, 'You're the White Team boss. Okay, your color is white. Let me make a white vest.' This became a tool to rally the people and give them a sense of identity. Sense of identity is very important to any organization, especially when you're in a high-risk business.

"Finally, some way, you start to put it together. You've become a high-functioning unit. You'd ask a question and someone would say, 'I don't know, but I'll sure find out.' There was complete give-and-take, without concern for ego and feelings. This was accepted within the whole team. This process, this power, this chemistry, this culture that was created was really marvelous. This leads to the development of people, but also development of a new skill set. The development of the relations between the controllers and the designers and the people on the plant floor there. Now it becomes a personal first-name basis."

PREPARATION AND TEAMWORK LEAD TO TRIUMPH

On July 20, 1969, four days after the launch of *Apollo 11*, Gene Kranz reported to Mission Control to begin his team's shift for man's first landing on the surface of the Moon. He addressed his team on a private communications channel in the Control Center.

Today is our day, and the hopes and dreams of the entire world are with us. This is our time and our place, and we will remember this day and what we will do here always.

In the next hour we will do something that has never been done before. We will land an American on the Moon. The risks are high . . . that is the nature of our work.

We worked long hours and had some tough times but we have mastered our work. Now we are going to make this work pay off.

You are a hell of a good team. One that I feel privileged to lead.

Whatever happens, I will stand behind every call that you will make.

Though today it's remembered as a resounding triumph, one of great technological feats of the twentieth century, for Kranz and his White Team the descent of the lunar module could not have been more heart-stopping.

"When we were going down to the Moon for the first time, just as we were about to crack the hill, we started having communications problems," Kranz recalled. First, transmissions became distorted and static-filled. Kranz resolutely issued a *Go* order. Static drowned out all critical data, and when the signals picked up again, radar revealed that the craft was moving too fast and might overshoot the landing zone. On board the spacecraft, a power meter failed; a computer program alarm flashed in the capsule and on the meters in Mission Control.

Kranz clearly relished the memory. "But then Charlie Duke in CapCom says, 'This is almost like a training run!' And all of a sudden everybody just snickered and said, 'Yeah, just like a training run! To hell with the first *real* landing, we're just going to *work* it!'"

Finally, with less than a minute of fuel remaining, the lunar module touched down on the Moon's rugged surface and Neil Armstrong uttered his immortal words: "Houston, Tranquility Base here. The *Eagle* has landed." Unable to control his emotions, Kranz slammed his forearm on the console. On July 20, 1968, at 9:56:20 P.M. Houston time, Armstrong made his historic descent from the ladder to the lunar surface. It was the most triumphant moment of Kranz's career, the culmination of decades of preparation, and his ears rang with President Kennedy's promise: "We choose to go to the Moon in this decade, and do the other things, not because they are easy, but because they are hard. . . ."

But long before the official accolades, the cheering throngs and ticker tape parades, Kranz enjoyed a more personal and more intimate sense of accomplishment, he said, reflecting back on his life's trajectory. "The day we were getting ready to go down to the Moon, I was sitting in the Ops Room, about thirty minutes before we cracked the hill and started powered descent. I began to wonder how the hell I'd got there. What was it that Kraft saw in me? That trusted me to lead this team in an event that you could say was, as a leader, probably the most incredible responsibility you could ever be given. Why did the crew trust me? Why did the program trust me? So you finally get into this conundrum where you almost go berserk thinking, *What was it* exactly *that brought me to this time and place?*"

From the boy whose high school thesis predicted a Moon landing to the accomplished NASA Mission Control director who helped make it happen, Kranz has savored a life blessed with many caring and gifted mentors, he said. "Leadership is a journey. You never stop learning."

A big part of leadership preparation for Kranz—and for me— was driven by the desire to always keep learning and growing. I wanted to become the most complete person I could be, the most authentic version of myself, which included becoming an expert not just in technical skills but also in human skills.

TEST OF LEADERSHIP

Gene Kranz's greatest test of leadership came not during the successful Moon landing but during the *Apollo 13* mission, an epic story of disaster averted. On April 14, 1970, Kranz and his White Team were slated to oversee the lunar orbit insertion and the ascent from the Moon, but at precisely 55 hours and 55 minutes—some 321,860 kilometers away from Earth—an oxygen tank in the *Apollo 13* service module exploded. Then came the ominous transmission, "O.K., Houston, we've had a problem here."

Kranz remained unflappable as he rallied his White Team into action, set the constraints for the consumption of oxygen, electricity, and water, controlled the three course-correction burns during the trans-Earth trajectory, as well as the power-up procedures that allowed the astronauts to use the command module for the trip home. As *Time* magazine later reported, "Quickly responding, [Kranz] made the first of the long night's many important decisions, ordering the astronauts to turn off a fuel cell, check their thrusters and power down the guidance and navigation systems. Though he may well have anticipated the worst, Kranz never faltered or showed signs of panic."

With scarcely a moment's rest, he and his team created, literally on the fly, the procedures necessary to return astronauts in a severely damaged spacecraft back to Earth. As a new day dawned, the White Team guided the *Apollo 13* crew. They jettisoned the lunar module *Aquarius,* leaving the command module *Odyssey* to begin its lone reentry through the atmosphere. After a complete communications blackout briefly stopped hearts around the world, *Odyssey* regained radio contact and splashed down safely in the Pacific on April 17, 1970. For their heroic efforts, Kranz, his White Team, and the astronauts received the Presidential Medal of Freedom.

The Mission Control director's leadership during the *Apollo 13* mission, later memorably reenacted by Ed Harris in Ron Howard's film *Apollo 13,* was marked by unwavering optimism and stalwart leadership. Kranz pushed himself and his team despite fatigue and sinking morale. He also exhibited a courageous decisiveness in the face of unfathomable risks, though he did not give the "Failure is not an option!" rallying cry made famous in the movie. A Hollywood screenwriter came up with that phrase because, Kranz confessed, "My real speech was too long."

His actual words were "O.K., this crew is coming home! You gotta believe it. Your team must believe it and we must make it happen!"

Still, many of his coworkers said the simple five-word declaration attributed to him in the movie was an apt credo for Kranz's stewardship during a life-and-death crisis. Kranz liked the Hollywood version so much that he chose it as the title of his autobiography.

In our discussion, Kranz refused to take much credit for what transpired during that crisis televised around the world. Still, I was impressed with the way this dynamic leader engaged each member of his team by making every one of them feel like an important contributor with a personal stake in achieving the goal.

"By the time we got ready to fly a mission like *Apollo 13*, this was not only the team in the Mission Control Center. This was the team out in the plant. This was the team out in MIT Draper Labs. There was this kind of mystique that we were able to create where we had everyone believing that they were personally responsible for the success of this mission.

"And once you get to that point, boy, you're dynamite. You get answers coming in for questions you haven't asked yet! At the time of *13*, I completely forgot about lithium hydroxide, crew atmosphere. I was more interested in working the power problem, getting them home, fighting the battle of where we're gonna land. All of a sudden, this group off to the side is saying they've come up with a solution to a problem I haven't even asked [about] yet."

"During those white-knuckle hours of the *13* mission, how critical was that sense of shared responsibility and that culture of collective ownership?" I asked Gene.

"The leader builds leaders," Kranz told me. "He expects his people to stand up. 'Hey, we need somebody to work the power resource problem. John Aaron, you're it.' John Aaron became a leader. 'Boom. Arnie Aldridge, you got checklist. Bill Peters, you're going to work on crew survival.' And the rest of the team said, 'Well, I don't think Peters is the best guy, but he's the guy, so we'll work for him.' There's a give-and-take that has to exist within the organization.

"The leader can't do all the jobs. And he has to have the capacity to assign responsibilities, and the team has to accept those responsibilities. Most of the time he's going to be right. And if he isn't right, the team's going to give the leader the benefit of the doubt."

"How does a leader articulate the necessary clarity of vision?" I asked.

"This is probably one of the most underrated skills of a leader. I describe leadership as the ability to focus [the] talent, energy, and imagination of a group upon an objective," he said. "We've talked about integrity. But yes, it's also the ability to clearly articulate this vision, this direction, that makes people want to follow. And I go back to Harry Carroll. It was his *passion*. If you have passion for the work that you do, articulating that work and that vision in Technicolor is no problem. Articulating it with absolute belief and conviction. I won't say it's easily acquired. But it is acquired. It didn't come naturally to me. It came to me because I'd been associated with Carroll and I'd seen how he was able to influence me as a young engineer. He communicated it to me, and I've never lost it through my entire life. I don't care if I'm speaking to a big crowd or to fifth-grade kids; you do this passionately and completely."

Other critical aspects of leadership are building confidence and providing hope, Kranz said. "You don't go out to a mission and say, 'Hey, we expect to fail.' Your job as a leader and as a team is to find solutions. During *Apollo 13,* this came about through all the training. The team was clearly focused on the objective. It was the same thing when we went down to the Moon. We didn't go down to abort the landing. We were going to land. Of course, it takes time to develop this set of skills, this intimate, deep-seated belief. It takes communication through the days, weeks, and months leading up to an event, where everybody becomes a believer. But it starts off with this thing called the passion for the job. If you have a passion for the job, you will find a way."

THE SHARED MISSION

To what degree did his experiences as a fighter pilot affect his development at NASA? I asked Kranz.

"To some extent, as flight directors, we were all competitive," Kranz remembered. "It was like being top dog as a fighter pilot. But at the same time, you would help these guys when they needed it. It was the point of saying, 'We're all in this together, and if one of us fails, we all fail.'"

Experience as a fighter pilot is great leadership training for NASA because it instills the confidence necessary to function in such a high-risk environment, he said, noting that three out of the four flight directors for *Apollo 13* had flown high-performance aircraft.

I mentioned that my own fighter pilot experiences had given me invaluable self-confidence because it was so satisfying and fulfilling to become proficient at the skills and teamwork required for what is considered by most to be the epitome of flying.

"Flying high-performance aircraft is an incredible confidence builder," Kranz agreed. "It's inherently risky. You learn to become comfortable in a high-risk environment."

He recalled one of his most challenging missions as a fighter pilot, flying into a typhoon between Formosa (Taiwan) and Okinawa. The flight leader had radio problems, so he gave Kranz the hand signal to take the lead for the four fighters in the formation. This was an intensely high-pressured situation for Kranz to be thrown into so early in his military career.

Suddenly he was in charge of navigating through the tremendous storm, with lightning all around them, analyzing the situation and deciding where they would go. On top of all those challenges, this also was the first time Kranz had ever led a formation in a "jet penetration," which means that the group had to stay at a high altitude to conserve fuel until relatively close to their destination; then, with Kranz in the lead, drop in a steep descent down through the storm while staying close enough to maintain visual contact with one another's planes.

During this intense flight, Kranz was well aware that if he made a mistake it could easily mean death for him and the other pilots on the mission. The fact that he held it together and rose to the occasion was a tremendous confidence builder, he said. This was a life-and-death situation. "I was in the lead with three other guys hanging on me, and if we didn't get down, they were going to end up punching out, over the water, in a storm, which is not good," he said with understatement. "It's accepting this responsibility that's thrown upon you. Having the confidence to go do it."

The key skill he derived from this experience, he said, was learning to be "in a comfort zone within a dynamic, constantly changing environment—and feeling that you can master any situation that's thrown at you while leading [your] people through this wall of water. . . . When you break out . . . you feel happier than hell. You feel like you're Mother Hen taking those chicks home. There's no question that you grow, you feel comfortable living and working in a high-risk environment. It becomes almost natural."

Handling such a challenge with skill, courage, and self-discipline changed his view of the world, especially the way he perceived risk from then on, Kranz said. "Everybody says, 'Did you ever feel stressed during *13*?' I say, 'Hey, I had the entire *world* sitting behind the viewing room. The media was sitting off to the left of my control room. We were reporting live as it was going on. But I didn't even know they were there!' "

This story mirrors my own military experience. When you're a fighter pilot there are very well-defined responsibilities. Great skill and great teamwork are required, and the risks are so great that even a momentary lapse can be catastrophic. The traits you develop in those situations stay with you the rest of your life, and you know that you have accomplished something that very few people have done. That sort of thing makes a mark on you and sets you apart from those who've never faced such challenges.

Technical mastery isn't the only challenge of leadership, of course. You also have to master your emotions and develop a high level of self-control, not just over your fears but also over your anger and outrage. Leaders can find themselves torn between the instinct to protect their team and the need to follow orders. Loyalty to one's team and to one's own people can put a leader in conflict when he is expected to put the goals of the organization first. This complex, often contradictory, dynamic has long fascinated me. Those who have seen combat often say that they are not fighting for a cause or a country but instead for their comrades beside them. As a pilot, my first priority was always the safety of my passengers and crew.

With those thoughts in mind, I asked Kranz to return for a moment to his days at Myrtle Beach, back to another of his early mentors, Colonel Francis Stanley "Gabby" Gabreski. After he was commissioned in the Air Force, Kranz came under the wing of the legendary ace fighter pilot, who "had all the components" of leadership, including the instincts of a great teacher or coach.

"A leader is a coach. When you're a young fighter pilot, to have an ace flying your wing, that's the way to go," said Kranz. "You're flying your first flight and he's going to be flying your wing. It's a two-on-two with hundreds out there. You're on top of the world as a young punk!"

Gabreski was well known for his intense devotion to those under his command, which sometimes put him in conflict with his superior officers. He was all about preparing his pilots to handle their responsibilities. This principled leader was not focused on climbing the chain of command, Kranz said. "I think it's the only reason he never made general," he added. "He was intensely loyal to his people. And basically, every outfit on base was equally important to him: his pilots, his flight, his equipment, the maintenance guys, every person in this chain was critical."

"Gabby remained true to his values and did what he knew was right even though he knew there was a price to pay in his career," I said.

"I think he did," Kranz agreed. "This is true for many leaders. There's a point at which every leader is going to be faced with a challenge of taking the more difficult road. I think Gabby was one. There's many other examples out there. He was one of those individuals who believe not only in their mission but also in their team. And there comes a point at which you get a direction to move that is counter to that set of beliefs, that set of standards, that you've established. You're faced with a choice to compromise and take the easier path. That is, again, one of the characteristics that the leader has to maintain among the members of his team: that he is always working in their best interests."

"Is that based solely on the strength of one's reputation?" I asked.

"Yes, reputation. People view him as without peer. They say, 'This is the guy that I want to work for. This is the guy that I want to be.'"

CONTROLLING EGO

"How, then, do we, like Colonel Gabby, show resolve when our personal values aren't always congruent with the task we're asked to undertake?"

"Now you're getting into a different component of leadership," Kranz said. "Ego is a leader's enemy. And when you get into this situation, you have to address it from a standpoint of 'Why do I not agree to this thing? Do I have solid legitimate reasons, or is it just because this is not the way I want to go?'"

The toughest thing a fighter pilot and any leader must learn is to override ego and to self-assess, Kranz said. "You need to have a selective filter," he added. "If you can now move ego out of it and say, 'Okay, I still got technical issues with this thing here, let me address this. Have I done my best at addressing this technical issue?' Virtually everything worthwhile that's to be done these days is done as a *team*. Because things are so complex, so fast moving, you need the total breadth in order to compete for the future. As a leader—as an individual—you have to learn to check your ego at the door every day when you come to work."

This self-control also extends to obeying orders even when you may not agree with them, or with the officer who issues them, said Kranz, who admitted that he sometimes balked at his orders if he felt the safety of his crew was being jeopardized unnecessarily.

"Operations is the art of the possible. You may say to yourself, *Okay, I don't agree with it, but I can accept it.* You accept it because there is a hierarchy; you accept that this guy is a leader. You understand that he is faced with the same challenges that you've got. When the time comes that you no longer respect that person for the work he's doing, if it gets to a point that you can't salute him, then it's time to go out and look for other employment. But you don't go out—I hate to say it—you don't communicate these thoughts to your people. This is something that's very personal."

MAKING TOUGH DECISIONS

Kranz noted that he was once "set to punch out" of his job at NASA because he disagreed with his superiors on a decision that he felt endangered the astronaut crew. He took a stand, but before the issue could come to a head, the astronauts raised similar concerns and won out. "Fortunately I was saved by the crew recognizing the same thing," he said. "But also, I had to eat crow in that process because I had popped off to my boss and said, 'You can take this job and shove it.' I had to go back in and eat a little bit of humble pie. That's another thing that leaders must sometimes do."

Those at the top often cannot share their emotions and concerns with their team members, Kranz said. "Leaders have to carry an awful lot of *emotional* burden," he offered. "You've got to keep it to yourself because your team . . . they've got their own problems. You've got to be prepared to accept some tough decisions."

Perhaps the greatest challenge for any leader, Kranz said, is to create an organization from scratch by establishing standards, values, and trust throughout. "This is the challenge we were faced with when we started off with the Space Task Group," he said. "Because we had marvelous chemistry in the Space Task Group. We had classical aeronautical engineers, generally in their late thirties or early forties, from Langley Research Center. We captured the entire Avro Arrow flight test team, who were in their early to midthirties. And then I came in with a group of other aviator types, young college graduates in our twenties, as the raw material. It was fascinating to watch this particular group establishing the culture necessary for success. And it's really the challenge of the leadership to establish this culture."

This is accomplished by first establishing a set of standards that are followed from the top all the way down, Kranz said. "And you can never violate those standards, because once they're established, this is the calibration point, the reference point, for performance of every individual within the organization.

"That's step one. The next thing, you have to articulate a set of values. Gabby did this, but when you're starting off in a new organization you have to articulate a set of values as to who you are, what you stand for, and what you'll be known by. That's the second step.

"Once you have that, then you can establish the trust, and once you have the trust, then you can establish the team. It starts off with this very strong set of standards that you've set for yourself. Gabby had it easy because he had this established team as opposed to starting a new organization."

If Chris Kraft was known as The Teacher, I asked, then what was Kranz's own moniker?

"General Savage!" he said, unleashing a booming laugh. "Remember *Twelve O'Clock High*?"

"Yes," I said. "One of my all-time favorite films."

With Kranz's professional reputation as an uncompromising, no-nonsense leader, he may indeed have resembled General Savage, the brigadier general portrayed by Gregory Peck in that 1949 war classic, but in his personal life the proud father and grandfather appeared much softer-edged. Indeed, he seemed the quintessential family man. On the wall in his living room hung a framed black-and-white portrait of his six children—five daughters and a son—all of whom live nearby in the Houston area. Four of his daughters still work in the space industry.

We'd been talking for nearly three hours, Kranz barely moving from his seat, rarely easing his intense focus. "Geez, the coffee," he said, noticing that the carafe, tray, and cups that Marta had set out on the dining room table lay untouched. The black brew had long since gone cold.

I had one final question for him. "During *13*, did you ever doubt that you'd get the entire crew home safely?"

"No, *never*," Kranz said, snapping upright. "Not for one minute. That was true for the entire team. We were so focused on the objective: let's bring these guys home."

FOUNDATIONS OF MISSION CONTROL

To instill within ourselves these qualities essential for professional excellence:

Discipline: Being able to follow as well as lead, knowing that we must master ourselves before we can master our task.

Competence: There being no substitute for total preparation and complete dedication, for space will not tolerate the careless or indifferent.

Confidence: Believing in ourselves as well as others, knowing that we must master fear and hesitation before we can succeed.

Responsibility: Realizing that it cannot be shifted to others, for it belongs to each of us; we must answer for what we do, or fail to do.

Toughness: Taking a stand when we must; to try again, and again, even if it means following a more difficult path.

Teamwork: Respecting and utilizing the ability of others, realizing that we work toward a common goal, for success depends on the efforts of all.

To always be aware that suddenly and unexpectedly we may find ourselves in a role where our performance has ultimate consequences.

7

TONY LA RUSSA

Pressure comes from caring and wanting to do something for the team. It comes from your sense of being held accountable, right? We often say, "If you're not nervous, you're not ready. If you're too calm, you don't care enough."

I FIRST BEFRIENDED RETIRED MAJOR LEAGUE BASEBALL MANAGER AND three-time World Series winner Tony La Russa over strays, and I'm not referring to stray fly balls. My family of dog and cat lovers raises puppies for Guide Dogs for the Blind and we take in foster kittens for ARF, the Animal Rescue Foundation, based in Walnut Creek, California, not far from our home in Danville. You might be surprised to learn that ARF, a "no kill" shelter, was created by the very same sports figure whom writer Buzz Bissinger once described as "intense, smoldering, a glowing object of glower."

Tony La Russa may project that imposing image on the ball diamond and in postgame press conferences, but that's not the thoughtful man of uncommon empathy and grace I've come to know. Nor does it sound like the softhearted guy who founded

ARF. La Russa, who retired as manager of the Saint Louis Cardinals after winning the 2011 World Series, was leading the Oakland A's in May of 1990 when a stray cat came prowling onto the playing field during a game with the New York Yankees. In front of television cameras with millions of fans watching, the game was delayed due to a feline on the baseline. Umpires and players tried to corral the cat without success. Finally, Tony did what managers do. He took charge, coaxing the cat into the dugout, where he kept it for the rest of the game.

After the game, he and his wife, Elaine, initially planned on taking the stray to an animal shelter, but they discovered that many shelters euthanized dogs and cats not adopted within a certain period and those that did not euthanize were overcrowded. The La Russas were not about to let that happen to their ballpark stray. They found the cat a home and then founded ARF to provide the East Bay area with a more benevolent animal shelter. Instead of euthanizing abandoned kittens, as many shelters do, ARF relies on volunteers like us to keep the kittens until they're old enough to be fixed, have their shots, and ultimately be adopted. We've really enjoyed doing this as a family activity, but we had never met Tony La Russa until he found us.

When my family and I were cast in the intense media spotlight immediately after the Hudson River landing, an ARF staff member mentioned to Tony that we were volunteers for the shelter. Tony called our home that same day. I was still in New York City, preparing for the first meeting with the National Transportation Safety Board investigators who would be questioning me for several hours about Flight 1549. Lorrie was home, but she was screening calls with the answering machine because we'd had such a deluge from the media and well-wishers.

When my wife heard, "Hi, this is Tony La Russa," she picked up the receiver and had a brief chat with him. Tony offered his congratulations for the safe landing of Flight 1549 and also his condolences for all the media attention, which included a fleet of television satellite trucks and swarms of reporters and photographers camped in our cul-de-sac. Tony, who also has two daughters, said that if he could help us through the media storm he'd be glad to share any contacts or resources we might need.

At the time, we were still reeling from the loss of privacy. The intensity of sudden scrutiny was overwhelming. Early on we were receiving 250 media requests each week, but it wasn't just the media knocking on the door and peering into our windows. Strangers were coming to the door seeking autographs and photos of us. This was a sudden, life-changing event for my family and me. We had to quickly rise to the occasion to fulfill our new roles as public figures. To face this media onslaught, I had to develop new skills and improve those I already had.

Tony has been through similar experiences. He'd managed under the glare of World Series pressure, handled the media frenzy over his Cardinals' star Mark McGwire when baseball's steroid scandal broke, and jousted with fans and reporters on a daily basis for many years. Tony understood that all the attention came with his job, but he also knew that a normal, private family like ours was ill prepared for such a life-changing event.

Once I got home, I returned Tony's call and we began having regular chats over breakfast or lunch. I was surprised at how much we had in common, including our appreciation of good coffee. My new friend was skeptical of my ability to brew my own until I played barista in my kitchen one day, whipping up a latte for him.

"Wow, Sully," he said. "This is actually good!"

"What were you expecting?" I asked.

"You know what?" he said, laughing. "On the way over here, to be honest, I was dreading it. Just dreading it. I was prepared to suck it up and hold my nose and endure whatever I had to."

WHATEVER IT TAKES

Like any great leader, Tony La Russa has learned to do whatever it takes to motivate and drive his players to perform at their highest levels. In a sport in which a batting average of .300 is considered a high level of achievement, baseball is often described as "a game of failure." Leaders like Tony also understand that experiencing failure and learning from it are part of success.

La Russa is widely regarded as the quintessential old-school "baseball man." In his midsixties, he accomplished what no other manager in the modern baseball era has, winning the Manager of the Year Award five times. In a time of rampant free agency, when owners and fans demand victories, La Russa has forged a career of remarkable longevity. He has managed major league clubs for thirty-three consecutive seasons. He led the Cardinals to their tenth world championship in 2006. That World Series win made La Russa only the second manager in major league baseball history to win championships while coaching both National and American League teams. In 2010 he finished his fifteenth season at the helm of the Cardinals, ranking third on the list of all-time major league baseball wins for managers, with 2,638 victories.

Tony's final year as the Cardinals' manager exemplified his remarkable career. After trailing Atlanta by ten and a half games in the National League wild card race in late August of 2011, his never-say-die team rallied. They won twenty-three of their last thirty-two games, rolling past the Braves in dramatic fashion on the final day of the regular season.

After winning their league's wild card slot, the Cardinals went on to defeat the Texas Rangers four games to three in a hard-fought, classic seven-game series. Fans and sportswriters alike hailed the Cardinals' gritty comebacks and teamwork in that series, in which La Russa's belief that every member of the team is a "go-to guy" was once again proven true. Often called the best manager of the modern era, La Russa already has "a ticket punched for the Hall of Fame," according to *Sports Illustrated*. Baseball experts have long noted that the most special thing about La Russa is his keen intellect and a leadership style that is at once instinctive and cerebral.

In a time of posturing and pampered multimillionaire ballplayers, La Russa, the son of a delivery truck driver, hails from a working-class background and still exudes a blue-collar bluntness. As many have noted, this Tampa native of Spanish-Italian parentage is a tough guy to pigeonhole, given that he also holds a law degree, speaks fluent Spanish, reads voraciously, follows a vegetarian diet, is an outspoken animal rescue activist, and has performed in two ballets, playing a sugar plum in *The Nutcracker* and Grim Reaper Rabbit in *The Mad Hatter*.

SUCCESS THROUGH FAILURE

On a sunny winter morning prior to the 2011 baseball season, I drove up to talk to La Russa at his ARF office in Walnut Creek. He greeted me in a green short-sleeved Kavu sports shirt and dark jeans. As always, he looked fit, tanned, and ready for any challenges that might come his way. We sat in his office surrounded by baseball memorabilia, autographed uniforms, balls, bats, and framed awards. His bookshelves were packed with a wide range of reading material, confirming my belief that, like me, Tony has a passion for always expanding his knowledge.

His journey to leadership in his chosen field was born of failure in that same field. He was a talented athlete growing up, and scouts offered him his first professional contract when he was still at Jefferson High School in Tampa. Tony signed the deal, which he now regards as a youthful mistake.

"I signed too young, just wasn't strong enough," he said.

He sustained injuries early and often but managed to keep playing at a high level for ten years. "When I was slotted as the starting shortstop my rookie season, it was the first time in major league history that an eighteen-year-old had started a game," he said. "There's only been *two* more since then."

I shot him a questioning look. Tony knew what I was wondering. "Trivia answer: two pearls and a turd," he said. "Future All-Stars Robin Yount and Alex Rodriguez were the two pearls. And then there's *me*."

He hit .250 as a rookie, but "sat on the bench in the big leagues for three and a half years, mostly in Oakland." This was a crucial turn of events for this future coach and strategist. Injuries cut short his playing career, but that failure eventually led to his career as a manager. Like many leaders who enjoy long-term success, Tony learned from his failures. I told Tony that if he had been a better player, he likely would not have been such a standout as a manager.

STAYING IN THE GAME

Tony knew his playing days were numbered, so in the off-season he began attending law school at Florida State University, where he completed his studies "after five winters." During his last three seasons as a baseball player, he also served as a player-coach and benefited from the sage guidance of coaching mentor Loren Babe, who "allowed me to ask him every question and never took it personally. He just took it as this thirst to learn. That was really the beginning of my understanding of leadership. I saw how the club responded to Loren. The first year I was still playing quite a bit, but I had some limited opportunities to coach, to lead, and people were looking at me differently. A lot of times as a player you lead by example."

I have seen throughout my career the importance and power of leading by example: by trying to personally and genuinely live the qualities that one believes in. Tony did the same in every aspect of his life. Around this time, he was also making a mark as a law student. One of his law professors, impressed by his performance in the classroom, suggested that he do a clerkship in federal court. The nearest federal circuit court was in New Orleans. Hoping to still keep a hand in baseball, Tony spent his last year as a player/coach with a Saint Louis Cardinals Triple-A team based in New Orleans.

Then Tony's life took another unexpected turn. In his first season with the minor league Cardinals team, its young manager contracted lung cancer and missed several games. Tony stepped in and managed in his absence. The team owners were so impressed, they made Tony the manager of the struggling team, which forced him to step up as a leader rather quickly. "Now I'm doing a crash course in my mind, almost overwhelming myself. Oh, wham! What was it that I learned from Loren?"

Tony let out a dry laugh. "Sure enough, I managed for two weeks, and the team responded to me. Bottom line: When it was over, the job didn't overwhelm me, which surprised me. I realized I could handle it."

In 1973, La Russa married Elaine and then entered law school in Tallahassee. He was still trying to choose between practicing law and coaching baseball, but since he had to wait for his bar exam results to get his license, La Russa decided to stay with baseball at least another season. "Elaine said, 'Okay, why not? Get it out of your system.'"

I laughed at that story and said, "And you haven't yet, have you, Tony?"

"No, I haven't," he said. "It's really kind of a fairy tale."

Now it was my turn to identify with him. After Flight 1549, my life changed dramatically in a similar "fairy tale" manner. Suddenly I found myself in the company of important leaders in government, business, entertainment, and other fields. Many of them and those in the media were interested in what I had to say on aviation topics. I decided to use my sudden fame as a platform for stepping up as a leader in that field, particularly on issues related to passenger safety and the plight of my fellow pilots facing pay cuts and the loss of their pensions. Like Tony La Russa, leadership was thrust upon me, but both of us were more prepared than we might have thought initially.

DEFINING MOMENTS

For Tony, the defining career moment came not in the media glare of the World Series, not even in the big leagues, but while he was playing Single-A ball in Modesto, California. It was 1966, and Tony was a talented young infielder caught in an emotional dilemma. He was dealing with mounting pressure in the hours before a big play-off game. His decision-making process that day and the strategy he devised to face his fears would become part of his successful managerial style.

"We were going to the ballpark around one thirty," he said. "And the whole morning, man, the pressure's getting to me, and a lot of times what happens when you're pressured and you're afraid to fail, you're tempted to call in sick."

Modesto was in a play-off series against their rivals, the Angels, and Tony didn't want to let his team down, even though he had a valid excuse, a sore throwing arm. His worry was that the sore arm would cause him to make a throwing error to lose the game. If he said he was unavailable to play because of the pain, he knew at least one person would never forgive him. "Right around noontime, it just came to me. I said, 'If I duck this one, how am I going to live with myself?'"

He was only twenty-one years old, and just beginning his playing career, but Tony grasped the ramifications of fleeing his responsibilities. Instead, he began psyching himself up, trying to "get rid of the bad vibes" and shed his overwhelming sense of dread. The strategy was deceptively simple, but enormously effective.

"I said, 'I'm going to be aggressive with everything I do.' So I drove into the park, got out of the car, slammed the car door, walked purposefully into the locker room. Everything, I mean everything I did, even the way I took my shirt off—POP!" His teammates stared. This was unlike the normally stoic, laid-back Floridian they'd known. He performed every action, right down to the way he buttoned his uniform and strapped on his gear, with exaggerated emphasis and aggression. "See, a lot of times, when you're playing every day, you pace yourself so that you're ready. You get loosey-goosey," Tony explained. "But I took batting practice and made sure I swung at everything and ran hard. All of a sudden, just through the sheer act of being aggressive, I felt the blood start to pump. . . ." Tony threw every ball with added vigor and launched his body at every grounder like it was a matter of life and death. "I could feel this new energy, and I was more focused," he said. "I had set a direction of something to do rather than something to avoid. I'd told myself to be aggressive. If I made a mistake, it would be an aggressive one. If I see something coming to the plate that's white and moving, I'm swinging at it!"

In his first three at-bats, Tony had two hits and scored a run to tie the score. Then, in the top of the ninth inning, he came to bat again with his team up by one run and three runners on base. Tony stepped up and hit a grand-slam home run over the scoreboard. He shook his head.

"Yes, that's a true story," he said, savoring the memory.

It's such a great story, in fact, that over the years it's been told and retold many times until it has acquired the glow of legend. Tony has often recounted the story to motivate his players, and he's called up the same golden memory to give himself a boost when faced with the challenges of major league games. All too often, he says, players find themselves paralyzed by fear, by thoughts of humiliation: "They say, 'I could embarrass myself—I could fail.'"

The abiding lesson of his ninth-inning grand-slam story is "learning about these reserves that we all have within us," Tony said. "If you commit to something, and you honestly try to do it, you have reserves of strength, a will, that you don't even know about. Let's say you're fifty pounds overweight and you commit to losing weight, and if you really commit to it, you'll do it. If you never worked out and you're going to the gym, as hard as it is at first, and as badly as you want to quit, you've gotta take the first step."

When his players and staff members are plagued by self-doubts, Tony counsels them: "Commit. Be aggressive. And *never* look back."

BECOMING A PRESSURE PLAYER

"I've been taught to make pressure your friend," Tony told me. "And we teach our players how to handle pressure and become pressure players. We have a three-step process, and that's one of our advantages as a team because when we play these big games, anybody might have to step up."

It's one of the primary leadership lessons he shares with his players. Baseball is unlike a lot of other team sports, according to La Russa: "If you're in a basketball game and you're down by two points, there's a couple of guys on the roster that you want to take that last shot. Well, in baseball, we teach every guy on our team that he can be the go-to guy."

Tony began each year with the expectation that his team would play for the World Series championship and that this pressure would be a friend, not an enemy, for his players. "You can't get to September as a team, playing for the first five months like, 'Hey, whatever happens, happens. . . .' No, it doesn't work like that. You need to make things happen, even during the early months of the season. Even during the spring. So pressure attaches," he said. "If you're a player on a team that's going to try to win, yes, you better believe: pressure attaches."

Tony said he has three basic steps for preparing his players to deal with the stress of each season. Call it his PEP talk, because it focuses his players on *preparation, exposure,* and *process.*

Step one is preparation: "If you know that you are prepared for whatever thing you're doing in life, then you'll feel less stressed out than if you were unprepared," he said. The classic example he gives is the student who has put off studying and doing assignments all semester and then crams just before the final exam. "You did all this cramming at the end and you've shortened that process, so you walk in there hoping they ask you stuff that you might get by on," he said. "Well, that anxiety felt walking into the classroom is due to a lack of preparation."

The much better scenario is the student who has prepared all semester by doing the daily assignments and learning the material over time so that on the day of the final exam there is less tension. "Then you walk into the test saying, 'Okay, ask me whatever you want, 'cause I'm as prepared as I can be.'"

This concept is completely transferable to any line of work, but "In baseball the lack of preparation manifests itself differently, in maybe the physical training you didn't do, or maybe the mental preparation was lacking. But however you cut it, if you shortcut the preparation, you're going to feel pressure. If you do the preparation, by definition you feel less overwhelmed."

The second component of Tony's PEP program is exposure. His belief is that the more someone is exposed to stressful situations, the better he or she becomes at handling them. Inexperienced ballplayers typically respond two ways in a pressure situation, he says. Some are gun-shy. They are so afraid of making mistakes that they can't help but do just that. Their fears overwhelm them. Others are so eager to prove themselves and so pumped up that "the minute the pitcher releases the ball, they swing at anything, chasing bad pitches."

But after enough repetitions of these pressure scenarios in practice and games, players can learn and master methods for calming themselves, such as controlling their breathing while monitoring their thoughts so that they don't give in to fears or become overexcited. Players who are exposed to stressful situations time and time again often gain so much confidence that they become *eager* for the opportunity to prove themselves.

The final step in mastering pressure is learning to focus not on the outcome or result, like winning or losing a game, getting a hit, or throwing out a player, but instead on the process of performing at a high level. Tony says this third step is "the Golden Rule."

"Pressure comes from *caring* and wanting to do something for the team," he said. "It comes from your sense of being held accountable, right? We often say, 'If you're not nervous, you're not ready. If you're too calm, you don't care enough.'"

La Russa said a batter must be thinking only about using his fundamental skills well and not looking ahead to the results. So a batter should not allow himself to be distracted with "hero versus goat" thoughts such as "Man, if I drive in another run we'll win this game." Or "If I strike out we don't have a chance of winning."

"You focus in on how, how, how, with thoughts such as 'Okay, this guy's a high-ball pitcher, here's how I'll adjust.' Once you get in the batter's box, your focus should be on the absolute basics. Your focus needs to be on your batting keys, especially see the ball, get a good pitch to hit, and hit the ball," he added.

Meanwhile, La Russa was doing the same, sticking with the basics pitch by pitch, play by play, inning by inning. Throughout the game, he used "self-talk" to maintain that concentration.

"If I stop doing that, my thoughts wander off to this or that happening, so I use that mechanism to stay focused," La Russa said.

As the leader of the team, the manager can't be thinking about the outcome of the game. Instead, he must remain in the moment, analyze each situation, and take appropriate actions, he said.

"My process needs to be, 'Okay, watch where the defense is. Make sure I've got the right pitcher throwing to the right guy.'"

Tony paused here and related his final step for dealing with pressure to my situation as the captain of Flight 1549. "When we first met, Sully—remember?—I asked you if you went through the litany of stuff you had to do—that 'boom, boom, boom, boom'?

And you told me it was exactly the same: focusing on the process, not the result. You told me, 'Tony, if I had thought about it at that time, the dire consequences, I might have done something wrong.' If you'd been thinking about 'Hey, I'm gonna land this plane someplace and I'll be a great hero,' you'd have been distracted, and you would have missed something fundamental. So you just went into this cocoon and remained focused: *No, this is what I need to do.*"

La Russa told me that even before we'd met, he'd thought of my actions on Flight 1549 as a great example of handling pressure through the same methods he teaches his ballplayers. He'd even told his team "that from now on, when we stay focused in a pressure situation, we're going to say, 'We Sully'd it.'"

I had to smile at that. They say you know you've made it when your name becomes a verb! "Thank you, Tony," I said. "It's a great honor to have my name attached to one of your coaching lessons."

He continued: "After I told the boys that story, I said, 'Hey, I'm talking about winning a *game*. But look at what Sully was dealing with. That's life and death. Still, it's the same ABCs. His process was totally pressure proof.' That's the best example I can give any of my players, or my coaching staff, of doing it right and making pressure your friend."

OVERCOMING A CULTURE OF ENTITLEMENT

One of the greatest challenges managers like La Russa must deal with is the more self-centered attitudes of modern athletes who've been raised as spoiled prospects rather than as team players. Like any leader, Tony has had to adjust his approach as times have changed. He began his professional career before the dawn of multimillion-dollar, multiyear player contracts. Back then, playing baseball was not a path to riches and fame as much as it was a sport played for minimum pay that allowed only for "basically, survival," he said.

"You knew if you played good today, you'd play tomorrow. If you had a good year you'd get some money and you'd keep your job. Survival is basic human nature."

Many managers today "forget that it's so different now than it used to be. The professional athletes you deal with today are often spoiled. They've not been held accountable. People have been protecting and caring for them," La Russa said. The average annual salary of a major league baseball player in 2010 was more than $3 million, with the top echelon of players earning $20 million to $27 million a year. Because of the stratospheric salaries and the twenty-four-hour media attention, baseball managers have challenges motivating their players and keeping them focused on doing their best day in and day out during the long season. "You'll give maybe the greatest leader's speech anybody's ever given. And if they pay attention to you, if you get their buy-in, the next day when you see them on the field you might have lost their attention for whatever reason," he said. "In fact, all coaches in major professional sports are challenged to deal with these distractions."

Baseball requires teamwork perhaps more than any other major sport, but the self-centered focus of modern athletes does not encourage the selfless attitude required of a team player. "They're raised in this culture of being constantly told, 'You're an athlete. You're entitled. You're always right.' They have these entourages. If they do something wrong they get protected. They have their families, their friends, and their representatives, and all these people are all telling them, with some rare exceptions, 'Get yours. Get yours. Get yours.'"

"How does a leader in any field cope with a culture of entitlement?" I asked.

Tony calls his strategy *personalization*. Initially, he reminded the members of his team that it was in their best interests to be viewed as winners, and the only way to win in baseball was to put the team's best interests ahead of the individual's. "When I think it's appropriate, I say, 'Hey, fellas, if you're going to listen to what your friends and representatives tell you instead of what your *team* needs and what your coaches and manager say, well, then you need to be either a tennis player or a golfer. But if you play a team sport, it really is about *us,* and you need to contribute, and if all your teammates contribute, you're going to be better and we'll all win."

INSTILLING CORE VALUES

Over his thirty-three-year career as a manager, La Russa also identified three important values, which he tried to instill in his players to overcome their sense of entitlement and to engage them in a team effort. Those values are *respect, trust*, and *caring.*

"The respect comes when I show them that I have something to contribute and that our coaching staff has something to contribute," he said. "You establish that respect through your experience and body of knowledge, by knowing something that can help them. But then you really bring your respect home because of the way you transmit your message. Are you there every day? Do you do it?"

I said, "Leadership by personal example."

"Exactly. Leadership by personal example. That's the science and then the art; the art of presenting your message earns your respect. 'Hey, this guy, he understands this game is hard. He understands me.' So they need to see that every day, see that you're as committed to the program as anyone in the clubhouse. You can't send out that message and then let them see you leaving early—'Hey, fellas, I'm going golfing.' They need to see you hang by the batting cage. That's what really earns the respect."

In my thirty-year career as an airline pilot, I've found that pilots are a proud bunch and they work very hard to be thought worthy by their peers. When you begin a flying career, you work hard to demonstrate competence. If you demonstrate competence and skill over a period of time, you begin to gain the trust of your colleagues. If you consistently demonstrate competence and trustworthiness over a long period of time, if you are particularly diligent and adept, and if fortune smiles on you, you may earn their respect.

Trust also is instilled as a team value when the leader walks the talk, La Russa said. "Leaders have a real opportunity to take the easy road, either bullshit, to use one term, or outright lie their way through tough situations. Well, as soon as the people you're supposed to be leading understand that you can't be trusted, you've got no chance. It's just like any relationship. This starts out as a business relationship, but then, at least the way we do it with my teams, it becomes a personal relationship as well."

"It's like a three-legged stool," I said. "The leader needs to model all three values to build a team mentality. If one is missing, it's going to topple."

The crucial third leg is the value of caring. "In our sport you can't fight through the distractions of media and money without the caring," Tony said, and he often needed to draw on all his reserves of caring or empathy as a manager. "Maybe they're buying into what their family and friends are telling them. Or maybe, while you're giving the team speech, they're thinking, 'Man, I wanna be on ESPN,'" he said. "If you really care, you understand that they are just human beings, and that's just the nature of things. And I'm going to work my butt off to make my own relationship be more important to them."

Building a team is time-consuming, challenging hard work and requires constant vigilance, La Russa added. "That means that every day, every stinkin' day, our coaches and manager, the trainers, the equipment guys, the traveling secretary—anybody that's involved, every member of the club—is supposed to watch each player," he said. "Now I only have twenty-five, but still, we're supposed to watch every player every day. We're supposed to observe everything: 'Hey, you know, he's getting a little too full of himself.

He's depressed, what's going on? Maybe there's a problem at home? Maybe his agent's telling him, "Man, you gotta get more money."'"

It's not enough just to show up at the ballpark focused on winning a game. All the technical preparation, all the attention to Xs and Os, will be for naught if the players aren't focused on their roles and committed to playing as a team. As manager, La Russa had to be alert to every player's attitude and mood. "Caring means paying attention every day. And as soon as you detect a difference, of course, that's still more time consuming. 'He's different; but *what's* different about him?' And then you need to have a conversation or draw up some action plan, which takes still more time. You've got to explain to him why you're doing this, then you've gotta do it, and then you've gotta evaluate it."

My profession demanded the same sort of constant diligence, and it was necessary to avoid complacency on every flight. It also required being aware and prepared. Flying a passenger airplane is demanding work, just as the process of building and leading a team is laborious. Tony and I agree that the key to any group is to instill the values of respect, trust, and caring; only then can our missions be accomplished.

"This respect-trust-caring triangle, this three-legged stool, as you said, is the reason why we have players, year in and year out, saying that this is the best situation they've ever had, our situation with the Cards," Tony said. "And you know something? I *know* they're right. That doesn't mean we're the only ones doing it, but not too many teams do. We understand that it goes beyond the money they make. It's this environment that we create, where it's very supportive, very positive, very caring. I mean, it's a professional sports club, but it's exactly what you'd want with your family."

The best pilots I've flown with, those I admire and respect the most, had two traits in common: they cared a lot, and they paid attention throughout their professional lives. These are the pilots who made it look easy.

MOTIVATIONAL METHODS

Another fundamental leadership challenge Tony faced on a daily basis was providing his players with "the *how,* the *what,* and the *why*" of motivation. "As a leader, you establish the *what* first," he said. "If you take a simple example in baseball, you'd say, 'We haven't been driving the runner home from third with less than two outs. What we have to do is improve dramatically at driving that runner home.' An *ineffective* leader just points out the problem, 'Now let's go do it!' Walks out. Anybody can point out the problems. Sometimes you don't even *need* to point out the problems."

I have long strived for a deeper understanding of the *why* as well as the *how,* and Tony's explanation offered insights that he has done the same. Once a leader has established that a problem exists, then it's necessary to provide the method for solving the problem, the *how,* as La Russa said. But it is equally important to establish the *why.*

"You used to be able to stand up there as a leader and say, 'Guys, we have to do X-Y-Z.' And then, if you're effective, you say, 'And this is *how* we're going to do it. Okay, let's go do it!'" he explained. "But now, in today's society, kids question everything. They question their parents' authority: 'What do you *mean,* Mom and Dad?' So an effective leader tells the team *what,* then he makes sure that he explains *why:* why is the *what* important? And of course the *why* connects directly to the *how.* The *why* gives them the reason to pay attention to the *how.*"

I sympathized with Tony, and with any leader dealing with a team of individuals whose focus is on their own self-interest rather than the group's goals. The key to engaging them in pursuing those goals, he said, is to build personal relationships, then to assure them that you are invested in their success and that there is a personal payoff for each participant if the team succeeds. Tony calls this "the power of personal relationships."

"If you know that I'm having this personal relationship with you, where I'm telling you that what you're doing is not good enough, and I'm holding you accountable in a *positive* way, and you know that I'm being honest with you, then it's really difficult to ignore," he said. "You have to be the biggest jerk that ever walked the face of the earth to neglect or ignore this personal attempt to relate to you. And that's how you fight through all the bullshit. That's why this personalizing is so crucial."

After building a trusting and positive relationship with each player, the leader or manager must then take it one step further by personalizing the incentives for overall team performance, La Russa said. "I'll tell a guy, 'Even if you are the most selfish player around, is that what you want to be? Don't even answer that; let's assume you're the most selfish player around. If you hit .270 on a losing team, you're gonna make a million bucks next year,'" he continued. "'You hit .270 on a winning team, you're gonna make five million bucks. So if you're the most selfish guy around, you'd better hope that your teammates play so well so that the team is successful and you get that bigger paycheck.'"

Focusing the individual on having a high-quality experience is another motivational method a leader can wield. "You also explain it to them on an even more basic level: 'You think it's gonna be fun to play this six months together. We're over here pulling together and being a true family, but you're gonna be coming to the ballpark just making sure you take care of yourself? Is that going to be fun for you?'" he said. "Again, I come back to that core principle: You have to appeal to their human qualities. You have to personalize the incentive."

The morning we spoke, Tony was in the midst of juggling a contract renegotiation with the Cardinals' undisputed star attraction, Albert Pujols, under intense media scrutiny. The Dominican-born first baseman is widely considered the most feared hitter in all of major league baseball. I wondered how Tony's technique of personalization worked in motivating a future Hall of Famer like Pujols, a player who seems to need no external motivation to succeed. "Is Albert an exception in this era of self-centered and unmotivated athletes?" I asked.

"He's an exception because Albert Pujols would be a great player for whatever leader he played for," Tony said. "I'm sure we've contributed something, but this is what works for him. He's very committed, religiously. He's not going to let God down for his blessed gifts. A lot of guys say that; he means it. He's very committed to his family. His wife is an important influence in his life. And he knows that he has a special gift in baseball and he has a certain self-pride about being as good as he can be."

Pujols's commitment to excellence is reflected in his high level of productivity over his career, including an overall batting average of nearly .330 that easily puts him among the top forty players in the record books, Tony said.

Pujols's outstanding rookie year with Saint Louis in 2001 ended with his team losing a tough five-game division play-off to the Arizona Diamondbacks, the eventual World Series champs that season. After their final game, La Russa signed a photo of himself and the young star with this high praise: "To Albert. Best player I have ever managed."

Tony also advised the National League's Rookie of the Year to never change his attitude. Pujols promised he wouldn't and he has kept that promise. A nine-time All Star, he helped the Cardinals win the World Series in 2006. "Mind you, he made that promise in his rookie year with a lot ahead . . . the fame and fortune," Tony marveled. "And sure enough, three or four years later he signed a seven-year contract with us that made him a millionaire. Yet he still comes to the park; first guy in spring training; still works hard. He has not changed."

Tony said that Pujols practices personalization to push himself to be the best player, husband, and community member he can be. Leaders who urge team members to do this must remember that they have to model it themselves. "The basic idea of personalization is this: it's all about *you* without being egotistical," La Russa said. "And if you're the leader—and this is really critical—you can't ask them to personalize it to the *n*th degree if you're not personalizing it yourself."

SHARING LEADERSHIP TO REINFORCE THE MESSAGE

I've always believed that the best leaders are those who teach and encourage their team members to be leaders by sharing responsibilities and investing in their success. Whenever I began a series of flights with a new crew of flight attendants, I gathered them together in the passenger cabin prior to boarding, introduced myself, shared my thoughts on the flight, told them I'm relying on them to be my eyes and ears on the plane, and assured them that I would do everything possible to help them do their jobs well.

With that in mind, I asked Tony how he worked with his team captains and on-field leaders to strengthen communication and unity. "As the manager, is there some sort of alliance, some necessary chemistry between the general and the captain on the field?" I asked my friend.

Tony replied that developing leaders was "the meat" of his job as manager, but then he corrected himself. "Well, I can't say 'meat,' because I'm a vegetarian, so that's the tofu of getting this thing right," he said with a laugh.

It's difficult for a manager to reach each and every player on a twenty-five-man roster with every message, so his goal is always to build a core of team leaders, or "cosigners," who relay his thoughts and instructions to the rest of the team, he said. The more leaders you have on the team, the more effective it becomes, Tony explained. "Let's say you have two leaders on the team. If they get hurt or if they struggle, and you're asking them to maintain the right message, that's really hard for them," he said. "If a guy's not hitting well or not pitching well, there's so much anguish—they're embarrassed."

Tony often met with the cosigners individually and occasionally as a group, welcoming candid comments, he said.

"Our policy here is that they can challenge anything that the coaches or me or anybody in our organization says. If the equipment guys or the trainers or the traveling secretary is doing something that takes away from what we're trying to do as a team, the core leaders are supposed to challenge me. 'Hey, Tony, you're working us too hard,' or 'Why are we leaving at three o'clock on a day off?' Anything at all," he said.

To encourage an open line of communication, the leader must be willing to provide explanations when questions are asked. Then, if the leader has empowered his team cosigners effectively, they will reinforce the message when the leader is no longer present.

"Soon as you walk out in the clubhouse, on the field, at restaurants, or on the planes, your core leaders are there to reinforce the message. They say, 'This is how we do things here.' When a young player comes in, he's mentored by the core. Pretty soon, this young player's become part of it. And four or five years later, then you pass the baton and he's one of the core leaders. It's a beautiful system when it works."

Tony was describing the culture of his team, and to me that is the attitudes each member has about the organization and all involved. Mentors model, encourage, and require their people to be true to their values.

The cosigners are the key component in making it happen, Tony said. "You get a group of guys that will challenge your message," he noted, "but if they believe your message, then they go out among their peers and spread it and then enforce it."

I gladly would have listened to Tony's leadership strategies for five or six hours, but word came to his office that a busload of senior citizens had arrived at ARF. They were waiting to meet him, hoping for snapshots and autographs. As I was leaving, I noticed the oversize rings he wore on each hand. They were as large as walnuts and I assumed they were World Series championship rings, but when I asked if that was the case Tony shook his head. "No, these aren't the World Series rings," he said. "I've got those at home. These are the pennant rings from Oakland in 1988 and Saint Louis in 2004, the years we lost in the Series."

I asked Tony if wearing those reminders of defeat was his method for staying hungry despite all his success.

"Yeah," he said with a nod. "They remind me to take nothing, nothing in this life, for granted."

After our talk, my friend, whom I now call "Champ," set about proving the power of his motivational methods one final time, leading his Cardinals to the World Series victory. The next time I see him, I plan on telling him that it's now safe to wear all three of his championship rings proudly. He's certainly earned that right.

8

ROBERT REICH

There's a huge difference between leadership and authority.
There are a lot of leaders around who don't have any shred of
formal authority at all. And there are many people with a lot
of formal authority and great titles who are not, in the slightest
bit, leaders.

IN JUNE 1964, THE SUMMER THAT ROBERT REICH TURNED EIGH-
teen, one of his best friends, social worker Michael Schwerner,
was brutally murdered as a result of his civil rights activism. The
twenty-four-year-old Cornell University graduate had mysteriously
vanished, along with two other volunteers who were registering
black voters in the South. Schwerner and another volunteer, Andrew
Goodman, were Jewish. The third, James Chaney, was African-
American. They were missing for almost two months before their
mutilated bodies were found in an earthen dam near the small, segregated town of Philadelphia, Mississippi, on August 4, 1964.

"This young man was a very close friend. I considered him a
mentor," Reich recalls. "We spent our summers together, his family

and my family. My grandma had a little cabin in the foothills of the Adirondacks. His family had a cabin nearby. He was about three years older than me. And I just admired him enormously."

The murders of Schwerner and his fellow civil rights activists, which inspired the movie *Mississippi Burning,* occurred just as Robert Reich was entering college. The racist killing by a group of white supremacists (eight men were eventually convicted) was a turning point in his life. "I was suddenly shocked there was that degree of evil in the world, and that people would go to such lengths to prevent other people from fulfilling their potential and that this kind of prejudice, fear, and violence could take the life of somebody who was an important person in my life."

The former Rhodes scholar says that his friend's murder instilled in him a hunger for social justice and compelled him to become a leader and advocate. Even after so many years, Reich still becomes emotional at the memory of his friend. "In retrospect, I believe that the death of Mickey Schwerner, along with the deaths of the two others, made me even more committed to the cause of equal opportunity and civil rights, even more committed to the importance of ensuring that everyone could get ahead in America."

This was a crucible event in the life of Robert Reich, much as Flight 1549 was for me. Such powerful events may present themselves as tragedies or moments of triumph. Usually it is an event beyond our control, good or bad. What makes it a crucible event is not so much what happens as how we respond to it. Our response, in turn, generally reflects how we've lived up to that point, how we've prepared ourselves.

We successfully landed Flight 1549 because we were a veteran crew. In my case, I had spent a good part of my career studying aircraft accidents and trying to understand what went wrong so I could manage risk. I was driven to understand not only what to do but what not to do. It was intellectual curiosity that drove me to always look for ways to grow and learn. I wanted to make a mark, have an impact, and contribute more.

Their experiences in the civil rights movement fueled the passions of many men and women, black and white, and propelled them into leadership roles in politics, government, religion, and business. This desire for social justice became a driving force in the life of Robert Reich. A graduate of Yale Law School, author of more than a dozen books, political commentator, and economist, Reich served as U.S. secretary of labor for four years under President Bill Clinton after previous government service under Presidents Gerald Ford and Jimmy Carter. His achievements as the nation's twenty-second secretary of labor, under President Clinton, were particularly impressive. He implemented the Family and Medical Leave Act, led a national fight to shutter sweatshops in the United States and halt child labor around the world, headed the administration's successful effort to raise the minimum wage, secured workers' pensions, and launched countless job-training programs and school-to-work initiatives.

As a scholar who has tested his leadership theories in the real world, Reich is widely regarded as one of the most influential labor secretaries in U.S. history. Millions tune in to hear his advocacy for progressive policies each week on NPR's *Marketplace*. He also does frequent commentary for MSNBC and other networks. Reich joined the faculty at the University of California, Berkeley, in 2006 and serves as the Chancellor's Professor of Public Policy.

I met with him on campus, in his humble corner office in the Goldman School of Public Policy, on the upper floor of a converted 1920s fraternity house. When I knocked, he greeted me warmly. Reich was born with a genetic disorder known as Fairbanks disease that limits bone growth, so he is not even five feet tall, though he has a strong presence, a keen intellect, and masterful communication skills. The son of a clothing store owner in Westchester County, New York, Reich attributes his early self-confidence to his stay-at-home mother, who instilled in him the sense that "I could do whatever I wanted to do, that there was nothing holding me back."

"Believe it or not, it wasn't until years later I discovered I was very *short*. Now that may be surprising, but the environment that I grew up in was so supportive—I went to a very rural public school—that I wasn't particularly aware of it," he said, smiling at the memory.

Reich learned early on to use self-deprecating humor to deflect attention from his short stature. During his unsuccessful 2002 run for the governor's office in Massachusetts, he joked about wanting to be the "first leprechaun governor" and began his speeches by promising "to be short." He also credits his public school teachers with encouraging him to focus on his gifts, develop them, and use them to benefit others. "I remember several of them talking about the poor, about the role of the United States in the world, about the challenge of equal opportunity in American society—and I took it all in like a sponge," he recalled.

After his stint as a Rhodes scholar at Oxford, where he met Bill Clinton, Reich enrolled at Yale Law School, where he met fellow law student Hillary Clinton. There he clerked for a federal judge, and one of his law professors, conservative Robert Bork, invited him to come work for him in Washington during the presidency of Gerald Ford. Bork had been appointed Solicitor General, and the young Reich immediately accepted his first government position.

"I spent a couple of years arguing and briefing Supreme Court cases for the Ford administration. And then when the Carter administration came in, I wanted to see how economic policy could affect the lives of ordinary people. I became the director of the policy planning staff at the Federal Trade Commission. That too was a great education. I learned huge amounts about the American economy from the ground up, the actual empirical reality of how it was organized, as well as who was winning, who was losing, who was falling behind, and why."

As a leader, writer, and advocate, Reich has expressed concern that "turbocharged corporate competition," fueled by investors seeking the best possible deals, has resulted in extreme social problems. He believes governments around the world have failed to address societal disparities because big corporations and Wall Street firms are constantly seeking competitive advantage through politics. As a result, the voices of ordinary citizens have been drowned out. He advocates for "corporate social responsibility" and laws that would keep corporations focused on making better products and services while limiting their efforts to influence politics through lobbying and contributing to political campaigns.

DRIVEN BY A DESIRE TO SERVE

Reich said that his principles, and the values and moral system that have guided his life and his leadership, were instilled by his parents, mentors, and guides, such as his sixth-grade teacher, Bill Gervain, who taught that "we each have a responsibility to make the world better, but that those of us who had particular gifts and particular capacities had even more responsibility."

His third grade teacher, Alice Camp, had already helped Reich define his talents and given him the confidence to step up as a leader. "I remember one day she was giving a lesson to the class, and she said, 'I'm going to write a word on the blackboard. You may not know what the word means, any of you. But I want you to know that Bobby exemplifies this word.'"

Much to Reich's surprise, the word she wrote in her big longhand was *ambition*. "I didn't know what it meant, but as she started talking about it, I was a little embarrassed, honestly," he said. "I never thought of myself as ambitious. In fact, I didn't think of myself as very much of anything. I had no adjective for myself. And she did, in more subtle ways, too, convince me I could positively influence other people."

The teacher's description gave Reich a new perspective. He wasn't driven to be a leader simply so he could be in the spotlight.

Instead, he wanted to make a difference by inspiring others to join him in taking action. "I was always organizing people," he said. "In high school, I wanted to get people to stop smoking. I thought it was dangerous, and I organized an antismoking campaign."

Reich and his recruits put up posters and created a library display featuring a plastic skeleton they'd burned and charred to make the point that smoking cigarettes would ultimately "burn your insides." His campaign was strikingly similar to modern antismoking advertisements, but way ahead of its time. This was in the early 1950s, when some advertisements actually promoted the health benefits of smoking, and long before the U.S. Surgeon General declared the dangers of tobacco and nicotine. In fact, some teachers were "very upset" with Reich and his antismoking campaign, because they smoked. "The librarian, who was a very committed smoker, was furious with me. She wanted me to take down the display, but I said, 'Look, I think it's important. Let's talk about the data.'"

His classmates, who elected him president of his high school class and its student government, acknowledged Reich's leadership abilities. He held the same positions in his college years. "But being 'president' didn't seem to me to be terribly important," he said. "It was what I could do."

MAKING A DIFFERENCE

Robert Reich is among those leaders who consider themselves primarily public servants, a term that he admits seems a little antiquated in times marked by so many self-serving leaders in politics, business, and other spheres. "People often talked in the fifties and sixties about public service," he said. "They didn't talk about becoming a government bureaucrat or becoming a cabinet secretary. They talked about public service. And what they meant was, quite literally, *serving* the public. Whether it was a not-for-profit group, whether it was a social movement such as civil rights or the antiwar movement, or whether it was working in a direct public capacity."

His generation witnessed the power of activism first in the mass protests of the civil rights movement. They saw that government could call people to action and accomplish amazing feats like landing men on the Moon. They also saw that individuals could make a difference by working together in organizations like the Peace Corps and Volunteers in Service to America (VISTA).

For this leader, "public service was almost inevitable," a course followed by him and everyone he admired, Reich said, noting that "social ideals were so dominant among people my age." He turned down far more lucrative positions as a consultant or lawyer in the private sector. His calling to public service and making a difference in the world was so strong that he never considered taking another path. "I don't mean to suggest that I had any kind of a negative opinion about the private sector. It just didn't come on my radar screen as something that would help me achieve what I thought important to achieve."

Like so many leaders I admire, Reich has the innate ability to take the long view, but when I commented that making a difference seemed to be a goal in his life, he rejected that term. "You said 'goal,' but it was more than a goal; it was an assumption. A goal is something that you strive for. You think, *This is something I want to achieve.* But an assumption is far more basic. I simply assumed that this is what I would do with my life. This was partly because of my mother's belief that I could do anything I wanted. If you really pressed me, I assumed that I would be a 'leader' because I believed in social change that created more opportunities for people and I was going to dedicate myself to it. And so, inevitably, I would lead people. Not a goal. I wasn't sure of how to get there, which is different. I assumed that's what I would do."

When Reich was twenty-one years old and in his final year at Dartmouth, *Time* magazine ran a story profiling him and his undergraduate peers, the class of 1968, calling them "troubled and troubling." The story cast those who had been high school seniors when President John F. Kennedy was assassinated as "The Cynical Idealists of '68." Reich's interview in the story demonstrates that he was a long-term, big-picture leader even then. The writer noted Reich's academic achievements, including the Rhodes scholarship, his starring roles in school plays, and his leadership in student government. Reich also showed himself to be someone who believed strongly that healthy societies and nations should not be afraid of challenges to the status quo, and that they should welcome diverse opinions and perspectives.

Reich smiles when recalling the youthful idealism captured in the *Time* article. "The only thing I remember about the [interview] is that they asked me what I thought I would do in my life. I remember being surprised by the question. And I said to them, 'I'll be sort of a cross between a philosopher and a political hack.'"

Admitting that this prediction provided him with a wide range of options, Reich noted that by "political hack" he really meant being an activist, which is exactly what he has done.

THE REAL WORLD AND THE CHALLENGES OF LEADERSHIP

Idealism is an important aspect of Reich's leadership approach. After all, he still is committed to making the world a better place. Yet, he noted that part of being a leader is being realistic about the challenges. In the late 1980s, I worked on a campaign with a couple of dozen other pilots at my airline to address safety issues with a program called Crew Resource Management. We developed a series of CRM courses that were taught to all our pilots and flight attendants with the goal of developing leadership and teamwork skills to encourage more collaboration on safety matters. One of the things we had to do was overcome resistance to change by creating a psychological buy-in from the pilots. We had to convince them that there were real and valid reasons for what we were doing, and we did that by showing how it affected each of them personally. We found that when we personalized these issues, the pilots not only bought into the changes we were making, they also took ownership of the process.

Reich noted that most individuals and teams tend to cling to "work-avoidance mechanisms" until they are given a reason to buy into a change or take an action. "Leadership, to me, is about helping groups of people focus on the most important things they need to do and then get it done," Reich said. "Or get them done. You know, we all use a variety of work-avoidance mechanisms in our lives because, after all, we couldn't function as human beings if we didn't have them. Take denial. If we were not in some state of denial—that is, if we really every day, every minute, were fully aware of all of the problems that are around us—life would be impossible."

Escapism is another temptation for leaders. "We may not be in denial. We may know that global warming is a true issue, but we have to escape from it," Reich said. "Sometimes we've got to enjoy our families, enjoy our work, enjoy our friends. Otherwise we'd go nuts."

A third work-avoidance mechanism for leaders is scapegoating. "We say, 'The problem is real. I'm not denying it. I'm not escaping from it. I'm aware that it's there. But it's not *my* problem; it's their problem. They brought it on. It's because of them.' The Chinese are to blame for our unemployment because they hold their currency down to levels that are too low. Or undocumented workers are to blame for unemployment because if they weren't here there'd be more jobs for Americans. That kind of scapegoating goes on all the time. That also is a work-avoidance mechanism."

The worst "and most flagrant" work-avoidance mechanism is cynicism because "it allows us the luxury of saying, 'Well, nothing will happen, nothing will change, why should I get involved?'" he said.

A true leader focuses not on the problems but on the solutions, Reich said. The leader says to his team, "'Look, the only way anything is going to improve is if you get together and you understand what has to be done for your survival, for the betterment of this institution. Don't dwell in denial or escapism or scapegoating or cynicism. And I'm going to help focus your attention: keep your attention, keep your energies directed at those key problems.'"

I asked Reich if his optimistic views of leadership and making the world a better place were as prevalent today as in his youth.

"No," Reich said. "I think there's much more cynicism now. But remember, we were still living off the huge positive feelings this nation had after surviving the Depression and winning the war. I was born just as World War II ended. There was an abiding sense in this country that this nation could do anything. In a sense, it paralleled my mother's lesson to me that I could do anything. Progress was a basic tenet of the American creed. And progress meant not just material progress. It was social progress. We would overcome the lingering effects of de jure and then de facto segregation. We would open opportunities for women. We would enable the poor kids who had the guts and gumption to make it in America. We would be the beacon of light for the rest of the world. We would be the moral authority for the world. Again, this was all taken for granted."

That faith in the power of individuals and government to lead positive change was greatly diminished by the failures of leadership during the Vietnam War and during the Watergate scandal that drove President Richard M. Nixon from office. "There's been a new understanding of America's history in the world, which is not nearly as positive," Reich said. "Most of my students here at Berkeley, I would say, are committed to public service, but not to a career that includes government."

Reich, like me and many other Americans of our generation, still believes that our nation and its citizens are blessed, and that our leaders are morally bound to promote social justice and freedom. "I still believe that we have a particular moral mission in the world; that we are unique," Reich said. "I still believe in progress. I still believe in social justice. I still believe that it's possible to effect a great deal of positive change. If I didn't believe that, how could I teach all the undergraduates I teach?"

FAILURES OF LEADERSHIP

As a former cabinet member and concerned American, Reich is troubled by recent failures of leadership in government and business, particularly those that led to the recession of 2006–2009, from which many Americans have yet to recover. He does not buy the arguments of those who claim the crash was caused not by greed or recklessness in the investment community but rather by consumers who overextended on their home mortgages, or by too much government interference in the markets. "I debate a lot of these people," he said, "and I honestly don't know whether they are fools or they are just ignorant. Whether they are knaves who know the truth but who have a financial interest in making sure the public *doesn't* know it."

I noted that they may have an interest in perpetuating the status quo and Reich agreed. "Yes, in perpetuating the status quo and perpetuating a set of mythologies that are very dangerous," he said.

Reich believes the economic crisis was caused by leadership failures at the highest levels of business and government. "Wall Street went on a binge. And Wall Street went on a binge largely because you had the toxic combination of almost free money— Alan Greenspan and company had lowered short-term interest rates to historically low levels right after WorldCom and Enron had eroded investor confidence—and a failure of the Fed and the SEC and others to adequately police Wall Street, and the evisceration of New Deal regulations such as Glass-Steagall, which separated commercial banking from investment banking. As a result, we saw these Wall Streeters having, essentially, almost free money and a green light to do whatever they wanted with it."

True leaders take responsibility for their actions, and they focus on what is best for the majority over the long term, but in this scenario, short-term greed trumped all, Reich feels. The recent Great Recession, as he calls it, serves as an example of cynical short-term leadership and leaders in denial. It is the responsibility of leaders to convince their followers to make choices that serve the long-term welfare of the majority, even when those choices are hard and unpopular.

OVERCOMING CYNICISM, DENIAL, AND DOUBT

I asked Reich how a leader overcomes the sort of ingrained cynicism, selfishness, and short-term thinking that he feels led to the Great Recession. He responded that when he took over the Labor Department in 1992, the bureaucracy was rife with cynicism and virtually paralyzed.

"This was after twelve years of labor secretaries who'd come and gone in rapid fire and who had no interest in the goals of the Labor Department, at least as far as most of the employees felt. Whether they did or not is another issue. But most of the employees felt that the string of labor secretaries was uninterested in the goals of the Labor Department. So I had to rebuild trust.

"One of the key elements of distrust and the cause of so much cynicism was the issue of delegation of real authority. They'd seen so many labor secretaries come and go that they didn't believe it when I said, 'If you come up with a good idea, I'm going to implement it.'"

He worked to overcome that cynicism toward leadership by demonstrating that he was worthy of trust, Reich said. "I would hold mass meetings of employees, a thousand at a time, and I'd have my deputy labor secretary next to me, the Solicitor General, the solicitor of the Labor Department on the other side, and a couple of other key people. Then I'd say, 'Listen, I want your ideas.'"

His employees were initially very reluctant to come forward because of their built-up distrust and cynicism. Finally, one man raised his hand and suggested getting rid of time cards for Labor employees. The man argued that time cards were unnecessary and easily falsified.

In front of those assembled, Reich put the question to his top lieutenants, asking if there was any good reason to stick with time cards. No one could come up with one.

"Okay, starting next week: no time cards," Reich announced.

The room went dead silent.

"Then there was this almost explosion of . . . well, it is hard to describe the sound of a thousand people letting their breath out at once," Reich said.

After two or three demonstrations like this, the entrenched cynicism within the Labor Department dissipated, and "some fabulous ideas" came out of those sessions, Reich said. These open forums with department staff also fostered a greater sense of ownership, and the feeling that every employee could make a difference in the organization.

"It spawned a minor revolution in terms of small-scale improvements in the delivery of all sorts of programs," Reich said. "Again, it wasn't hard. That's the point. It was not difficult to do. It was just unleashing the capacity that was already there. In the end, people want to do their jobs. Everybody wants to do their jobs. But they're just beaten down due to cynicism, so many of them ultimately just give up."

As Reich demonstrated within the Labor Department, leaders can overcome that cynicism by giving employees a voice, listening to them, and allowing them to have an impact. This builds loyalty and trust, as well as the enhanced sense of ownership. Reich recalled that a few years after the time card solution was worked out, another Labor Department employee suggested profiling individuals immediately after they'd been fired or laid off. His idea was to determine whether each individual who'd lost a job was in an industry that might allow for him or her to return someday. The Labor Department employee thought that if they could identify those individuals who weren't likely to return to their old jobs, and immediately get them into job training and job placement programs, Labor might be able to bring down unemployment or at least shorten the period in which these people were out of work. The employee thought that this sort of program would save so much money over the long term that those funds could be used for job training programs.

"We tried it on a pilot basis and it turned out that employee was exactly right," Reich said.

"That must have been a huge step in beginning to build the trust that you talked about," I said.

"It was essential . . . *essential*," he replied.

I asked if it engendered more loyalty in his organization, and Reich replied, "It certainly engendered more of a sense of ownership."

"Every social movement, every successful company, every successful institution has leaders who understand that basic principle," Reich added. "In terms of overcoming cynicism, denial, or escapism, it's a matter of providing dramatic illustrations. . . . But I've come across a lot of institutions where people are willfully ignorant, in deep denial about the problems of the institution, where the institution is heading toward death either because its costs are too high, or it's not providing what people want, or it's so wedded to the past and to past successes that it can't see that the environment has changed."

212 / MAKING A DIFFERENCE

ENGAGING THE WORKFORCE

Reich believes that most people in every profession and field want to do a good job, but leaders too often fail to engage them by getting them personally involved. You accomplish this by actively listening to them, building a shared sense of mission, and giving them the power to make a difference. Reich once did a series of management tapes with W. Edwards Deming, the pioneering management expert who is considered the father of the Total Quality Management movement. Deming was then in his eighties. He had schooled an entire generation of Japanese managers after World War II on his philosophies for engaging the workforce. They listened to him, but American managers didn't, and he was angry because nobody was listening to him. He was right and he knew he was right, Reich said.

"He knew the Japanese were eating our lunch because they understood his principles," he noted. "We started to listen to him only when he was very old. But he thought and understood that the elemental truth was that most people wanted to do a good job, most people wanted to be engaged, most people were desperate to have a fulfilling work life. But most leaders had no idea how to engage them and how to give them that fulfillment. And it wasn't complicated. It was easy. It had to do with some basics: listening, walking around, giving people a sense of engagement and ownership, and enabling them to define what the central problems were."

Some leaders don't listen to or interact with employees because they get too caught up in being the authority figure, but Reich notes that "There's a huge difference between leadership and authority. There are a lot of leaders around who don't have any shred of formal authority at all. And there are many people with a lot of formal authority and great titles who are not, in the slightest bit, leaders. Leadership may be a little easier if you have formal authority, but sometimes formal authority puts too much of a constraint on you. When I was secretary of labor, for example, I had a very big megaphone as a cabinet member. But I was very constrained in what I could say through that megaphone. Before and after I was secretary of labor I had a much smaller megaphone, but I could say whatever I wanted. So formal authority can actually, in some ironic and paradoxical way, constrain leadership."

Sometimes, Reich said, a leader needs to step back and allow the group, or the institution, or the nation, to define the problem for itself. "Sometimes the leader's job is less direct. For a leader to simply get out there and hold a poster up and say, 'This is the problem'—that itself lets people off the hook. They don't take personal ownership. That kind of leadership actually is dangerous, because it allows the group to say, 'It's *his* or *her* project—it's not *ours*.' The minute it stops succeeding or the minute things slow down or the minute that you hit the first big stumbling block, that leader becomes a scapegoat. No, you've got to enable people to see for themselves what must be done."

Reich suggested that leaders dealing with resistance practice "shock therapy" in the form of open-book management, a philosophy that calls for treating employees as partners rather than hired hands by sharing critical information with them, challenging them to make the organization or business better, and sharing the rewards with them.

"One of the beauties of open-book management is [that] everybody can see the truth," Reich said. "There's not any question of trust: you see the numbers. One thing I used to do a lot of—and I still do—is to use graphs, particularly graphs that show trends, because they can be very powerful tools." The leader who uses graphs and stories that serve as examples can persuade his followers to reexamine assumptions, just as a teacher does with students, Reich said. "I teach seven hundred and fifty undergraduates this term. I constantly play the devil's advocate. I never teach them what I necessarily believe. I always teach against what *they* believe. Because what I really want them to do is learn to think harder."

I've always believed that storytelling is a very powerful tool, especially when you draw from your own personal experience and the story is told in a genuine and compelling way. A good personal story can illustrate important thoughts and concepts.

Humor is another useful tool for both leaders and teachers, Reich said. "Humor is the great disinfectant. Humor is the vehicle through which people begin opening their minds. . . . You remove the threat if they know that you share the same sense of humor and you can laugh at something together. And suddenly you're no longer on opposite sides. You're actually united."

SHARING RESPONSIBILITY AND REWARDS

Reich and I discussed the fact that the growing income disparity between top executives and their employees presents a challenge to any leader trying to unite and motivate his team, and it may also threaten the stability of our democracy. He noted that that 1 percent of the population is taking home 23.5 percent of the total income in our country now, compared with 9 percent of the total back in the 1970s—and the median wage has gone nowhere since 2001 based on inflation. He said that even the most ideologically conservative person can look at where we've been and where we are going and say, "We've got a problem here."

I expressed my amazement at the number of people who don't make that connection and demand change. "One of the few ways I can explain this behavior is that they are more dogmatic than pragmatic. It's an ideological necessity for them to think that there should not be government intervention in what they consider free, perfect markets, or for some other reason that we should all just make it on our own wits—or not—and that they don't necessarily see a problem with that. I'm not sure that there is a particularly good answer for that, or I don't know one," I said.

"Well, in my experience, there are always a certain number of people that are so dogmatic they clutch to their belief system regardless of the facts," Reich said. "It's a theology. Basically, I don't have enough time in my day. I suppose I could crack their theology given enough hours, but I don't have enough hours and it's not worth it."

"It seems that there is a vast number of people who really have not thought deeply about a lot of things but who are open-minded, who may have predispositions in one direction or another but are intellectually honest," I said. "And if presented with a good argument, and good graphs, and good illustrations and good examples, they will reexamine their assumptions."

Reich noted that CEO compensation right now is averaging about three hundred fifty times the salary of the average worker. "In the 1950s, it was fifty times the average worker. In the 1960s, it was up to about eighty times or ninety times the average worker, and we've seen it steadily notch up. Is this because CEOs are greedier than they were? No, human nature doesn't change over time. People are just as greedy as they ever were. The question is: What are the incentives operating upon them to either contain that greed or let it go? Indulge it?"

Reich believes that the major factor at play is Wall Street's insatiable demand for short-term profits, which has driven demand and escalated compensation for executives who've shown they can increase the value of stock shares. "What changed was that Wall Street and investors, desperate for high short-term share prices, want the most talented, proven stars that they can get," Reich said. "And they will pay top dollar for them. Everybody right now is essentially a free agent. You know, it's like sports and entertainment. The stars are commanding huge amounts of money."

I told Reich that I find this growing income disparity alarming. It affected me personally as a pilot whose salary was slashed 40 percent and whose pension was terminated (due to economic conditions and corporate bankruptcy at U.S. Airways) even as the compensation of top executives escalated. On a larger scale, I'm worried about what it means for our nation when so much wealth is being accumulated by such a small percentage of people, endangering the middle class that has been one of our greatest resources. I asked the economist if this was a systemic fault and, if so, where it was taking our country. What ultimate price would we pay as a society?

"We're already paying a price in many ways," Reich said. "Support for international trade has fallen dramatically. A majority of Americans now don't think trade is good for America. If we had a more prosperous country and people felt more that they had a greater share of the benefits of the gains from trade, we would not have that consequence."

The same holds true with immigration, Reich said. The United States once welcomed all immigrants, but now so many citizens are scared about job security that "they are becoming easy prey for demagogues who want to point a finger of blame at immigrants.

"If we continue to see widening inequality of the sort that we are seeing—that is, a very small number of people at the top, relatively speaking, claiming a larger and larger share of the national income and wealth—then we're also threatening to undermine the bonds of trust that we have in this society. A society depends on a fundamental notion that we're all in the same boat together. That's the connective tissues that enable us to make common decisions. But if people start thinking we're not in the same boat—they're in one boat and the rest of us are in another boat—that begins to erode trust."

"Or not even in a boat," I said. "We're in life vests out here somewhere in the water."

"That's right," Reich said. "We're in a sinking dinghy. It begins to erode social trust and confidence in the integrity of institutions. Look at the significant drop in public confidence as expressed toward businesses, toward Congress, toward all major institutions of society, and look at the graph of declining public trust. Now put it against the graph that shows median income."

I asked Reich what this growing disparity in incomes and the lack of job security meant for the vast majority of workers who are not top executives, not the stars, not the twenty most sought-after people in each organization. If they were better educated, if they had more marketable skills, would they be able to fare better in this environment? Or is it such a large and complex systemic problem that even better education would be insufficient?

"No, no, that would be helpful," Reich said. "If they were educated better, had more marketable skills, and also took upon themselves the responsibility for continuously upgrading their skills, that would be helpful. But job security is gone. They would not have job security; they would have *employability* security. In most environments—the Great Recession is an exception—but in most environments they'd be able to continue to land on their feet. But even the best of them, who've kept up with the right skills, had every bit of education that was relevant, will occasionally fall flat, and there's no real safety net. Though I don't think *safety net* is the right metaphor. I think it should be—what do you call those?—*trampolines*."

THREE KEYS TO SECURING AMERICA'S FUTURE

I asked Reich what leaders in this country could do to make the United States more competitive in the global marketplace and to provide greater job security for the next generation of Americans.

"What we did beginning in the 1940s and through the fifties, sixties, and much of the seventies," he said. "That is, invest substantially in education and in infrastructure, and in basic research and development. You know, those are the three keys. We had a free ride as a country for much of that period of time because of the unfortunate fact that women did not have many professional options other than teaching. So we didn't have to pay very much to get very talented people in the classroom. Now if we want talented people in the classroom, we need to pay men or women as much as we pay talented people anyplace else. The law of supply and demand is not repealed at the classroom door."

Reich believes that the current structure of our capital markets discourages the sorts of long-term strategies that are needed in both government and business to get our country back on track. Visionary leadership will be in short supply until that structure changes, he said.

"I think that the capital market that we have right now in terms of publicly held corporations is absolutely inimical to long-term visionary thinking," said Reich, who noted that he'd have no interest in being a CEO in business these days. "The capital markets demand quarterly profits. The stock analysts are impossible in terms of the demands that they are placing on CEOs. Wall Street runs the game almost entirely. Who would want to be a CEO under those circumstances?"

"What about a private versus a public company?" I asked.

"Even that's difficult, because most CEOs who are working for private equity groups are still under huge pressure to turn things around very shortly. They can't make long-term investments. So essentially we need a new set of laws. For example, the longer you hold a share of stock, the lower your capital gains tax. Patient capitalists should be rewarded; impatient capitalists should be penalized. If you had that kind of a structure, that would enable CEOs to think over the long term. I would also link CEO pay to long-term stock performance rather than short-term performance, because again, the whole thing now works against any kind of visionary leadership."

Reich and I agreed that there are perverse incentives in play in today's business climate. "Every incentive is perverse," he said. "But the point I'm making is that markets are organized by laws and rules and regulations. There's *no* free market in the state of nature. This whole notion that we have a choice between government and market is silly."

"It's not something given by God," I said.

"No, it's something given by legislatures and courts and a huge number of regulatory agencies and others," Reich said. "And if we get the incentives right, then CEOs can do a job that is not only good for short-term investors but, more important, good for all of the stakeholders: good for employees, good for communities, good for the country, and the national economy over the long term.

"But if we get the incentives wrong—as they are now—no CEO is going to be able to do a good job, because the entire system works in the opposite direction. That's why I come back to my point about public service. Public service isn't just about doing 'good things.' Public service is about organizing society in a way that provides the right incentives for people to do jobs that, ultimately, will have very positive public outcomes."

THE THREE DANGEROUS SEDUCTIONS OF LEADERSHIP

The leader who does aspire to be a visionary and to work for the long-term benefit of his organization or business must contend with what Reich calls "three dangerous seductions," which he has either experienced or witnessed firsthand.

The first seduction is martyrdom, he said. "I have seen leaders and I've felt in myself occasionally the desire to work so hard that you essentially burn yourself out. Or you take on so much of the institution's, or society's, responsibilities that you indirectly cooperate in the institution's desire not to take responsibility."

The great irony, Reich said, is that the sense of martyrdom "feels great. To be a martyr, to go down with all your energy and kill yourself for whatever cause, does feel great. But it does nobody any good at all. And in fact, martyrdom is a sign that you're a bad leader."

The second seduction is a first cousin to martyrdom that he

calls messiahism. "I came into the Labor Department after twelve years of labor secretaries who people felt weren't listening to them. I came in with Bill Clinton. It was the first Democratic administration in twelve years. I had something of a reputation. When I came in, it was like I was liberating Europe from the Nazis. True, the people didn't trust me, but I was still treated as if I was the answer to everybody's problems. As if I would change the world."

That is a dangerously seductive feeling for a leader to have, and it doesn't serve the organization either, Reich said. "I love the idea of being the messiah, but anybody who believes that they are the answer and can change everything on their own is deluding themselves and dangerously deluding everybody else. Again, it's a tacit cooperation in work avoidance because the group says, 'Well, you're going to do it all and we don't have to do anything.'"

The third seduction of leadership, which Reich admits to succumbing to on occasion, is to take on the role of "truth teller." The danger here is that there are always those who don't want to hear the truth, so they follow the kill-the-messenger strategy and do whatever they can to marginalize the truth teller by making that individual the issue. "They ask, 'Why are you doing what you're doing? Why are you saying what you're saying?' They will go after you in an ad hominem way," Reich said. "But the seduction comes in wanting to be a truth teller who will tell the truth even if he or she is marginalized. In other words, there's a certain pleasure in being marginalized and telling the truth. 'Well, nobody's listening to me. I'm a prophet. I know the truth, but nobody has ever listened to me or will ever listen to me.'"

Leaders know that point has been reached when you say something and nobody responds, because they've heard it before, Reich said.

"They've compartmentalized you out of existence. They're mentally rolling their eyes," he said.

The danger for truth tellers lies in becoming so predictable that people automatically discount whatever they say, considering them extremists, rabble-rousers, troublemakers, or cranks, he said.

"The attempt to marginalize you, your willingness to be marginalized, is *very* dangerous," Reich noted.

A true leader who wants to make a difference by speaking the truth has to avoid becoming so predictable that people tune out the message. You can do this by picking your battles and speaking against type. Reich does this by speaking truths that defy efforts to pigeonhole him as a liberal, such as his opposition to the corporate income tax, which he has often spoken out against.

"I think [the corporate income tax] is crazy. You don't even know who pays it, and it actually is one stepping-stone to corporate personhood—no taxation without representation—which is nuts," Reich said. "But most people who are politically in my camp hate it when I start talking about getting rid of the corporate income tax. I'm still speaking truths. I'm just picking a few things that are against type. It throws people off. It makes it harder to put me in a box and harder to marginalize me."

Leaders who are pigeonholed by the media as either conservatives or liberals run the risk of losing their effectiveness because their potential audience is diminished, Reich believes. "I do this program for public radio, *Marketplace,* and I noticed one day that when they introduced me, they said, 'Robert Reich's presenting the liberal point of view. Next week we're going to have so-and-so presenting the conservative view.' I called them immediately and said, 'What are you doing? You know you are putting me in a box.'"

The polarization of politics so evident today was not such a factor in his formative years, Reich said. Back then there was not such a deep divide even between Democrats and Republicans. He detests those who seek to pigeonhole him and others with a social conscience. For example, he's often targeted as a liberal, yet one of his early mentors was legal scholar, former judge, and onetime Supreme Court nominee Robert Bork—"and you can't get more conservative than Robert Bork."

THE NEXT GENERATION OF GREAT POLITICAL LEADERS

It was now late afternoon, and the winter sun had lengthened the shadows outside on the Berkeley campus. Before I let Reich return to his scholarly work, I asked for his thoughts on the dysfunctional nature of our political system and the fact that it has become increasingly difficult to get our "best and brightest" to run for elective office. This was another aspect of leadership that Reich had experienced firsthand. He'd run a spirited if ultimately unsuccessful campaign for governor of Massachusetts in 2002. It was a campaign remarkable for both its honesty and its good humor. He'd released perhaps the best-titled campaign book in history: *I'll Be Short*. He'd also distinguished himself as the first Democratic candidate for a major political office to support same-sex marriage while also supporting abortion rights and condemning capital punishment.

Though his campaign was poorly funded and his staff made up almost solely of his Brandeis University students, Reich came in a close second out of six candidates in the Democratic primary and garnered 25 percent of the vote. Playing devil's advocate, I asked Reich if running for office is almost impossible for the average person to do, either for financial reasons or in terms of staying true to one's value system.

Reich rose to the topic, his eyes gleaming. "I will say yes to the former, no to the latter, having done it. It's very difficult to run for office if you're not rich. I was never rich, and I ran for office, and I ended up spending five hours a day on the phone trying to raise money. That's not only humiliating—it's no fun," he said. "If I had known that I was going to do that for a year, I would not have run for office."

Reich lost his bid to become governor of Massachusetts in part because he didn't have the funds to go up against his Democratic primary opponent, who was the state treasurer and had more "bargaining chips."

"We still went into the final week of the primary neck and neck. Out of a field of six, she and I were neck and neck. But the last week, I ran out of money. My campaign manager said, 'Bob, you've got to take out a second mortgage on your house.' I said, 'No way. I'm not going to do that. I'm not going to jeopardize my kids. If we run out of money, we run out of money. If she wins, she wins.' And she did.

"I was sad about that. I thought that I could have beat Mitt Romney—who was the Republican candidate," Reich said. "I would have loved to debate him. I thought I could have made a pretty damned good governor. But it wasn't to be. And that was my one try at elective office."

More qualified leaders might be willing to step up and run for public office if we had a system of public finance that provided a public dollar for you for every private dollar raised by your opponent once you achieved a certain level of credibility, Reich said. Credibility might come from getting a nomination or a certain number of petitioners. This system would eliminate any advantage of private fund-raising, he suggested.

I agreed that it would certainly end the ever-increasing amounts spent on political campaigns, stopping the arms race in fund-raising.

"In its tracks," Reich agreed.

But it would not deal with another major impediment to attracting qualified political leaders: negative advertising by independent groups, Reich said. "To get control of that, you've got to change the laws. And we've got to have Supreme Court justices that understand that there is a difference between freedom of speech and the opportunity to spend unlimited amounts of money on a campaign," he said. "This is all a matter of systemic improvement."

While acknowledging that financial challenges are a concern for any leader who aspires to run for public office, Reich said he does not think a true leader has to compromise his values to win elections. "I actually believe that you have a better chance running for office and winning if you stay true to your values than if you don't. I learned this from someone who became a good friend of mine named Paul Wellstone," Reich said.

Wellstone was a senator from Minnesota. In 2003 there was a vote on the Bush administration's resolution to go into Iraq. The polls showed that the majority of Americans felt we should go into Iraq, but Wellstone voted against the resolution, Reich recalled. "I talked to him the next morning and said, 'Paul, I admire what you did. I happen to personally agree with it. But you're killing yourself electorally. You're in really grave danger now. You're not running that far ahead of your opponent.'"

Wellstone's response was to laugh, Reich said. "He said, 'Wait till you see tomorrow's polls.' I said, 'What are you talking about? Have you seen them?' Paul said, 'No, but I know them.' Wellstone was confident his poll numbers would rise after his dissenting vote on Iraq because he knew that although Minnesota voters might not always agree with him, if they feel that you have the courage of your convictions and if you make a sensible case to them, even if they disagree they will support you."

Reich said that in his sole run for office, he sensed that voters appreciated when he was candid about his beliefs. He believes that the election was not lost because he was truthful.

"I believe it was lost because I didn't have enough money," he said. "My opponents all had a lot of money."

Reich had made up his mind to remain truthful even when it was not politically expedient, he said. "There was a speech in which I was asked about my support of gay marriage. And the question was: 'You've already come out in favor of recognizing the rights of gay couples to have the same legal rights—civil unions—as every-one else. Why not take the next step and support gay marriage?'"

Reich said he responded, "'You know, you're absolutely right. I *do* support gay marriage.' Then I remember going back to the campaign headquarters, and my campaign manager was almost suicidal! He said, 'Bob, you know you've just given away the elec-tion.'" But Reich felt that he'd provided "as cogent a reason as I could, and people appreciated it. They may have disagreed with me. But in the end, they appreciated my honesty."

Robert Reich is a man after my own heart. He believes that ideas are important and that important ideas can make a difference in the world.

9

MICHELLE RHEE

I think my strength as a leader is not knowing more or being smarter, but just being able to bring together talent and then being able to see, "Okay, what are the barriers they're going to get?" Then I'm going to go and knock those things down so you can do your job.

OF ALL THE PEOPLE I APPROACHED TO PARTICIPATE IN THIS PROJECT, none was more on the cutting edge of the national dialogue, none was more talked about and admired—or as polarizing a figure—as Michelle Rhee. Not long after Rhee took over as schools chancellor in Washington, D.C., in February 2008, she announced a plan to shut down almost two dozen schools in the capital's dysfunctional public education system. Irate parents showed up at one local school meeting to scream and throw things at her. Within just a few months, Rhee had polarized the entire city. Her detractors dubbed her "The Terminator," "The Hammer," and most famously, "The Dragon Lady."

The feisty former second-grade teacher stood her ground.

"When I came into the District, eight percent of the eighth graders in the city's schools were on grade level in mathematics," Rhee said. "Eight percent. That means ninety-two percent of our kids did not have the skills necessary to be productive members of society. But when I looked at the performance evaluations of the adults in the system at the same time, I found that ninety-five percent of them were being rated as doing an excellent job.

"How can you have a system where all of the adults are running around thinking they're doing great work for kids, and what we're producing for them is eight percent success?" asked the ardent school reformer.

I spoke with Michelle Rhee in the offices of her latest venture, Students First, a not-for-profit advocacy organization dedicated to education reform, which is located in a chic loft space on Seventh Street NW in the nation's capital. The forty-one-year-old Rhee was smartly dressed in a silk dress printed with swirls of lavender, mauve, and royal blue. She wore diamond stud earrings and a tasteful engagement ring given to her by Kevin Johnson, mayor of Sacramento and former three-time NBA All-Star.

Though she was nursing a head cold, Rhee was gracious in our talk, belying her reputation for steely determination. One of her criteria for leadership, she noted, is "You have to be okay with not being liked. When the endgame becomes popularity or approval ratings or being liked by folks, it's very easy to lose your way."

Between sips of her Starbucks venti, she said, "When I was in the chancellor job, there was a columnist at the *Washington Post* who said, 'I like Michelle and she's doing all the right things. I just wish she would be nicer and more accommodating.' I called him and I said, 'What's this about?' And he said, 'I think your tenure here will be elongated if you are nicer and you play the game better.' I told him, 'You have to figure out what you think the most important characteristics of a schools chancellor are. If you think it means being nice and accommodating and getting everyone to like what I'm doing, then you should be advocating for my ouster. If you want warm and fuzzy, I am not your girl. That's not my strength. The person who's going to do that may certainly be here a lot longer, but they're also not going to get as much done. Because if you're trying to keep everybody happy, that means you're not really doing a whole lot that's different.'"

NOT AIMING TO PLEASE

Rhee's forceful personality, unflappable nerve in the face of criticism, and willingness to speak her mind won her accolades from the likes of Oprah Winfrey and former New York City schools chancellor Joel Klein. "She is without guile," Klein, who considers Rhee a protégé, said in a *Newsweek* interview. "So rare in public life." When she made a 2010 appearance on *Oprah,* Winfrey glowingly referred to her as "the warrior woman for our time."

Her raucous tenure as head of the District of Columbia Public Schools (DCPS) certainly required the will of a warrior. It all began on June 12, 2007, when newly elected mayor Adrian Fenty appointed the reform-minded Rhee to lead a sprawling school district serving more than 47,000 students in 123 schools, widely regarded as the worst-performing major school system in the nation. Almost immediately, Rhee, then just thirty-eight years old, stirred controversy. The *Atlantic* magazine described her as a "lightning rod," as well as "the most controversial figure in American public education and the standard-bearer for a new type of schools leader nationwide."

Yet in a field often known for dogmatic theorists and faceless bureaucrats, Rhee became one of the nation's few education celebrities. Her face graced the covers of both *Time* and *Newsweek,* and she was one of the stars of the documentary *Waiting for "Superman."*

In 2011 she was named to *Time*'s list of the hundred most influential people in the world.

For Rhee, the new watchword of education reform is *accountability,* specifically teacher accountability. Rhee and her generation of reformers overturned the long-standing Left-Right political dynamic by going head-to-head against the teachers' unions, a longtime Democratic power base, and instead embracing traditionally conservative programs like school "choice" through charter schools and vouchers, as well as the national testing standards of George W. Bush's No Child Left Behind Act.

By eschewing the status quo, Rhee achieved remarkable results: Under her leadership, the worst-performing school district in the country became the only major city system to see double-digit gains over three years in both state reading and state math scores for seventh, eighth, and tenth graders. Graduation rates and enrollment rates rose for the first time in forty years.

As chancellor, Rhee was responsible not to a school board but only to Mayor Fenty, who gave her the power to fire central-office employees. Rhee fired nearly a hundred of them. In her most controversial and contentious move, she negotiated a radical performance-based compensation contract with the teachers' union. The contract had the potential to completely revolutionize the way teachers are paid.

Under Rhee's stewardship Washington had become "ground zero for education reformers," according to the *Atlantic,* which reported: "Young graduates from Harvard and Stanford were streaming to work as interns in her office, and she'd received blank checks from reform-minded philanthropists at the Gates and Broad foundations to fund experimental programs."

Such radical change drew opposition from teachers' unions, parents, and politicians. The 2010 Washington, D.C., mayoral election was interpreted as a referendum on Rhee's brief tenure as schools chancellor. When Mayor Adrian Fenty lost in the 2010

Democratic primary, Rhee took the defeat personally, calling the results "devastating for the schoolchildren of Washington, D.C." Still, rather than backing down from her stance, Rhee encouraged education reformers to "be more aggressive and more adamant." On October 13, 2010, Fenty announced that he'd accepted Rhee's resignation as schools chancellor.

I understand how Rhee felt. As I became more of an advocate for safety issues in aviation and in health care, I felt a moral obligation and a mission to do so.

DRIVEN AND UNCOMPROMISING

As we sat in her conference room, Rhee reflected on her headstrong and outspoken leadership style. She admitted that she'd stirred up trouble for herself when she publically said, "Collaboration is over-rated." Her uncompromising attitude bucked the historical way that the political establishment treated education professionals.

"We don't have an environment where we say, 'Yes, reform-ers disagree with the unions—vehemently disagree—and so let's duke it out,'" Rhee told me. "Instead, we've got a dynamic where people are saying, 'No, let's focus on what we all agree on.' That's like telling a married couple with problems, 'Let's go to counseling and talk about all the good times we had.' It's not actually going to move the ball forward; it's not going to get you to where you need to be."

Rhee, who grew up in Toledo, Ohio, believes controversy or conflict may be necessary when the stakes are so high and the need for reform in education is so great. This daughter of Korean immi-grants has never been afraid to take a stand and challenge the status quo, especially when it comes to helping others and her commu-nity. Her physician father instilled in Rhee and her two brothers "a real desire to help others," and she was particularly drawn to working with children, Rhee said.

"I've always had an affinity toward kids," she told me. "Even when I was in high school, I used to volunteer my time with terminally ill kids. One year I went to run a summer camp on an Indian reservation in Saskatchewan, Canada. I also volunteered at an inner-city school where my high school boyfriend's mother taught."

Her mother, who owned a clothing shop, was stricter than her laid-back father. She was a demanding "Tiger Mom" parent who passed on her competitive nature, willful determination, and focus on excellence and accountability to her only daughter, Rhee said. "When we came home with As, she'd say, 'Why wasn't it an A *plus*?' recalled Rhee. "One time my younger brother did poorly on his grades, and I got grounded because it was my responsibility, as his older sister, to help him and tutor him."

Shy and an average student, Rhee "had to work a lot harder than my peers did. It just didn't come naturally to me. Again, I grew up in a household where all through my high school and college days the mind-set was I could never be good enough. Nothing was ever good enough. I think this is the big difference between Asian families and Americans. In an Asian family, we weren't being congratulated for mediocrity or even for doing well. Unless you were the best, you were going to get no kudos whatsoever. And because I was never the best at anything—I was decent, I was good—I had this constant mind-set of 'I've got to work harder, I've got to do more, and it's not good enough.'"

Being the Boss

Rhee described herself as "a utility player" in high school: someone who could do most things "decently well" but "not particularly well." She had no concrete career goals, though she realized that she had some organizational and leadership skills.

"I figured out that I was a talker, meaning that I honed my

public speaking. And I was elected student council president. We had assemblies two or three times a week schoolwide, and I'd have to run those. I'd have to get up and ad-lib and that sort of thing.

"Starting from high school, a couple of things became clear to me. One, that I was a pretty good public speaker, and two, that I could be a leader. I was somebody who could get everybody motivated and could communicate with folks."

She also discovered that "I was a little bossy, yeah. I always had a plan for how things were going to play out, whether it was on the social scene, or on the field hockey team, or academics, or whatever. Then I would just execute the plan, and I would just tell everybody where to go and they would go."

Those who've worked with Rhee in more recent times would not be surprised to learn that from a young age she also had strong and clear-cut opinions. "In fact, that's probably one of my biggest challenges: I am a very black-and-white person, and there are very few gray areas in between," she admitted.

In college, first at Wellesley and then at Cornell, Rhee went through a "radical Asian woman phase" where she learned to be even more assertive, she said. "I took lots of classes on being oppressed. We did trainings for student groups on racism and sexism and all this sort of stuff. I went from being completely assimilated to pretty militant, but I ended up balanced somewhere in the middle."

GRUMPY MANAGEMENT TRAINING

Rhee received real-world training in running a business from her summer job at Grumpy's Deli. The irascible and demanding owner, who lived up to his nickname, would prove to be an important mentor, she said.

"Grumpy taught me very early on that you have to cut bait quickly with people. If people don't have what it takes to be successful, even making sandwiches, you gotta just cut bait. Grumpy would fire people all the time, often in front of me."

When her short-tempered boss opened a new location, he made Rhee the manager and passed her the Grumpy baton, telling her to run her shop just as he ran his. "It was never hard for me firing people," she said. "I've since managed thousands and thousands of people in my life, and I realize that for some people it's really painful to do. For me, I never had that level of angst. And today—this sounds a little crass—I'm very good at firing people, because when I fire people it's not ever about 'You're a bad person or you're not good.' It's always about fit.

"My thing with employees is always: You, as an individual, should be happy in your job. You should like and trust your boss. You should enjoy coming to work every day, and you should be adding value to the organization," Rhee said. "If that is not a fit, if those things are not happening, then you are going to be happier being in a different place with a better fit. And we will be happier having somebody who's a better fit. I'm always amazed at people who are unhappy with their jobs but keep them. If you're not happy, move on. Do something else. I mean, life is too short to be doing something every day that you don't like."

"It sounds like you have high expectations of others," I said, "just as your parents had high expectations of you."

"Yes," she said. "I have a very low tolerance for incompetence."

TIGER TEACHER

After graduating from Cornell in 1992, Rhee joined Teach For America, a then-new nonprofit organization created by the young Princeton graduate Wendy Kopp, whose mandate was to recruit fresh Ivy League grads to work in underperforming inner-city schools. Rhee's first assignment was to teach second grade in a crime-plagued Baltimore neighborhood. Hers was one of the city's lowest-performing schools. Yet, under these seemingly bleak conditions, Rhee's latent talents as an educator blossomed.

"From the moment that I had that experience in Baltimore, with the kids in that school, I could not imagine doing anything else with my professional life than being involved in public education," she told me. "In my first year, I just was not a good teacher at all, and then my second and third year, I got better. I took a group of kids who were at the absolute bottom on standardized tests and took them to the top. And it was such an obvious thing. It wasn't rocket science. We didn't do anything crazy other than what I felt my parents had done with me: build a work ethic and discipline in kids."

Using her mother as a role model, Rhee became a Tiger Teacher. "My students came in early. They stayed late. I made them do stuff on weekends. I made them do two hours of homework a night, which people back then thought was crazy. I mean, second graders doing two hours of homework a night! In my mind, it was sort of obvious: it's not like these kids are going straight to soccer practice or taking piano lessons right after school. These were inner-city kids: they were going to go back home and sit on the stoop or play Nintendo, right? Obviously, it would make more sense for them to be doing their homework and catching up."

Today, as the mother of two school-age children, Rhee has a different perspective on expecting that level of afterschool commitment. "Now I have a third grader, and I can barely get through twenty minutes of homework with her, now I understand how crazy it was. But back then, it just made perfect sense to me."

"What response did you get from their parents?" I asked.

"At first I got a lot of pushback because we were demanding a lot every day," she said. But, no surprise here, Rhee kept pushing her students to meet her lofty expectations despite the low expectations of others.

"By my second and third year of teaching, I had this group of kids who were, again, at the bottom and I took them to the top," she said. "It was just the same things that any kid needs to learn: discipline, hard work, time management, structure. I saw that when you put kids in an environment where you had superhigh expectations for them, you provided them with a lot of rigor and a lot of discipline and all those structures, they excelled. It didn't matter that, you know, Tiffany was sexually abused when she was five. None of that mattered when we actually got in the classroom.

"As teachers we were incredibly influential in their lives, and based on the environment that we were creating for them in school, we could literally change their trajectory in life."

TURNING POINT

In her early days as a teacher in Baltimore's poorest neighborhoods, Rhee was discouraged that few parents showed up for conferences. At first she thought they didn't care, but as she came to know the families better, she realized that those mothers wanted the best for their children, too.

"They didn't want anything different for their kids than what I wanted for my kids," she said. "Perhaps they weren't as savvy as I was, they didn't know how to navigate through the system, but their desires for their kids were not different.

"That was the major turning point in my life," she said, "the moment where I became obsessed with this notion that for kids in America today, their life chances and their life outcomes are dictated by things that they have no control over."

It was a shocking epiphany, Rhee said, to realize that children's fates depend so much on "who they happen to be born to and what neighborhood they lived in and therefore what schools they went to. This is the most un-American notion in my mind.

And I'm sad to say that we are still no better off today for poor and minority kids than we were twenty years ago when I got into this game. The whole notion was just completely un-American and unjust to me."

"It was an alien notion to you," I said. "It made no sense."

Rhee came to believe that the only thing stopping poor minority kids in inner cities from being academically successful was the adults in their lives, and "what we are doing or not doing, the environment that we're creating or not creating, the expectations that we have or don't have."

Thus began Rhee's new life. She had become a committed take-no-prisoners and leave-no-child-behind education reformer.

"That's when it locked in for me," she said, her eyes glowing with passion. "Back then there was this saying that all the educators liked to use: 'All children can learn.' It got coined back then, it was this big thing, everyone used to say it. But I'd think, *You know what? Half the people, or more, who are saying this say it because it's a politically correct thing to say, but they don't actually believe it. In their heart of hearts, they wonder, 'Well, can the kid succeed if the mom's on crack?'*

"I lived it. I'd seen it firsthand and I knew that they could, so I just had a different passion about it. It's the injustice that kids are going through every day. It's the low expectations, it's the excuses, it's all that crap. It just pisses me off to no end."

No Excuses

Rhee bristles at those who make excuses for children or write them off because of their difficult circumstances at home or in their communities. "That's the last thing that our kids need. You talk to any of the kids and they'll tell you that, and I saw that with my kids," she said. "After my second year of teaching, the Baltimore newspaper printed this article about test scores in the city. And our school was at the bottom, or in the bottom two, on test scores. I showed this article to the kids, and I said, 'What do you think people think about us when they see this?' They said, 'People think we're dumb.'

"'Right, are we dumb?'" she asked.

"They're like, *'Noooooo!'*

"These are eight-year-olds—second graders—shouting, 'No, we're not dumb!' People criticized me back then because they said it was inappropriate to have that conversation with kids. And to this day I believe that you've got to be honest with kids."

Rhee described a trip to Harlem where she met with a group of schoolchildren and told them, "There's a big debate going on in education reform right now about you—about poor kids of color. Some people say that because of the home environment that you live in that you can't learn at the highest levels. And other people believe that you can. So let me ask you, What do you think?"

The children in Harlem shouted in unison. "Yes, we can."

"And then one little girl said to me, 'I want you to tell the people of America that it is not where we come *from* every day, it's where we're *going* to that makes the difference in our lives.'"

"That's a great way of putting it," I said.

"Perfect," she said.

"It's about having high expectations," I said.

"Right," she said. "They crave that—my kids and any group of kids that I know. They want the structure. They want the high expectations. I have a belief in all children, but in particular poor minority kids, because I think they're given the raw end of the deal, that they have the biggest gap between what their potential is and where they are currently performing. Whether they close that gap or not has absolutely nothing—or very little—to do with things that they can control."

Taking Responsibility

"Do you think it's not only possible but also imperative that we close this gap in achievement?" I asked.

"No doubt."

I asked Rhee if a child's learning potential is unaffected by the quality of life at home and in the community.

"Here's the thing," she said, "if you have a substandard diet and substandard health care, and the electricity in your house went off because your mom couldn't pay the bill, of course that stuff matters. I'm not saying that it doesn't have an impact. It makes it a lot harder. But my point is, they're still overcomeable. And that's our job: to ensure that kids can overcome that, versus just sort of abdicating responsibility."

Good leaders take responsibility for the success of their people. They find ways to help their followers achieve success, and in Rhee's case, that meant recognizing that she had to provide what her students' parents and home environment did not. Doctors, lawyers, and other high-achieving role models that she grew up with were in short supply in Baltimore's impoverished neighborhoods. One of her students said that his cousin, who delivered pizzas, was his role model because he had a regular job. To help counter that, Rhee tried to help them connect the dots between getting an education and having a better life. In a move that brought her some criticism, she also gave her students daily incentives to work hard and strive for success.

"The kids I taught did not have relatives who had gone off to college, who were lawyers and doctors. So you're asking an eight-year-old to make all of these calculations about their life based on something that is so far away from their reality that they don't even know what it looks like," she said. "That doesn't happen magically. That only happens through somebody, every single day, saying, 'This is what you have to do. This is what it means to have something else, to go to college.' That is not something that happens overnight."

One of her more controversial classroom strategies was to reward her students for doing their homework.

"My classroom was big into rewarding kids," she said. "You did your homework every day, you got a ticket. At the end of the week, if you had so many tickets, you could go to the classroom store and buy things like pencils. The kids really responded to that. A lot of people said, 'You're teaching them the wrong things; you've got all these extrinsic motivators instead of the kids learning intrinsically.' I'd say, 'But you don't go to work every day for free. You get paid to go to work, right? There's a reward. Why should we expect the kids to be operating in any different way?'"

THE UNCOMPROMISING CHANGE AGENT

Rhee has always pushed herself to be her best every bit as hard as she pushed her pupils. She left Teach For America after her three-year tour to complete a master's degree at Harvard's Kennedy School of Government. Just before Rhee graduated from that program in the spring of 1997, Wendy Kopp asked if she would return to Teach For America to launch a spin-off of Kopp's creation.

Rhee took the helm for the New Teacher Project, which contracted with school districts to find and train people interested in becoming teachers after extended careers in professions such as science, journalism, law, or other fields.

Rhee became the driving force for the New Teacher Project, which at its ten-year mark had recruited some twenty-eight thousand new teachers to serve in more than two hundred school districts, including those in New York City and Washington. Rhee was so effective leading the New Teacher Project that she caught the attention of politicians and civic leaders trying to reform their school systems.

Washington, D.C.'s Mayor Fenty had campaigned on a promise to fix the District's chronically dysfunctional public school system.

He saw Rhee as the dynamic and fearless young educator who could actually get things done. Almost immediately, Rhee's confrontational style drew both admirers and vocal critics, but few doubted her passion for improving educational opportunities for all children.

Like Bill Bratton and his approach to traditional law enforcement, Rhee saw herself as an agent of change in the educational field. Just as she once had offered incentives to her students to push them to succeed, she did the same with Washington, D.C.'s teachers. She proposed a revolutionary contract that rewarded the most effective teachers instead of those who had the most years on the job. Teachers could opt to make up to $140,000 pegged to their effectiveness, but to get that money they had to give up tenure. Or they could keep tenure and accept a smaller raise.

The contentious battle with the teachers' union over that proposal lasted two and a half years. I asked Rhee if she would have handled the negotiations with the union any differently in hindsight.

"I don't honestly know that I would have done anything differently from the bargaining side other than try and communicate better with the teachers," she said. "I will tell you this: Had we taken the stance that most school districts do—which is 'We're going to get along with the union; we should find the common ground'—we would not have ended up with the contract that we did. Had I taken a softer stand and been more accommodating and more willing to collaborate and all that kind of crap, we would not have ended up with the contract that we did."

That contract, she noted, provides no tenure, no seniority, no lockstep pay, and "is actually good for children now."

As a leader who placed her responsibility to students above any desire for personal or professional gain, Rhee said that doing what was best for students was far more important to her than winning over critics who lambasted her as a "Dragon Lady."

"Because I'd said to those people, 'Look, when it comes to kids,

I'm not compromising,'" she said. "'This is not a negotiating position that I'm staking.' I think that at the end of the day, for what we were able to accomplish, it was worth it. All the controversy, all the heartache, all the bad press; everything was worth it at the end of the day for what we were able to get for the kids in this contract and protecting their rights first and foremost."

CONTROLLING THE MESSAGE

Unlike Bratton, however, Rhee did not control the message in the media as she pushed for change. She admitted to me that a vocal minority of teachers fighting her efforts to replace tenure with pay incentives did a better job than she did in that regard, which helped to prolong the battle.

"I made a lot of mistakes while I was here, but one of my biggest mistakes was that I did not do a good enough job communicating directly with teachers," she said. "I assumed that everyone knew where I was trying to go. I just thought it was obvious: 'Yes, we want to close the achievement gap between white and black kids. We want every kid to be achieving at the highest levels.' That, to me, was just 101. How could you believe anything else? And what I realized over time is not everybody believes that, that's not everybody's aspiration.

"The press would come out and write some crazy story, I would read it and say, 'Nobody's going to believe that. Who would believe that?' So we didn't proactively go out and try to say, 'Actually, no, that's not the case.' I was so incredulous about it that I assumed everybody else would be too."

In hindsight, Rhee said that she would have been more proactive and more diligent about "sending our own consistent messages" and "explaining why we were doing things and when we were doing all this. If I had to do it all over again, that's definitely one of the things I would have at least tried to do. What happened was, in the vacuum of not having the direct message or communication from me, the blogosphere and the media filled the void, and that's all that people were getting. So then it just became 'fact.' Even though it was crazy, dumb stuff half the time, it just settled into people's heads as 'fact.' It was because I was very naive, I think, when I took the job. I thought, 'You know what? If we produce results, then people are going to like them and want them to continue.'"

Rhee smiled as she recalled that her then husband-to-be, Kevin Johnson, had often said, in reference to the forming of public opinion, "One of the saddest things and lessons I learned from my whole experience is, results don't matter that much sometimes." Her point was that even though most agree that her changes have improved the Washington, D.C., school system, there is still lingering resentment about her methods and her personality.

"People didn't like the *way* that we were doing things. Forget the fact that, in a three-year period of time, we saw more academic gains than the District had ever seen, that academically we went from being at the bottom of everything to actually leading the nation in gains," she said. "That didn't matter, because people didn't like the way we were doing things. And that just was so foreign to me.

"Personally, if I'm living in a city, I don't give a crap what the mayor's personality is like as long as you pick up my trash and the schools are good and the streets get shoveled. I'm very results oriented, and that's all I care about. I don't care if somebody's nice as long as they get the job done."

STAYING FOCUSED ON THE MISSION

Because of her battles with the teachers' union, I asked Rhee whether public employees should have the right to organize and to collectively bargain.

"I am in favor of employees' rights to organize and to bargain on *certain* things," she said. "The problem that I see, within education, is that the role of the public-sector employee unions has now changed, and they now are driving and bargaining over things that are actual policies, which is absolutely an unhealthy dynamic."

Rhee's argument with the teachers' unions is that their focus, in her opinion, was on maximizing the pay and privileges and priorities of their group, and that focus determined their approach to crafting policies for educating children.

"Sometimes what's good for adults in the system is good for kids," she said. "In those cases, I have no problem. But at other times, those two things come into conflict with one another. And when they do come into conflict, meaning what's good for the adults is not good for the kids, that's where I draw the line. I don't think that we can expect the public-sector employees' union to want what's good and right for the kids. I just don't think that's reasonable. That's not their job. That's not how they're oriented."

When the union fights to retain tenure so teachers can't be fired, it is only doing its job, but from her perspective, tenure does not serve the best interests of young people, who deserve the best possible education.

The Need to Lead

I asked Rhee if most of her life had been a preparation for her role as a reformer, given her passion, drive, skills, and knowledge of her field. Rhee said that in fact her upper-middle-class upbringing, Asian heritage, and private-school education might seem an unlikely background for an inner-city education reformer. Yet the leadership role does suit her compelling need to right wrongs and to bring order out of chaos.

"It doesn't make sense in people's heads that I would be a champion for the neediest kids, but from the leadership standpoint, I've always had very strong opinions. I've always been really vocal," she said. "My nature is such that when I see something that's not working, maybe others would let it play out and see how it goes, but that drives me nuts."

I noted that Rhee seemed to have little tolerance for inefficiency, and she agreed. I asked her if she was impatient.

She said, "In some ways I'm very impatient." Then she laughed and offered a vivid illustration of her need to restore order to dysfunctional situations.

She and her former husband went to a restaurant when she was pregnant. Rhee was very hungry but there was a wait, one much longer than she had the patience for, especially when she saw empty tables. "I sort of cased the joint out, and then I went behind the counter, and I started telling the busboys, 'Go clear that table, go tell the hostess to take these people there,' and I cleared out the backlog like that," she said, snapping her fingers. "Now, I didn't do that because I cared about the business, but because I wanted to eat, right? It was all so I could eat my pancakes.

"But the crazy thing is, these people worked for the restaurant and they're listening to me, right? They're not supposed to be taking direction from me about what to do or what not to do. My ex-husband says, 'That's vintage Michelle. They were looking for leadership. They wanted somebody to tell them what to do, and they were excited about having somebody tell them what to do to solve the problem.'"

I told Rhee that the restaurant story seemed to mirror her experience in education. Everyone agrees that the system is dysfunctional, but few are willing to step up and take command of the situation and fix it, as she and Wendy Kopp and others have endeavored to do. "You've become an education messiah to some," I said. "There are a lot of people who really care about education, who want it to work. They're not quite sure how to get there, and you've given them this drive and this direction.

"Do you feel like you wouldn't have been able to do what you ended up doing without the experiences you had earlier in life?" I asked. "Or was it such an innate part of your nature that you probably could have done it anyway? In other words, are leaders born or made?"

"I think that the raw material of being a leader is just there," Rhee said. "Then that can either be molded so that you become a leader or not, but, I mean, I see this with my kids. When they're working on a group project, my twelve-year-old takes control. She tells everybody what to do and assigns everybody a role. She's been that way since she was in second grade. My little one is like that, too. She started a business making these origami frogs and she has all these people working for her with the business. And she's like, 'I have to fire Isabel.' I don't think normal eight-year-olds are starting up businesses and trying to figure out how to fire their friends."

"No," I said with a laugh. "Not too many."

"A certain part of it is just innate in people," she said. "Then I think that those skills can either be developed or not, depending on the experiences that you have. But I've had the good fortune of working with so many incredibly talented people through my years, and some of them, some of the smartest, most determined, dedicated people, don't want to be in that leadership role. They don't want the conflict. They're almost *allergic* to it. That's not who they are; that's not the role that they want to play. Every fiber of their being tells them that. That's why I think that *raw* piece has to be there."

DEVELOPING HUMAN CAPITAL

I encouraged Rhee to talk more about developing the raw talents of others, such as teachers. "What kinds of things should we be doing—could we be doing—to make all teachers better?" I asked. "Is it possible for somebody who's been a fifteen-year veteran and minimally effective to actually get better? If so, what does it take?"

"The people I love are always those who have the will and not the skill," she said. "Because I believe that if you've the will, there's something to work with. But at the same time—and, again, this is from my Grumpy roots—there's a part of me that says, especially when you're doing work as important as we are, 'How long are you going to wait? How much time are you going to give them? How much of an investment is worth what kind of an incremental difference?'

"I believe in creating an environment of constant improvement, one of professional development, investing heavily in that. But I also think that you can't have an endless amount of belief that people can get better, because I think that some of them probably, despite all of the will in the world, will not be able to do it."

I asked what role trust and loyalty play in her concept of leadership. "Is that important to you? Is that something you worry about? Is that something you work on?"

"Yeah, it is," she said. "It is something that I think is very important. I have certain strengths and I have a lot of weaknesses. I think that as a leader and as a manager I set my organizations up in a certain way. One of the things I'm actually good at is I can sniff out talent, and I have no problem with hiring people who are a whole lot smarter than me. Some people don't want to hire people that are smarter them because they want to be the smartest person in the room."

"They're threatened," I said.

"I don't have any problem with that. I like when everybody else is smarter than me," she said. "And then my job, as the leader, is to block and tackle, and to do all the stuff that they don't want to do, that makes their lives hard or whatever, so that they can do their jobs."

"So you can remove barriers?" I said.

"Yes. And that's where I feel like my strength as a leader is, in being able to do that, not in knowing more than everybody. President Obama is so smart that he actually probably knows more than a lot of other people on the staff, and that's one of his strengths as a leader. I think my strength as a leader is not knowing more or being smarter, but just being able to bring together talent and then being able to see, 'Okay, what are the barriers they're going to get?' Then I'm going to go and knock those things down so you can do your job."

Although she admits to not being a warm and fuzzy person or leader, Rhee still considers trust and loyalty to be very important. "For a really long time I ran my own stuff, so I never had a boss per se, and that was one of my difficulties," she said. "One of my things that I wasn't sure about, my uncertainties coming into this job in D.C., was 'I'm going to have a boss for the first time.' But what I realized was that I didn't have any problem having Adrian Fenty as my boss, and I was sort of deathly loyal to him to the end. That's just the way my brain works."

Michelle Rhee can be very charming, yet she has an iron will and a driving sense of purpose. With that thought in mind, I asked if she is driven by anger over injustices she sees in the educational system.

"Without a doubt. I get my energy every day from kids. I love kids. My oldest daughter says, 'The difference between you and most adults is that most adults like their own kids, but you like all kids.' To a certain extent, that's right. I feel passion about all kids. And when kids are getting screwed, it just pisses me off. And to listen to these people who are making excuses for why the system can't work, why we have to slow down the process of change, nothing makes me madder."

Unlike so many elected officials in Washington, including most senators, congressmen, and even President Obama, Rhee sends her own children to public schools in the District. This is one of the reasons she grows so impassioned when talking about the issue of teacher accountability. Rhee noted that if her daughter's school principal assigned a bad teacher to her class in hopes that the teacher would improve with experience, that would not be okay with Rhee.

"There's no way that I would accept that for my kid," she said, her voice rising with passion. "There's no way that any of us would ever accept that for our kids. But we have scores of children in this city and across the country who don't have adult advocates who know how to navigate through the system and say no and get them into another classroom.

"We literally have kids languishing in the classrooms of ineffective teachers every day, kids who have no rights whatsoever. We're telling those kids, 'We don't care that you only go through first grade one time. Suck it up with this bad teacher because this is about their "employment rights" and whatever.' No! That's crazy! There's no way that we are going to have a higher-quality education system, one that's focused on kids and their academic growth, if we have rules in place like that: rules that are prioritizing the rights of employees over the needs of our children."

10

SUE SHERIDAN

I can't change what has happened to my son or my husband,
but I do hope that by telling our story, I can make a difference
and help prevent it from happening to other babies and daddies.

SUE SHERIDAN AND HER HUSBAND, PAT, FELT THEY'D FOUND THEIR
little corner of paradise in May 1992. The young married couple
had moved from Dallas to the idyllic mountain town of McCall,
Idaho, on the southern shore of a pristine lake near the heart of
the Payette National Forest. The town of two thousand people
was so small that it had not a single stoplight. McCall was their
refuge from the frenzied pace Sue and Pat had kept up early in their
marriage and courtship. Both had worked in international banking
and finance, and before that they had served together in the Peace
Corps.

In search of a calmer life and hoping to start a family, they'd
moved to Idaho after disposing of most of their possessions and
packing what remained in their 1966 Crown Victoria for their move
to one of their favorite places. Once they'd settled in, Pat worked

part-time as a financial consultant, but they adapted quickly to the more relaxed pace.

"And then we got pregnant," she said.

They made a fateful decision to have their first child at the larger St. Luke's Medical Center in Boise rather than the tiny rural hospital near McCall because "we thought it was safer and better," Susan recalled.

Their son, Cal, was born on March 23, 1995, in a normal delivery. Everything seemed to be going according to plan. Yet within days, that "perfect" life they'd seemingly found was shattered. Stoically and without much preamble, Sue recounted for me the life-changing series of events that began with the complications surrounding her son's birth.

"You have to understand, Pat and I had lived a *huge* life for ten years before we had kids, and when we moved to Idaho, we decided it was a good time to have a family." For more than two years they'd tried without success. "We found that I had complications, endometriosis," she told me. "And my doctor said, 'It's probably just not going happen for you guys.' So we considered adopting. Then my doctor said, 'Let me try one surgery.' That surgery was successful. We got pregnant a few weeks later."

After all the challenges they'd overcome, Sue and Pat felt their son was a miracle baby, beautiful and perfect. Sadly, their joy was short-lived. At first Cal's symptoms seemed innocuous enough. He was just sixteen hours old when a nurse noted on his chart that he was jaundiced. One doctor said his jaundice was normal and suggested placing him in the sun. A nurse jokingly called him "canary baby," the mother said.

The blood test that would have measured the severity of the condition was not done, and the mother and child were sent home. The medical staff at St. Luke's was reassuring. "We were told in the hospital that jaundice was normal and not to worry. So I didn't."

Almost as soon as Sheridan returned to their home in McCall, her newborn's behavior began to alarm her. Cal had been feeding normally, every three hours, but on his fourth day home, she couldn't wake him for his normal feeding. "I jiggled him and he would wake up and fall back to sleep," she said. "I called the hospital and said, 'There's something going on with my baby.' I told them, 'He's still yellow.' They told me, 'Don't worry, that's normal.'"

Sheridan was not satisfied with that response. She made an appointment with her pediatrician. Pat drove her and Cal into Boise for an office visit. Cal still would not respond, and he was not sleeping as usual either. He was also "a pumpkin color," she recalled. "We were told to go home and wait twenty-four hours. It was almost like 'Mom, don't worry your pretty little head off.'"

Meanwhile, Pat's mother, a registered nurse, was alarmed over her grandson's worsening condition and told Sheridan, "This is an emergency. Take him to the hospital immediately." Sue followed her mother-in-law's instructions, but the staff at St. Luke's Medical Center remained "very laid-back about Cal's jaundice," according to Sheridan. "On the second day they put him on phototherapy, which is standard treatment for jaundice. And then Cal started arching backward, making this really bizarre, high-pitched cry."

She felt something terrible had happened to her baby. "And again, we alerted everybody, but I was categorized as kind of a neurotic first-time mom."

As she watched in horror, her baby's legs "got really stiff and his head kind of turned to one side," she said. "I watched my son suffer brain damage in the hospital. . . ." The mother's voice trailed off, and her eyes moistened as grief briefly took hold once again.

Initially, the medical staff did not pick up on Cal's condition. Instead, they sent mother and child home again. "We were told he was fine: 'Go home; live your lives.' But after that Cal couldn't breast-feed. His body was twisted in strange ways. He never slept, though normal babies sleep all the time. His neurologic system was just totally damaged. So it was a struggle for Pat and me, as a couple, to have this baby that was so hard to manage. And so I started thinking, 'There is something going on here.' I started doing research on the Internet. I reached out to a long-lost friend who is a neurologist in Kentucky and said, 'I need help here.' Locally, the physicians were ignoring my concerns and my challenges."

Cal was unresponsive and severely underweight. Finally, his parents decided to go to a hospital in Salt Lake City. "When he was admitted to the hospital, this doctor very matter-of-factly said, 'What kind of cerebral palsy does he have?' I said, 'We've never been told he has cerebral palsy.' They brought in the social workers, and then the neurologist. 'We hate to be the ones to tell you this, but your son has cerebral palsy.'"

Confused and frightened, Sue and Pat next took Cal to the University of Washington in Seattle to see a specialist, who asked within thirty minutes of meeting them whether an ultrasound had been done on Cal after he was diagnosed with kernicterus. The parents said no one had mentioned that. "Your son has *classic* textbook kernicterus," the specialist advised them.

Neither had even heard of kernicterus. They sat speechless as the team of specialists explained that kernicterus is the specific kind of brain damage that results from advanced jaundice.

Now Sue and Pat stared at each other, confused, disoriented, and devastated. How could their miracle baby have developed a complication virtually unheard of in the United States, in any developed nation, for that matter, a form of irreparable brain damage found only in the poorest Third World countries?

SEARCHING FOR ANSWERS

The parents were reeling from concerns over Cal's mental and physical problems in the summer of 1995, but they remained determined to make a great life for their newborn. Sue Sheridan spent weeks with Cal at the Child Development and Mental Retardation Center on the University of Washington campus in Seattle. When medical experts repeatedly asked her why an ultrasound for kernicterus had not been performed on Cal when his jaundice appeared, the realization hit Sheridan that her son's condition was not some unavoidable complication but instead a medical error.

When his new doctors delved into Cal's records, they found that an MRI had been done on her son at the Boise hospital. It showed abnormalities in his brain, but no one had shared the results with her or Pat.

The doctors at the Child Development and Mental Retardation Center told her, frankly, that her son faced "a hard life." The mother refused to give up hope. She immersed herself in medical research, trying to learn as much as she could about her son's condition, his outlook, and the cause.

"That was the beginning of my advocacy," she said. "I was so shocked that this could happen to a baby born to an educated mom, a mom who did everything she could possibly do, read everything she could possibly read. I mean, no one had ever told me that jaundice could cause brain damage."

Sheridan learned that in the 1990s, most hospitals stopped testing newborns for kernicterus because it had become statistically rare. She discovered, to her horror, that a simple procedure—the bilirubin test—was not performed on Cal. The medical community had decided that kernicterus was no longer a threat, that it had been eradicated, like polio.

Bilirubin is a blood toxin. When a baby is born and separated from the mother's blood supply, the child's body must break down old blood cells and build its own. That destruction of red blood cells, which every single baby goes through, creates the bilirubin toxin that causes the skin to yellow. All babies experience jaundice at some level. An inexpensive bilirubin test measures the range. A normal range is 7 to 8 after birth. Cal's had soared to 34.6.

As she delved deeper into her research, Sheridan learned about some shocking changes in the national hospital policy: Prior to the 1990s, most hospitals kept newborn bilirubin levels under 20 to prevent brain damage. If the level neared that range, the infants were put under phototherapeutic lights, which reduced the bilirubin in the blood. But by the time Cal was born, since the medical profession felt that kernicterus had disappeared from the general population, "they stopped testing and treating for jaundice," she said.

I asked her if that change in policy was strictly a financial decision.

"A lot of it was financial, yeah," she replied. "It was the perfect storm brewing, because HMOs were coming in then. And with the HMOs came a different billing and payment structure. You also had doctors and nurses who had never seen kernicterus because they supposedly got rid of it in the 1970s, so it really was off the radar. You now had a population of parents totally oblivious to the dangers of jaundice. And probably the biggest confounding factor was when Congress passed the early discharge laws in the 1990s."

Suddenly, longer newborn stays in the maternity wards were deemed too expensive, and a new phrase, "drive-through deliveries," entered the lexicon.

As Sheridan recounted her experience, I couldn't help reflecting that, once again, our leadership in government and the medical community had forgotten very important lessons. An inexpensive and routine test that could have saved so much pain and suffering was no longer done simply because of cost cutting that overrode public health and safety concerns.

Even in aviation, where these hard lessons have often been learned only at great cost, literally bought with blood, sadly we have had to relearn too many of them. I was struck by the fact that some leaders failed miserably in their duty to protect the public; in this case, however, another leader with a great social conscience came forth as the result of this tragedy. Sue Sheridan could have let her anger and grief consume her. She could have focused on her own child's needs and shut out the rest of the world. Instead, she stepped into a much bigger role. Working doggedly and on her own, she pulled back the curtain on a stunning systemic failure.

"I felt betrayed," she told me. "I felt betrayed by our health care system for withholding information from moms. I started thinking of all the other mothers out there that this was going to happen to; that there could be a whole population of kids like Cal. I knew I could not change Cal. I could *never* change what happened to Cal. If there were *any* way, I would have figured it out. But I could help prevent it from happening in the future."

Sheridan had identified the problem, but she could find no organization or agency that would take responsibility for finding or implementing a solution. She'd thought that there was some group responsible for keeping the medical system safe, but she now realized that was naive.

Her nagging suspicion that the nation's entire health care system was broken was confirmed by a *USA Today* article that detailed the relationship between hospitals and the Joint Commission, which accredits hospitals but is also paid by the hospitals that it reviews. Even though Sheridan had no formal medical education, her financial training and common sense told her "this interrelationship between agencies didn't add up to safety."

She channeled her frustration and anger into a plan for positive action. Instead of being overwhelmed or wallowing in self-pity, Sheridan wrote "countless" letters to every federal agency she could identify that had responsibilities in the health care field, saying, "'This is what's happened to me and my family.' I told them that I'd witnessed some glaring gaps in our health care system. And that I wanted to be part of solutions.

"I didn't get a single response."

MORE THAN MOST COULD BEAR

If at this point in her story, you've come to admire Sheridan for her perseverance and her strength, be prepared to stand in awe, as I do, at this "accidental" leader's capacity for enduring personal tragedy and her incredible ability to combat her grief by working for the greater good.

She was still working out her plan for taking on the medical establishment when her forty-two-year-old husband began experiencing mysterious symptoms. Pat's severe neck pains were first diagnosed as related to the stress of dealing with their son's health challenges, but further examination detected a mass in Pat's neck that proved to be a tumor in his cervical spine. They flew to specialists in Arizona, where a neurosurgeon removed the tumor. A biopsy report said it was a benign growth often found in middle-aged men.

Pat was not provided with the final report on the tumor, which the family would later realize was a deadly mistake. Six months later, the pain in his neck returned. Doctors found a much larger tumor in his spinal cord that was growing so fast it caused a bulge in his neck. As Pat lay intubated and recovering from the second surgery, a physician whom his wife had never met entered the hospital room.

"We only have one question," the doctor asked. "Why didn't your husband begin cancer treatment after the first surgery?"

"Because we were told the tumor was benign," Sue Sheridan said.

Now, to their dismay, Pat and Sue were told that the new tumor had been a malignant sarcoma. "Can a benign tumor become a cancerous tumor?" she asked. The oncology team told her that was possible. Still, the surgeons were optimistic and confident that they'd removed all the malignant tissue. "We've got clean margins," one surgeon said.

Then a second specialist came into the room. "We have nothing to do with your husband. We're on the tumor board. We just want to know why your husband didn't get treatment after the first surgery."

"Because it was *benign*," Sheridan said again, wondering if they were confusing Pat's chart with that of another patient.

Later that same day, a third doctor came in and asked the same question, which prompted her to ask, "Wait a second. What was his pathology on the first surgery?" When the doctor claimed he did not have access to that information, Sheridan marched down to the medical records department and checked her husband's chart.

"Right there was the final pathology, which was signed twenty-three days after his first surgery. I read, 'malignant sarcoma,'" she said. "I'm standing by myself in medical records reading this. I mean, my knees buckled. I remember standing there, my back against the wall, saying, 'Oh my God! This is not for real!'"

The initial failure to treat the cancer resulted in a second surgery, six months of out-of-state chemotherapy, and experimental clinical trials at MD Anderson Cancer Center; moreover, it had undoubtedly reduced Pat's chances of survival. Remarkably, Sheridan still did not succumb to depression, nor did she accept defeat.

COMMITMENT ATTRACTS FOLLOWERS

The family relocated to Houston, where Pat began undergoing intensive chemotherapy. His wife kept furiously writing letters about Cal's condition, and now she included Pat's story as well. Finally, her efforts to grab the attention of the medical community were rewarded in 2000, with her husband still fighting cancer.

In response to her campaign to be heard, Sheridan was the only "consumer" invited to address the first National Summit on Medical Errors and Patient Safety Research, held September 11, 2000, in Washington, D.C. The title of the conference may have sounded mind-numbing and coldly bureaucratic. Sheridan's presentation was not.

Righteous indignation and outrage have rarely been expressed with such dignity and class. Before the assembled medical experts and dignitaries, she told the heartbreaking story of her son and her husband, and then she called upon those present to take responsible action to see that no one ever again endured the same fate as her two loved ones.

Sheridan called out the medical community. She demanded answers to the questions that had driven her, despite her grief and her exhaustion. She questioned why there was no reporting system, no mandatory disclosure, and no place where she could report these problems so they would not happen to others.

She testified that failure to disclose information to patients was, in her opinion, "criminal behavior, and should never be tolerated." She compared the minuscule cost of the bilirubin test that Cal should have received to his current "life care plan," estimating that his "medical costs will be between four million and seven million dollars. What costs are being saved?" she asked angrily.

In her testimony, she said:

Our biggest disappointment in the health care system has been the intolerable lack of integrity and blatant dishonesty, which appears to be an accepted practice throughout the industry, ranging from individual doctors up to the level of top executive officers of hospitals. . . . I can't change what has happened to my son or my husband, but I do hope that by telling our story, I can make a difference and help prevent it from happening to other babies and daddies.

The power of the Sheridan family's tragic story had immediate and far-reaching repercussions. After learning of her testimony, *USA Today* wrote a front-page article about Pat and Cal. The response reinforced Sheridan's growing suspicion that her son and her husband were just two of many to suffer because of flagrant and systemic medical errors.

Before that point, she'd had little evidence that kernicterus was a problem anywhere other than in the Third World. Several "experts" had actually told her that kernicterus was wiped out in the United States in the 1970s. After Cal's picture and the family's story appeared on the front page of *USA Today,* the Sheridans were flooded with phone calls from others with similar stories. They discovered that there were numerous victims of the same sort of medical errors, and many other individuals and families who had suffered as a result.

The media quickly picked up on the bigger story. Within ten days, *USA Today* ran a follow-up article about Sue Sheridan and six other mothers whose children suffered kernicterus gathering at an American Academy of Pediatrics symposium where she was scheduled to show a video of Cal as a "classic textbook case" of kernicterus.

"All these other moms converged," Sheridan told me. "We had no money, so we got two rooms for all of us. And we decided we needed to do something. We didn't sleep. We stayed awake for thirty-six hours and formed our nonprofit Parents of Infants and Children with Kernicterus (PICK). We recruited the nation's top published physicians, who would later join us as our advisers.

From then on, we were formidable. We were unstoppable. The Seven Moms. It went to eight, to twelve, to twenty-eight, thirty-six, sixty-eight, and then just started piling on."

Thanks to their compelling testimony and a video demonstrating the cruel and debilitating impact of kernicterus on their children, the mothers' grassroots beginning grew into a national and international movement that brought profound change to the health care system. Their efforts to raise awareness alerted doctors and parents. Many more cases of kernicterus were reported. Hospital staffs took the symptoms more seriously.

The group kept the pressure on the Joint Commission, which invited them to speak to a workshop. Sheridan made certain that representatives from the most important organizations were in the audience, including the federal agency that deals with Medicare and Medicaid services, the March of Dimes, and the Centers for Disease Control.

"Before long, we had twenty-five agencies gathered around the table," she recalled. "My background, of course, was business. But we had a mom who was a Ph.D. neuroscientist. We had a mom who was an OR nurse. We had a mom who was an event planner. So we threw a pretty good event! And now we weren't just these Seven Moms. We had the top doctors, basically, in the world, supporting us."

THE MESSAGE OF LEADERSHIP

With her formidable team assembled, Sheridan displayed the finely tuned communication skills that mark a true leader. She presented her case with a passion and power that could not be denied.

"I said our kids were getting brain damage from the omission of a test that costs *one dollar*. And, in the early nineties, because of cost cutting and economics, hospitals stopped doing some routine testing, one of them being for jaundice. We called for universal implementation that all babies got this dollar test before discharge.

"In a way, our naiveté and ignorance was a blessing. We didn't know that you just do *not* give the Joint Commission a to-do list! And we had huge expectations," she added. "We gave everybody a list of what we expected them to do."

Within two months, the CDC had issued a massive public health alert, and the drug commission issued its own. The National Quality Forum campaigned for Cal's injury to become what they call a "Never Event."

Sheridan paused for a moment to reflect. "It took *ten years,* but we changed the standard of care," she said. "The standard of care today is that all babies will get a jaundice test. We went to the Hill and got funding for focus groups and surveyed the U.S. population. And we did it in a relatively scientific way; we tried to make it bulletproof. . . ."

DRIVEN BY A GREATER CAUSE

For Sheridan and her group to have had such a powerful global impact attests to the power within all of us to effect change, but it takes commitment and passion and incredible perseverance, as her story illustrates. Sue Sheridan's experience also offers proof that leadership qualities live within all of us.

She had not set out to be a leader of any sort, but today Sheridan is renowned as one of the world's foremost patient advocates. Through tireless traveling, lobbying, and speaking to groups and organizations around the world, she has recruited an army of fellow champions who have convinced hospitals worldwide to adopt procedures that would have saved her baby, Cal, from his tragic fate. Today, Sheridan is the cofounder and past president of Parents of Infants and Children with Kernicterus, which works in partnership with private and public health agencies to eradicate this rare neurological condition. She is also the cofounder of Consumers Advancing Patient Safety, a nonprofit organization that seeks a safe, compassionate, and just health care system through proactive partnership between consumers and providers of care.

Sheridan was asked to take an even larger leadership role in 2004. Because she had become such an effective advocate, she was recruited to lead the World Health Organization's Patients for Patient Safety initiative. In announcing her new role with WHO, its chair of the World Alliance for Patient Safety, Sir Liam Donaldson, said, "She's a wonderfully articulate voice for patients and families and an inspiring motivator for us all."

Nothing in Sheridan's childhood could have prepared her for the tragedies and challenges that would consume her life in the mid-1990s. Indeed, she says, it was an "unremarkable" upbringing. Her parents were teachers in the small midwestern town of Adrian, Michigan, and education was emphasized. Her Spanish teacher, who'd been a lawyer in Cuba before fleeing the revolution, took Sheridan's class to Mexico and opened her eyes to the greater world, giving rise to her wanderlust. Later, she studied in Spain, where she and Pat, also an enthusiastic traveler, who worked for Texas Instruments, returned to be married in a small village. The couple later served two years in Ecuador with the Small Enterprise Development group of the Peace Corps. There they helped weavers in small villages market their products to companies like Pier One.

Sheridan exudes empathy and compassion, and as I listened to her, it seemed that working among the impoverished people in Latin America had been a formative and defining experience, as well as a rewarding and empowering one, for her. It helped shape her worldview as well as her sense of self. She and Pat changed the lives of those villagers. In return, seeing the positive impact she had on them changed her.

Her emergence as first a national, then an international, leader was powered both by profound emotional pain and by the sense of duty that exists in all of us. "We absolutely had to make sure this couldn't happen again to other babies," she told me.

Sheridan's experiences reminded me of that famous century-old George Bernard Shaw quotation, later paraphrased by Robert Kennedy: "You see things; and you say, 'Why?' But I dream things that never were; and I say, 'Why not?'" Sue Sheridan brought change in the world because she articulated a vision of a better future. Her optimism and her sense of belief became infectious, almost a force of nature.

CHANNELING ANGER INTO POSITIVE ACTION

I asked Sheridan how she had managed to come out of nowhere, as far as the medical community was concerned, and bring about such incredible change in the often imperious medical establishment.

"Yes, you're right—after all, I was just a *mom*!" she said. "I had *no* medical background. What was I thinking? When I got in front of an audience, I shared with them my belief that we *will* be successful. And we started out on Day One thinking we would be successful. I would get up and say, 'Join us! I challenge you, c'mon, I invite you.'"

In a sense, the negativity from medical groups and their condescension helped to fuel her passion. "Sure, I got mad," Sheridan said. "But I always took the high road. I'd never write letters to the editor that were, you know, calls to battle. I was not going to go to battle. I would step back and . . . just get fueled. And some of the people that I worked with would tell me, 'Go out. Go for a bike ride. Go swimming. Step away from it.'"

When she expressed her outrage with self-control and intelligence in public forums, she was seen as the leader of a worthy cause. "Suddenly I had these wonderful, great partners at the CDC, at the Joint Commission. I mean, these people who *ignored* my calls at first are now my partners," she said.

Anger can be harnessed as a positive, motivating force. Sheridan had become so incensed and her sense of justice so offended that her emotions could have triggered despair and depression. Instead, she used the power of those emotions to motivate herself, in part because she had always remained an optimist who believed that eventually the medical community would see the merit of her arguments. She took the long view and created a vision of a possible future. She described this to me as "the power of believing."

This inspired others, but it also helped her stay on track even when dealing with her second family tragedy. "I was invited to speak at a symposium, and there were seven hundred people in the audience. Meanwhile, my husband was in the ICU. He'd just had his spinal tumor taken out the day before. So I was pretty fragile," she said. "But I got up there and gave a call to action. 'It's not me against you; it's us together. Let's make sure this can't happen to anybody else.' Somehow, innately, naturally, my message would inspire people to take action."

Nowhere was this ability to inspire others more evident than in a speech Sheridan gave to a huge conference of the Hospital Corporation of America, the largest for-profit hospital system in the United States. Her speech that day was so passionate, so transformative, that it drove thousands of people into action.

"Sometimes when I speak, something just takes over," she told me. "I mean, it is from the absolute depths inside of me. When I had a chance to convince two thousand people, it turned into a revival. At one point, a doctor got up to the microphone and he said, 'Susan Sheridan, I don't know you,' but he told us that he was the CEO of a hospital in Texas. He said, 'I'm on my cell phone right now calling my hospital and, as of Monday, we're testing all babies for jaundice.'" Other hospital administrators promptly stepped to the audience microphones, waving their cell phones and making similar pledges.

"I was onstage and I started to cry, and this woman came up from the audience—the woman from HCA who organized the event—and now she was choked up, because it was her brainchild to bring me there," Sheridan said. "All of her affiliate hospitals deliver 225,000 babies a year. And she announced, 'For all of those of you in the audience who are running our affiliates, those of you who aren't going to start a bilirubin test, please stand up.'"

No one stood up.

A groundswell spread through the audience as more and more hospital executives made the commitment. "Within a very short period of time, all of their one hundred twenty-four hospitals implemented a new universal bilirubin test," Sheridan said proudly.

This determined mother was undergoing a metamorphosis. With every speech, every appearance, every conversation, she was growing as a leader. She confessed that in her corporate career and in graduate school, she'd often had difficulty speaking in public. She'd be nervous and almost tongue-tied. But this emerging leader discovered that her passion drove her beyond fear and self-consciousness. The importance of her mission was just too great to allow such minor concerns to impede her.

When Sheridan met with resistance from hospital executives or government officials, she developed a method for persuading them by applying a technique known as appreciative inquiry, which repositions problems as opportunities and uses past successes as the basis for developing solutions to current challenges. In working to convince those in authority who didn't agree that there was a problem or didn't want to change procedures, she did not put them on the defensive by confronting them. Instead, she would say things like "This is not about challenging your authority. This is about safety."

That approach accomplishes two things. It acknowledges that

the authority figure has the power, and it asks him or her to use that power for good, in this case by improving safety, because it better serves the patient. Her approach was to emphasize their shared goals, not their differences, and then to suggest ways to accomplish those goals.

Sometimes in meetings with hospital executives or government officials, Sheridan would encounter stronger resistance. In those cases, she would say, "It's okay to disagree." Then she would give them her research data, demonstrating clearly that issues needed to be addressed because of systemic failures. She would challenge them respectfully, and she would say that they had an obligation to make changes. She usually found that over a period of time, those who had resisted her would recognize that she knew what she was talking about, and they would yield to that expertise because she demonstrated that they shared her goal of protecting patients.

This is very similar to the approach we took in aviation to persuade captains and pilots to use Crew Resource Management (CRM). When captains were reluctant to use CRM, we would talk to them and their crews about having a shared sense of responsibility for safety. We didn't make it about *who* was right. We made it about *what* was right. This method of persuasion is not about holding hands, singing "Kumbaya," and then returning to the old ways. It's about solving problems.

Sue Sheridan has amazing skills of persuasion. In evidence-based endeavors like medicine, we often focus on the *what* and the *how*. Her story convinced hospital and government officials that they *should* do something and explained *why* they should do it.

I told her that I've often spoken to health care conferences too, because so many of the safety methods used in the aviation industry can also be applied to the medical field. What we have in health care now are islands of excellence in a sea of systemic failures. Sheridan is helping to enlarge these islands and to create new ones. To those who caution patience and say that these things take time, I say that I wish we were less patient, because the amount of preventable harm is so large.

I said I'd found, with my own public speaking, that it's always easy when it's from the heart.

"Yes," Sheridan said, nodding, "when it's from the soul."

Empowering Others to Lead

One of Sue Sheridan's most impressive contributions as a leader may be the fact that she inspired and nurtured an entire army of impassioned champions for change, most of them "ordinary moms," just like her, who are accomplishing extraordinary things.

She built this army. She delegated, shared information, encouraged others to step up, and then passed the baton, increasing her reach many times over. I have found this strategy effective in every industry. It was certainly true in aviation, where we improved safety by using these methods to lead culture change. Leaders need to prepare and encourage others to step up so that they too can make their marks. In a sense, Sheridan was able to advance by leaps and bounds because she tapped the talents of others who shared her mission.

As she traveled the globe, giving lectures and seminars to patients, mothers, and caregivers, she recognized the value of nurturing other voices to join her own. "I've met some powerful, wonderful people around the world," she said. "Often, when I met them, they were at the early stage of their journey. And I saw that the grief, and the hopelessness, was taking over their lives. I'm thinking of one especially in Mexico, a woman named Evangelina Vázquez Curiel, who also has a son, like Cal, with kernicterus.

"I traveled with her in Latin America and I mentored Evangelina, not *knowing* I was mentoring her," Sheridan said. Initially, she would ask Evangelina to join her onstage to share her son's story, but over time Evangelina became so confident and effective that Sheridan sent her on speaking engagements across Latin America. Evangelina now heads up PICK's programs there.

"That's been wonderful," Sheridan said. "It gives me goose bumps, actually, because she'll send me a picture of herself and the secretary of health in Mexico doing a presentation together. Evangelina is about four foot eight. She's a single mom. When I first met her, she was so shy that she wouldn't make eye contact. But now she is this robust woman, a powerhouse in Mexico!

"It's just so heartwarming to see others get the chance that I've had," she added. "And they are making differences in their own countries."

Leaders have a responsibility to create a culture that outlasts them, and everyone needs to embrace the changes necessary to improve the safety and reliability of the systems in which they work and upon which their patients, customers, clients, and passengers rely. To drive change, leaders must convince their organizations *not just that change is necessary, but that it is possible.*

When the status quo has failed us, we need to reject it and find another way. Like Sue Sheridan, I believe emphatically that quality health care is a fundamental human right.

"Our country endorsed the human rights declaration for health care at the United Nations," Sheridan told me. "But we don't practice it. We like to say it in writing, but we just don't practice it."

Her global impact and the fact that her organization has changed the standard of care for newborns worldwide reminds me of a letter I received after Flight 1549. The writer said that my crew and I had saved 155 lives but he added that we might never "know how many other people will live or what they might accomplish" because of our actions. The number of people Sue Sheridan has touched worldwide is exponentially greater. It may be impossible to calculate how many children will live healthy lives as a direct result of her work.

"Yes, I would imagine that's true," she said, smiling, when I mentioned the millions of people she'd helped, but she said that sometimes thinking about a single specific child had a more intense emotional resonance. For Sheridan, it's more a sense of the ancient Talmudic proverb:

WHOEVER SAVES ONE LIFE SAVES THE ENTIRE WORLD.

"Honestly, when I got that first phone call from a mom, saying she'd read an article on Cal, that was enough," she recalled. "I mean, that still chokes me up. . . ."

She took a moment to wipe away a tear. "She read the article and told me that, because of Cal's case, she demanded to have a delivery room test. Her hospital wasn't doing it. She demanded it and took her baby back to the hospital for the test. Her baby's bilirubin was in the ninety-fifth percentile. Had she not demanded that test, had she not read that article, the baby would have suffered."

"You saved her child," I said.

"Yes, one baby. Just to know that you saved *one* life. Not me, personally, our group and the others that opened the doors did it," Sheridan said. "But that one phone call was sufficient."

THE COURAGE TO CONTINUE

When you consider that this wife and mother conducted her international crusade for medical safety while caring for her severely handicapped son, for her daughter, MacKenzie, born two years after Cal, in 1997, and for her dying husband, you have to just marvel at her courage and strength. She told me that when Pat was in his final hours, he asked that his family remember him in the happiest moments, not wasting away in some hospital, connected to tubes and IV drips and monitors.

"At the time, Pat was undergoing experimental treatment at

MD Anderson," she said. "And on March 8, 2002, he was told that he had ten days to live. Pat and I had always planned that if he wasn't going to make it through his cancer, we were going to get a boat, get all our friends, some wine, live and laugh, and that's how he'd spend his last days. But when he was told he had ten days to live, he said he'd changed his mind. Instead, he wanted to go to Disney World, watch his friends and kids have the time of their lives."

Sheridan worked with the staff at Disney World to set up the March gathering of fifty-three friends and family members in Orlando. Pat's final weekend was spent surrounded by his wife and children and those he most cared about.

"Disney put us in the presidential suite of the Bay Club, which was something like twenty-four hundred square feet," she said. "We rented a La-Z-Boy recliner for Pat, because that's where he was most comfortable. He stayed in that chair for those last three days."

In Pat's final hours, the couple had what she calls that final "husband-and-wife planning talk," a sober, unsentimental reflection on what her life was going to be like as a single mom raising Cal and MacKenzie.

"You know, Pat often called me by my maiden name. And when we were talking about what I was going to do as a single mom, he said, 'Brown, whatever you do, just don't give up on patient safety.' Of course I promised that I wouldn't give up that fight. You didn't know Pat, but one thing about Pat: he wasn't somber and he wasn't earnest. He was sitting there in that La-Z-Boy, kind of smirking, even in those final hours. Then he said, 'And, Brown, go out and kick some ass.'"

Pat Sheridan died a few hours later in that rented recliner, on March 18, 2002.

For a decade now, his widow has kept her promise despite all her other challenges, including financial struggles due to the astronomical cost of caring for her son and husband. Because Cal's condition was misdiagnosed originally, he didn't qualify for Medicaid, and his parents' private insurance policy soon reached its million-dollar cap.

"Thank God for our corporate jobs, because we had saved some money," Sheridan said. "And then when Pat's bills started mounting up, I started playing the float. I was a banker. I was panicking because we didn't have enough money. But I told Pat, 'Don't worry. I'm taking care of all the bills.' I would open up one credit card and use it to pay off another. I got a home equity line. I was ashamed. But I didn't have a choice."

In the end, she managed to repay all her debts. "Yeah, it was very difficult. We've talked about people mortgaging their houses to pay their medical bills—I know what that's like."

"The cost of health crises is one of the major causes of bankruptcy *even for those with health insurance*," I noted.

"I know what that's like," Sheridan said. "But do you really have a choice? If you're looking at a baby who needs medical care every three days and a husband who needs cancer taken out of him, what is the choice? It was very, very frightening. When we were at MD Anderson, that's a cancer factory. There's a whole community of people who are basically homeless [because] most have passed their million-dollar cap with their insurance company. Pat did that about four weeks before he died. So [because of their financial burdens from medical bills] they lived in this trailer park; these patients who had nothing lived in a trailer park, just trying to pay for their medication. Just trying to *survive* together."

GRATEFUL TO DO GOOD

Despite all the suffering her family has endured, Sheridan said that in some strange way, she feels like one of the luckiest people in the world.

"I surprise myself, but yes, I feel that," she said. "I think everybody has tragedy in life. What happened after Cal and Pat, and the remarkable opportunities and the soulful human beings that I've connected with . . . I never would have had those opportunities. I do feel very lucky about all of that. We couldn't have stopped Daddy's cancer or anything, but the three of us are, today, we're a little team. And we're very grateful.

"To be sitting at the World Health Organization or to be empowering a woman in Mexico, telling Evangelina, 'Now you are the leader. You are the rock star. You get up onstage. You do it.' I feel lucky to have been part of another human being, a woman who had been in my shoes, getting the chance that I had. At the end of the day you do say, 'God. That was great!' Yes, I've had tragedies in my life. But without them, in some way, I never would have had these opportunities."

We'd been speaking almost without a pause for more than two hours when Sheridan offered a final, astonishing anecdote. She described the birth of her daughter, MacKenzie, who, just like Cal, had developed severe jaundice in the maternity ward.

"Right before MacKenzie was born, I wrote out the care instructions," she recalled. "And I said, 'She *will* be tested.' So when she was sixteen hours old, exactly when Cal developed jaundice, the nurse came and she said, 'Mom, we have a jaundiced baby.'

" 'Okay,' I said. 'Let's put the plan into action.'

"They called the doctor and did the bilirubin test. MacKenzie's levels were in the hundredth percentile. And a neonatologist came in, put her under the lights, gave her an IV for four days," Sheridan said.

"I'll never forget that when they took MacKenzie away, I had time to take a shower, and it was my first shower after giving birth. I thought, *I'm just going to go take a long shower, stand here and let hot water run over me.* I started crying, and I was in the shower too long, I suppose, crying so loud, that the staff got concerned about me. They sent a chaplain in, a female chaplain. She said, 'Mrs. Sheridan. Mrs. Sheridan, I'd like to talk to you.' So I got out of the shower and she said, 'I understand you're really worried about your daughter.'

"'No, I'm not worried about my daughter,' I said. 'I'm crying because I'm seeing how easy it was to prevent what happened to my son.' I was grieving, just to see that there was no emergency, that it was so easy, this peaceful intervention. And MacKenzie was fine. That's all they had to do for my son."

II

JIM SINEGAL

How do you define who's a leader? Derek Jeter is a leader. . . .
Everybody respects him and understands that he is a leader. Patton
was obviously a real leader. I think Clinton was a leader. . . .
That doesn't mean they're not flawed. Many times leaders are
flawed, including in the Bible—David. But they are leaders.
They get people to follow them and to do things. And I guess
that's the description—when you get people to understand and
want to follow you in whatever direction you're going.

IT WAS SLIGHTLY BEFORE 9 A.M. AT THE COSTCO OUTLET IN DAN-ville, California, where my family and I often shop. On this special visit, I'd entered by invitation through a back loading bay, amid the beeping of forklifts and the bustle of employees preparing for a rush of early-morning shoppers. Even though this is a cavernous, 140,000-square-foot superstore, it is "small by our standards," Tim, a manager, told me. The warehouse store was filled with fifteen-foot-high stacks of merchandise ranging from everyday goods such as breakfast cereal and multivitamins to big-screen televisions, home computers, and furniture.

Inside the store, near the checkout register and the brand's trademark $1.50-hot-dog-and-Coke stand, I took a seat at a picnic table with a gregarious seventy-five-year-old who bears a strong resemblance to the white-haired character actor Wilford Brimley with his rimless glasses and somewhat neater mustache. But this is Costco's famously low-key cofounder and CEO, Jim Sinegal, who is wearing his store's own brands of khaki pants and striped button-down dress shirt—stacks of which were on sale for $17.99 nearby.

A former retail store bagboy, Sinegal and his cofounder, lawyer Jeff Brotman, built Costco Wholesale Corporation from a single warehouse into a $78 billion empire with nearly six hundred big-box bargain stores. Though he announced his retirement in September 2011, Sinegal will remain on Costco's board, and I have no doubt he will continue to make sure that the hot dog and Coke never cost more than $1.50 as a symbol of the retail chain's commitment to providing quality goods at great prices.

"We're sitting in this food court here where we sell the hot dog and Coke for a buck fifty. That hot dog and Coke has been a buck fifty ever since we started. Now it's taken an enormous amount of ingenuity for our people to figure out how in the hell to keep that thing at a buck fifty," Sinegal said. "A reporter asked me, not so long ago, 'What would it mean if the price of the hot dog ever changes?' And I said, 'It means I'm dead.'"

Ego-Free Leadership

Sinegal is known for keeping frills to a minimum in his stores, but the fact that he has no public relations team is more a reflection of his policy of rarely granting interviews. It's not that he's modest, it's just that Sinegal doesn't believe in the CEO-as-superhero myth perpetuated by some of his counterparts and certain media.

"The reason we don't do interviews is that the tendency in all of these things is to try to build the CEO of the organization into somebody who leaps tall buildings in a single bound and is faster than a speeding bullet. That's what all the magazines do—*Forbes* and *Fortune* and all of them," he said. "I got involved in doing a story on *20/20* one time, which they promised me was going to be all about Costco and not about me, and it turned out it was all about me and very little about Costco."

He also declines most interviews out of respect for his leadership team and his employees, Sinegal told me. "It's a negative aspect relative to the balance of the team," he said. "We're an organization. As much as *Fortune* magazine and *Forbes* or the *Wall Street Journal* don't want to agree with this, an organization has to be built with a lot of people, and they're all part of the story. When one person is picked out as the reason that the whole thing is successful, it's a little shallow. And it's really insulting to the people who are part of the organization."

Sinegal said he built Costco into the nation's fifth-largest retailer by "selecting a team that can run a business this size, and working with them over the years, I mean that's really the contribution . . . I feel proudest of."

PAYING ATTENTION

Sinegal has a worldwide reputation for putting his employees and customers above quick profits or stockholder demands, and for his old-school approach to retail. He comes across more as the folksy proprietor of a local mom-and-pop store than as a typical profit-hungry captain of industry. Still, a business feature in the *New York Times* noted his "ferocious attention to detail" and added that Sinegal "just might be America's shrewdest merchant since Sam Walton."

I had noticed when walking through the store with Sinegal that he'd questioned a manager on whether an item's price was correctly marked, and he'd also talked about his habit of picking up any trash he sees dropped on the floor. "You obviously know and care about this business intimately, and it's clear to me that you believe in leading by example and setting high standards," I said to him. "How important is that to you?"

"First of all, one of the nice things about only carrying four thousand items is it's a lot easier to control than a hundred and twenty-five thousand items," he said, smiling. "If I had a hundred and twenty-five thousand items in this building and Tim and I were walking around, neither of us could tell you what the price was on anything."

For such a massive big-box operation, his stores have a small-town feel, I said.

"We try to create a small atmosphere—all of us," he said. "And again, it takes everybody. It takes more than one person to believe that this thing works; otherwise it'll start to deteriorate. One or ten of us or twenty of us can't control everything. It really has to be something that is ingrained as part of the culture of the company. All of us believe it. And we think that will sustain us."

Sinegal noted again that he didn't want me to focus too much on his personal charm, charisma, or powers of persuasion. "You would be amazed at how much time we spend on succession planning," he said. "Not for me—well, part of it is for me, but that's just a part of it."

SMALL-TOWN VALUES

This unique business leader is proud of Costco's success but concerned that it doesn't become too big and lose its employee- and customer-friendly approach. "Unfortunately, we don't *like* to be a big company," he said. "We really want to think of ourselves as a small company, that we're adroit and we can make decisions quickly, that we can do things and get things done, and that we know all of the employees, like the old days when it was a lot of fun."

Costco began with a single store in Seattle in 1983 and as of 2011 had just fewer than six hundred stores, mostly in the United States, but also in Puerto Rico, Canada, Britain, South Korea, Taiwan, Japan, Mexico, and Australia.

Walmart, by contrast, has 642 Sam's Clubs in the United States and abroad. Under Sinegal's leadership, Costco has become the nation's leading warehouse retailer with about half the market, compared with 40 percent for second-place Sam's Club. But as the *Times* also noted, "Sam's is not a typical runner-up: it is part of the Walmart empire, which, with $288 billion in sales last year, dwarfs Costco."

Sinegal credits his success as a business leader to his mentor, Sol Price, a pioneer in the retail warehouse store industry, who was the founder of FedMart and Price Club, which merged with Costco early in its history. The son of a Pittsburgh coal miner turned steel-worker, Sinegal moved to California after high school to attend San Diego Community College. A friend who knew that Sinegal was looking for a part-time job called him one day to help unload a shipment of mattresses at a newly opened FedMart discount ware-house store owned by Sol Price.

"That happened between Christmas and New Year's, during my school break, and I went down and it was a buck and a quarter an hour. At the end of the evening, when we got the mattresses put inside, they didn't pay me. They said, 'You'd better come back tomorrow,'" Sinegal said.

"So I came back the next day, and they still didn't pay me, but I stayed twenty-three years."

I had to acknowledge the question he left on the table: "I hope they finally paid you."

"At one point about twenty years back I joked, 'One of these days they're going to say, "The mattresses are put away, we don't need you anymore." ' "

BAGBOY BEGINNINGS

Sinegal started as a bagboy at FedMart in 1954 and quickly rose to a management position. FedMart's dynamic owner became his mentor and the inspiration for many of his leadership methods. Sol Price, who died in 2009 at the age of ninety-three, was the son of Russian immigrants, a lawyer, and a retail genius whose big-box retail store concepts were imitated by Sam Walton to create his Walmart and Sam's Club stores.

"Sol Price was legendary in the retail business," Sinegal said. "He was considered to be one of the most original and innovative people in the business. To give you an example, Sam Walton made the comment once to the effect: 'I have over the years stolen more ideas . . .'—and then he amended it—'I prefer the word *borrowed* . . . from Sol Price than any man I've ever known in the business.' That's pretty high praise coming from Sam Walton."

As a college student, Sinegal was intrigued by the savvy Bronx-born retailer, who operated his company with guiding principles that Sinegal later adopted and used as his own. Price also inspired loyalty in his employees that was remarkable in the high-turnover retail business. The turnover rate at FedMart was only 10 percent, a figure that Costco has matched under Sinegal's leadership.

"I think Walmart at one time had an employee turnover rate in excess of sixty percent. That's pretty typical. Some of these fast-food places turn their people two hundred and fifty times during the year," said Sinegal.

I told Sinegal that this turnover issue was one I'd witnessed firsthand. I've noticed that at the Costco near my home I see the same faces time after time, their silver name badges proudly announcing their starting years. Many have been there twenty to twenty-five years, which is an indication that Costco is a pretty good place to work. He passed the credit on to his mentor.

"Sol was a real leader," said Sinegal. "I am diminished in his memory and presence, and I mean that. I'm not trying to be unduly humble, but he was a guy from whom I learned everything. A reporter called me one time and said, 'Gee, you worked for him for all these years. You must have learned a lot.' I said, 'No, that's inaccurate. *Everything* that I know about this business I learned from him.'"

Sinegal rose from bagboy to executive vice president as Fed-Mart became Price Club, and then, after five years with other companies, he was recruited by Brotman, who'd been impressed with "hypermarkets" in Europe, which were a combination of discount supermarkets and department stores. Using their credit cards, personal funds, and investments from friends and family, they opened their first Costco store in 1983.

Core Values

I asked Sinegal to outline some of the core business values that he learned from Sol Price and brought to Costco.

"We have a saying around here that in our business we have *four* things to do," Sinegal told me. "Our mission statement is very simple. We say you've got to obey the law, you've got to take care of your customers, you've got to take care of your people, and respect your suppliers. And if you do those four things pretty much in that order, you're going to do what you have to do as a public company, which is to reward your shareholders.

"Eventually, if you slip up on one of them—not obeying the law, not taking care of your customers, not respecting your suppliers, not caring about your customers and thinking you can fool them at every turn . . . you're going to fall apart."

More than anything else, Sinegal knows his clientele and their expectations, he said. Customers don't come to his superstores expecting to find pianists playing in the store as in Nordstrom or elaborate displays like those at Macy's.

"We don't have any illusions of why customers shop with us," he told me. "They don't shop with us because of the fancy window displays or the Santa Claus that we have at the front of the business. They come in and shop with us because we have great prices on great products. If you lose that discipline and don't understand *why* it is that your customer shops with you, pretty soon you're the same as everyone else."

FOCUSING ON QUALITY

The Costco cofounder said that one of his main goals is to never disappoint a customer in the quality of a store's merchandise. "So you know that if you're coming to buy a forty-seven-inch television set, we're not going to sell you a stripped-down model," Sinegal said. "We think probably you have in your mind an idea of how much money you are going to spend, say seven hundred dollars for a television set. We don't want to disappoint you. We want you to be able to spend seven hundred dollars, but we're going to give you a much better set than you would have purchased elsewhere for seven hundred dollars. We're going to give you one that has all of the full features, and that's the way we gear the business. We always go for the quality."

Costco is sometimes the butt of jokes about its supersize product offerings, but Sinegal takes big-box-store jokes with a grain of salt and a good-natured laugh.

"Look, because we don't do any advertising, it's easy to make fun of Costco. Conan once did a bit on his show: 'Costco was just rated the number one place for Christmas shopping.' He says, 'Isn't that going to thrill the kids when they go downstairs and open up a twelve-gallon jar of olives?' We're easy to make fun of because of that, but it's always done good-naturedly."

Sinegal's business leadership model is one of serving the customer and rewarding employees. He often hearkens back to the era of the ubiquitous Sears & Roebuck catalog, which for almost a century was a fixture in so many rural American homes. "When I was a boy, Sears & Roebuck was the Costco of the land. All of America shopped there," he said. "They shopped there for great prices on great products. Sears delivered consistently for decades.

"About fifteen or sixteen years ago I was sitting down with an executive from P&G, and we were discussing the changes in the retail business. He said, 'Look at the SG&A of Sears (SG&A being all your operating costs, costs of the business), so if you're looking at SG&A for Sears, it's 32 percent. And then Kmart is about 25 percent, and then Target at that time was about 20 percent, and Walmart is 15 percent.' Well, it didn't take any Rhodes scholar to figure out who was going to win that battle. There was just no way that Sears would ever be able to bring their operating costs down anywhere close to where Walmart was.

"This is important because of the traditions and history in retailing," he said. "The evolutionary process in retail is that you have people who start off at very low prices and pretty soon get caught up in what they're doing and think that they can raise the prices. They say, 'Maybe we can get another dime here and another twenty cents here and another fifty cents here.' And pretty soon you're like Sears—you've gotten yourself to where a competitor can come in and slide right under you and deliver a better value. You create an umbrella, so to speak, for everybody to come in under you."

The Costco retailing philosophy, borrowed directly from Sol Price and FedMart, put a spin on the conventional wisdom of salesmanship, he said. "In traditional retail the thinking is, 'Gee, I'm selling this thing for ten bucks, I wonder if I can get eleven for it?

The customer's never going to know the difference.' We look at it and we say, 'Selling this thing for ten bucks, how do I get it to *nine*? And then if I get it to nine, how do I get it to *eight*?' How do I create as big a gulf between Costco and the other retailers as possible so that people look at our prices and they say, 'They're not just better; they're demonstrably better.'"

GIVING VALUE FOR THE LONG TERM

In the last few decades, Costco has also attempted to distinguish itself from its rivals by stocking mostly high-end merchandise, Sinegal said.

"Quality is a significant issue. Anybody can sell goods for low prices. The trick is to be able to do it and make money, to be profitable and build an organization that succeeds. We took on the attitude very early on that we're not building this business to be here just today or next year or until 2015. We want to be here fifty and sixty years from now.

"We could have sold this business fifty times during the years if that's what we were after. We could have sold it and gotten a place in Scottsdale or someplace. But that was never on our minds. My partner and I always agreed that we wanted to build a long-term business."

This business leader tries to serve the best interests of and provide security for both his stakeholders and his stockholders, he said. "We think we owe that to all of the people that you see in this building and their families, to the suppliers who bring goods to us, to the communities where we do business. Our going dark in this facility would not be very good for the community. And so you've got stakeholders in the business who are very important, and you've got to continue to think about them."

STAYING FOCUSED ON A SHARED MISSION

Sinegal tries to instill the members of his Costco team with the feeling of a shared mission that makes them proud to be a part of the organization and focused on the same goals. And he has learned to take criticism and turn it into constructive action, he said.

"When we were starting in business up in Seattle, we applied for a beer and wine license," he recalled. "The alcoholic beverage control board came out and they started questioning us about everything. 'Why are you guys a *club*?' Our name at that time was Costco Wholesale Club. 'We don't like that, and what's the deal with the membership?' Eventually we agreed to drop 'Club' because they objected very strenuously to that."

The board filed other objections, along with an audit, and it became obvious to Sinegal and his partner that the intent of this group was to "stop us from getting in the business." Sinegal often claims he owes that Alcoholic Beverage Control Board auditor "a note of thanks because it made us focus on our business." The goal was to operate a retail store with such a high level of quality and service that there could be no objections from anyone.

"We decided that we were going to do what was necessary to overcome every objection," he told me. "And we were going to establish a rule: first of all, *no* seconds or irregulars. We're going to have the greatest refund policy in the world. We're going to say, 'If you're unhappy with the product, you bring it back to us. We'll give you a refund right at the front door.' We're going to pay our employees the best wages in the business. Nobody's going to be able to say that we're making money off the backs of our employees. We're going to provide great health care for them. We did an awful lot as a result of our looking at not just the Alcoholic Beverage Control auditor but the way people were going to view our business in a general sense."

Another very important attribute in business, Sinegal said, is discipline. "You look at this building and you would say, 'Boy, they must have *tens* of thousands of items.' We have four thousand items. If you went into a Walmart superstore, which is essentially the same categories of merchandise, they probably have something like a hundred and twenty-five thousand items. We really preselect the best quality and the best price that we can find. Then we try to bring value. And it's a lot easier to concern yourself with the value of the products when you've got four thousand items than when you have a hundred and twenty-five thousand."

BUILDING A CULTURE BASED UPON VALUES

I noted that Sinegal seemed to have created a corporate culture based on genuine values that he embodies. His actions and his words are in alignment, and therefore Sinegal engenders trust and loyalty from both his employees and his customers.

"Sure," Sinegal said. "I mean, every company headquarters you go into has some sort of a plaque up that says, 'People are our most important asset.' And then they shut down a factory and fire two thousand people because they didn't want to figure it out. And that doesn't mean that closing factories isn't necessary sometimes, but sometimes it's done because it's very convenient. It's very convenient to take off and move the jobs overseas. It's convenient to get rid of a factory because the wages got too high in a given place. Business leaders who cut and run lose out on the rewards experienced by those who fight and stay.

"We probably have fifty executives in the company who go back to FedMart and through Price Club and to Costco," he said. "Why is that important? It was a gauge of the type of leadership that Sol provided. He was an easy guy to believe and to trust, and he set up some very, very significant disciplines of our business that we felt proud about staying with. Now we try to do the same thing at Costco. We try to make our employees proud of our company."

Walking that talk is "very, very important" when dealing with employees if you want them to trust you, remain loyal, and follow your rules, said Sinegal. "These people are not fools. They know if you're bullshitting them. They understand if you're saying one thing and, in truth, their job doesn't mean a hill of beans and that you'd shit-can them tomorrow at the slightest provocation. They get it. They're also smart enough to see if you're cheating the customers, and when they see that, they will lose respect for you immediately."

Sinegal has zero tolerance for cheating either his employees or his customers, he said. "One of the ways you can get in trouble around this place is cheating. If the guys in the meat department put a little too much fat in the ground beef, they're going to get in serious trouble. It's not something that's tolerated," and Sinegal clenched his fists for emphasis. "We don't pay lip service to that. We expect to have the best ground beef and the lowest fat content. Nobody's allowed to equivocate on that. Nobody is allowed to take the fish and say, 'Gee, the code date expired today. Let me put a new code date on it.' But those are the types of things that happen in retail."

CUSTOMER RELATIONS

Just then, Sinegal paused as he noticed that an elderly couple was watching us as they stood nearby. "Yes, sir?" Sinegal said, rising.

"Excuse me," said the fellow, who was wearing a dark-blue ball cap. "I was just at the stockholders' meeting."

"Oh yeah?" Sinegal said.

"You did a hell of a good job. I'm Ben."

"How you doin', Ben?"

"This is my wife, Jean."

"Hi, Jean."

"We always go to the [stockholders' meetings] in San Leandro," Ben said, referring to a nearby community.

It was interesting to watch Sinegal interact with his customers. He warmed up immediately and engaged with them as if he were the owner of a hardware store on the town square and they were customers he'd known all his life. He gestured to their empty shopping cart and teased them about it— "Where's the stuff, guys?"— unleashing a barrage of laughter. Ben and Jean were obviously charmed that the Costco cofounder was so down-to-earth.

"You knew Sol Price?" asked Ben, who had done his homework on Sinegal.

"Yes, I knew Sol since I was eighteen."

Ben realized that he was interrupting our talk, so he offered one more comment before continuing his shopping with his wife. "You had a good shareholders' meeting up there."

"Thank you. We appreciate your support as a shareholder." Sinegal shook their hands warmly, wished them well, and then rejoined me at the picnic table.

"What a wonderful example that is of what we're talking about," I said. "Your customers are shareholders, and they know you and they appreciate what you've done."

Sinegal leaned closer and said in a half whisper, "He stopped by to tell me he loved the shareholders' meeting. We do about ten minutes' worth of films, and we're not afraid to poke fun at ourselves." Shareholders are served Costco muffins, hot dogs, and other treats at the meetings, which are conducted in the same folksy manner that Sinegal just displayed.

"Then my partner, Jeff, and I get up and tell them about the business and take questions. We typically answer questions until there are no more. We could be up there for an hour and a half answering questions, whereas at many shareholders' meetings they insist that you write down the question and submit it.

"I hope that our business is always user-friendly enough for everybody, including our employees. They like to see that, too. When they see us answering questions it suggests an openness, that we're not afraid of anything, there's nothing that we're trying to hide."

THE MANAGER AS A TEACHER

Since the couple who'd stopped by had mentioned Sol Price, I asked Sinegal to talk more specifically about the leadership principles he'd learned from Price and made part of his own management style.

"One of them was the fact that if you're a manager, you have to understand that you're a manager of people, not a manager of things," he said. "You're a manager of people. And if it were possible for me to chase every shopping cart on the parking lot and ring every register and stock every shelf and buy every item and pay every bill, I would do it, because I have this lofty view of my skills. I think I could get that done. But obviously you can't do that. You need to hire somebody else to do it. You want to hire somebody who's going to do it just as well as you would—a kind of alter ego—and who would handle every customer just the way you would handle them yourself."

When done well, management is "at least ninety percent teaching," Sinegal said. "Now, that doesn't mean teaching in a formal classroom setting. It means interacting with people, getting their feedback, giving them feedback, displaying the little things. If the people walking through the warehouse with me see me picking up a piece of paper, they pretty soon get the idea we're trying to keep these places clean.

"It's the same thing as if my manager, Tim, is walking around and a customer comes up and says, 'By the way, where are your pumpkin pies?' If Tim says, 'In the back someplace,' that's the way our other staff are going to react to a customer. But if he says, 'Just a second, let me take you back there,' or, 'Let me show you, it's back at number 18. You'll run right into it, it's on an endcap,' if he takes the time to take care of that customer, then the other people in the building are going to have the same attitude about it. So teaching isn't always just in a classroom with books. It's the way you're con- ducting things on a day-in day-out basis."

DOING WHAT IS RIGHT

Sinegal said he also learned from Sol Price that "you should try to deal with things head-on and correct them and not allow them to fester. And that it's okay, as the boss, to get mad occasionally as long as you're not vindictive. There's no question I have a temper, and I display it. But I don't take it out on people. I don't fire somebody on the spur of the moment. As a matter of fact, I very seldom fire people. Over the years I've had to, obviously, but that's not a pleasurable experience. You look at it from the standpoint that probably we failed as much as that person failed. Somehow we didn't give the right guidance."

In fact, if an employee has been with Costco for more than two years, they cannot be terminated without the approval of a senior manager, Sinegal told me. "That says to an employee, 'I can't go into work someday and, if my boss happens to have had a bad night, all of a sudden I'm fired and I'm out of a job. There's somebody else who has to review it in that process.' We try to provide that type of safety net for our people."

During the devastating recession of 2006–2010, Costco was able to keep that safety net intact while maintaining a remarkable equilibrium. "We were pretty successful," Sinegal told me. "We didn't have any major layoffs during the downturn. The only layoffs that we've ever had are when we open new places and then, after the first three or four months, if it hasn't succeeded as well as we thought, we may have to lay some people off and then bring them back later. We do some seasonal hiring during the holidays, but we explain to them, 'This is a job that's good through Christmas. If you want to stay with us and if we lay you off, we'll call you back in March or April, whenever we're hiring again.'

"We've very seldom had to cut into anybody who'd been with us a year. Very seldom. And hopefully," he said, knocking his knuckles for luck on the wooden picnic table, "we'll continue on that basis. There's no guarantees for that, obviously, but who would have thought that we were going to have the type of financial setback that we've had as a nation? I think it snuck up on all of us."

I asked how successful Costco was in accomplishing that goal in 2008–2009. He said they'd not laid off any full-time employees in stores that remained open.

"That's amazing, given the poor economic conditions during those years," I said.

The lack of layoffs or firings wasn't the result of charity or altruism, Sinegal explained. "What we did was, we continued to build our business. If you look at our numbers through that period of time, we continued to show good comp sales, meaning units that had been open for more than a year continued to grow positively. Just this past month, our comps on a company-wide basis were nine percent, which is very healthy. Typically during those tough periods we went through, those increases were in the three and four percent range, but they were still positive. We think that if we can hit three or four percent, we can get by without any layoffs."

PROVIDING SECURITY TO EMPLOYEES

Like most businesses, Costco has been challenged by the rising costs of health care as it tries to take a benevolent approach to employee benefits, Sinegal said. "We've experienced the same as every major company in America—double-digit increases in health care over the past eight, ten years. It's kind of crazy. I may be misquoting the number slightly, but I think when we started, a pregnancy cost us about five hundred dollars. Today it's over five thousand dollars, and that's without any complications. And there are always complications today. Doctors are so nervous that they run all kinds of tests."

Costco is known for its relatively generous medical insurance, life insurance, and other benefits. "We had a very comprehensive health care plan—health, life insurance policy, prescription, optical, hearing, dental. Our plan was so rich that we had employees whose spouses were working for other big companies and would come on our plan because our plan was so good.

"Of course, it's costly to do that," he said. "In the past, we were paying ninety-five percent and the employees were paying five. And the five was paid through deductibles, so we reached a point after these double-digit increases where we said, 'What the hell are we going to do? We can't go on paying ninety-five percent.' We altered the plan, so that we were going to pay ninety percent. And we went out to the employees and told them, 'Costs have grown so much, we have no choice but to review the plan and to redesign it in a fashion. Our promise to you is, you'll pay no more than ten percent.'

"Well, in the first year we discovered that we had adjusted a little too much and the employees paid twelve percent. So we gave every employee who was in the plan, I think it was a hundred and fifty dollars—put that hundred and fifty toward their 401(k) plan to make up for the difference. Why? Because that was the promise we made. And we said that's the promise—and no guarantee it's going to happen again—indeed it didn't. Costs went up a little further. And probably where we're at right at the moment, my guess is that we'll wind up exceeding the ninety percent. We'll probably wind up ending up at about ninety-one percent this year, but we think we can live with it."

I asked if looking after employees' health would in fact make them better and happier employees.

"Absolutely," he said. "But we think they deserve security. Why should people in retail not be able to have health care for their kids and buy homes and send them to good schools? We think they're entitled to that, and we think health care is a very important part of that. If you don't have health care—dental plans, for example—look at what you're doing to yourself.

"As a matter of fact, we're spending a lot of time now on preventative stuff, and that's really the secret to cutting down costs," he continued. "We've started antismoking programs, smoking-cessation programs, and we offer every employee a free physical. We want them to go get a physical examination on an annual basis. If we don't get enough of them doing it, then we're going to do some things to try to encourage it because we think it's in their best interest. We offer a mammogram. If you catch things and nip it in the bud, you'll get a hell of a lot smaller bill than you do if somebody has a very serious problem."

Providing security for employees and their families is part of the benevolent philosophy of business leadership that Sinegal formed early in his career. "These are all concepts that I learned from Sol. I started working for him in 1954, so it was a long relationship, and I was fortunate to see him just a couple of days before he died," Sinegal said. "That's a person who I still speak of with awe today, after all those years. And you could ask the same question of a lot of people in our organization who worked for him over the years, and they would say the same thing."

Sinegal laughed now. "If you'd have looked at me as an eighteen-year-old when I went to work for Sol, you'd probably wonder why in the hell he kept me! I was a smart-assed kid. I always thought I knew everything. And if I had ever said to him, 'Sol, you're my mentor,' he probably would have said something really elegant like 'Cut the crap and get your ass back to work!'"

A MERITOCRACY

Working with Price inspired Sinegal to lead his own company not as a dictatorship but as a meritocracy in which employees move up based on their achievements, hard work, and talents.

"In our company, we have a rule that we promote eighty-five percent from within the company. In truth, it's about ninety-nine percent," he said. "We very seldom hire managers. We would never hire a manager to run one of our Costcos. They would have to have been with us for a period of time. We've had people come to work for us that were vice presidents of Albertsons who came in, and we made them train for two years before we would make them a manager of one of our Costcos."

One of the keys to being the head of the type of meritocracy that Costco aspires to be, Sinegal said, is for the leader of the organization himself to remain down-to-earth: "Trying to keep your feet on the ground, trying to make sure that you're not so full of yourself and that you recognize you can make mistakes."

As he watched shoppers pass by with loaded carts, Sinegal offered his favorite example of leadership for me. "Classic example: Earl Warren when he was on the Supreme Court. He'd been the governor of California, and then he was chief justice of the Supreme Court when the case of *Brown v. Board of Education* came up. Warren was a conservative, appointed by Eisenhower, and the guy who everyone thought would take a very conservative viewpoint on this issue. He had several Southerners on the Court. He decided this issue was so important that they couldn't just make a ruling, like, with the majority, it had to be unanimous. So he led that court through that process in what he considered to be one of the very important issues of the time, and insisted that it be unanimous. He told them, 'We have to be unanimous. We have to have a common voice when we go out to everybody on this.' *That,* to me, is a leader."

"That takes amazing skills of persuasion," I agreed.

"Yes," he said, "and guts, because there was a major proportion of the country that did not agree with the ruling at that time. And a major proportion of the government. Again, Warren was appointed by a Republican president and considered to be a conservative, and yet he made the decision, and made the right decision."

Although he'd struggled earlier in our talk in trying to define a leader, Sinegal came up with a couple of varied examples.

"How do you define who's a leader?" he said. "Derek Jeter is a leader. I mean, obviously, everybody respects him and understands that he is a leader. Patton was obviously a real leader. I think Clinton was a leader. I mean, that doesn't mean they're not flawed. Many times leaders are flawed, including in the Bible—David. But they are leaders. They get people to follow them and to do things. And I guess that's the description—when you get people to understand and want to follow you in whatever direction you're going."

LEADERSHIP COMPENSATION

Given his own humble approach to leadership and Costco's relatively benevolent reputation for paying, promoting, and providing benefits to its employees, I asked Sinegal to offer his views on sky-rocketing executive compensation packages and CEO salaries that are often huge multiples of the average worker's salary.

"I think the same message that you send after a period of time, if it's always the CEOs standing up on television and saying, 'Look what I've done!' it starts to become a one-man gang that is running the business, but a disregard for the other 150,000 people. In a way, it's not a fair question, because I'm the founder of a business, so my partner and I have very low salaries by today's standards.

"Our base salary is $350,000 a year, which is very, very low when you measure it against companies like ours. But I've been very well rewarded in this business. I mean, I'm a big stockholder in the business, so it's not fair to compare me with somebody who is hired to go into Hewlett Packard, to go into Ford, or go into another company and have to run it."

Indeed, though he does take a relatively low annual salary, some estimates have placed Sinegal's personal wealth in excess of $150 million thanks to his Costco stock holdings.

"Having said that, I think some of these packages are outrageous," Sinegal told me. "Tens and hundreds of millions of dollars in some instances are—they're *outrageous*. There's no other way to describe it."

"Are you saying that there's just nobody who is worth that much?" I asked.

"I don't think so."

"I don't know anybody!" I noted.

Sinegal smiled broadly. "If I were a point guard for the Lakers, maybe—ten million, I guess. Or if I were Derek Jeter . . ."

"If some executives are able to completely insulate themselves and their wealth from the consequences of bad outcomes for their organizations, then it sends the clear message that 'We are not all in this together,'" I said.

"I don't think there's any question about it," Sinegal agreed. "I think it raises the unions' expectations too. When they go in, they say, 'Listen, this guy made $40 million last year. We're gonna get ours.'

"I'm also convinced, Sully, that an awful lot of what's happened with executive compensation has been driven by Alex Rodriguez getting $25 million a year. Or a rock star who makes $50 million a year or $60 million a year," he added.

Sinegal said that Steve Jobs, cofounder of Apple, the highest-valued tech company in the world, was "certainly worth at least as much as Alex Rodriguez and maybe more."

"That's true, especially if you look at the innovations he led his team to make and the stockholder value he created," I said.

Sinegal noted that another respected business founder, Warren Buffett, "only takes a basic salary of $150,000. But he's also worth $38 billion. I mean, it's much easier for Warren Buffett than for somebody who's hired to go into General Motors and fix a bad situation and to know that he might not be there two years from now."

A Delicate Balance

One reason so many top executives can demand extraordinary compensation packages these days is because of Wall Street pressures for ever-rising quarterly profits. The executives who produce those short-term profits and satisfy Wall Street and the stockholders have become highly valued superstars, which has driven up the price for CEOs and other top managers.

The pressure for short-term gains to satisfy Wall Street's insatiable demand for quick profits disturbs many executives even as they have to deal with it daily. Wall Street analysts have often annoyed Sinegal with their claims that he doesn't put shareholders' interests first, through Costco's being so generous with employees' pay and benefits compared to its competition. I asked him how he deals with those pressures while still trying to manage with a long-term perspective.

"First of all, you deliver," said Sinegal. "If you deliver consistent profits, they also want to set their own targets. They never agree with your targets. They always think that you can do better. And the question over the years has always been the same: Why do you have to pay so much? Why do you have to have such rich health care plans? Why can't you raise the price on these things? Wall Street analysts always think they can run the business a little better than you, and they have better ideas on how you can do it."

"Many have probably never run a business," I noted.

"Most of them haven't got an idea how to run a business,"

he agreed. "But I don't want you to think that I'm knocking the system, because some of these guys asking questions do make you think. You don't like the question at the moment, particularly if you're in the spotlight when it's being asked. But when you reflect on it, you say, 'It wasn't a *bad* question. It deserves some consideration, and we should take a look at it.'"

Since Costco is a publicly held company with stockholders, I played the Wall Street devil's advocate for a moment, noting that compared with other American corporations, Costco's employee benefits, for example, are considered very generous. According to statistics from a *New York Times* story: "Costco's average pay, for example, is $17 an hour, 42 percent higher than its fiercest rival, Sam's Club. And Costco's health plan makes those at many other retailers look Scroogish. One analyst, Bill Dreher of Deutsche Bank, complained last year that at Costco 'it's better to be an employee or a customer than a shareholder.'"

Sinegal dismisses such criticism with a cursory shake of his head. "We've always had the feeling that if you hire good people and provide them with good wages and good jobs and an opportunity for a career, then good things will happen in your business," he told me. "We think that, generally, has been the key to our success. Just to come back to square one, the greatest contribution has been to continue to bring people in who understand that and run this business. The company now has 151,000 employees, so it's difficult to be small when there are 151,000 employees. Very difficult. It's the bane of business. You get so large and it's like turning an aircraft carrier around—or landing a plane in the Hudson."

Sinegal said he has run Costco with a long-term perspective but always with an eye to making it as efficient as possible while staying true to his leadership values. "So number one, they're not running the business. We want to be here fifty years from now. We're going to run the business in the way we think is proper. That doesn't mean that we're not going to have to adjust things at some point in time. But we're going to do everything possible to make sure that, as in that example of health care, we're presenting the best plan; as in the case of the wages, we're presenting the best plan; as in the cases of the prices, that we've got the best prices; as in the case of quality, we've got the best quality. We're going to stress those things because that's what makes us different than everybody else. And we don't want to wind up being Sears & Roebuck. We want to wind up being here. *I* won't be here, but there are going to be a lot of other people who count on this company."

Sinegal said that Costco's stock has fared well in comparison with that of its competitors, like Target and Walmart and Sam's and Lowe's and Home Depot and other big-box merchandisers. "Our stock sells for a higher multiple of earnings than any of them and has consistently for the last eight, ten years. So that's a bunch of chatter from Wall Street. They like to hear themselves talk. They understand the quality of our company. Again, I'm not knocking the system. The system's been very good to us. The system works. Companies that don't perform are going to wind up getting slammed. That's the way business is."

"Have there been cases where analysts have threatened to downgrade your stock?" I asked.

"Sure, they do it," Sinegal said. "They've done it."

"Does it force you ultimately to do things that you really would not want to do?"

He shook his head. "We've got to stand the pain. Again, that doesn't mean we don't look at some really good questions that are coming our way, but in the final analysis, if the answer is to raise prices, it's not going to happen."

"Have they forced you to be more aggressive on your salaries or your benefits?"

"No, but I think they've probably forced us to run our business better."

"To be more efficient?" I asked.

"To be more efficient," he said. "The question always comes

down to how much money did you earn and what should you have earned, and how well are your sales going, how well are those comps going? When you miss your target, you have a right to be criticized. It's a business. Shareholders have a right to expect performance.

"And as I mentioned to you earlier, we think that the performance over a long period of time is what counts," he added. "Unfortunately, all of us in American business are judged on quarterly reports. In retail we're judged on comps every month, which is too bad, because I think it's forced an awful lot of managers to make those kinds of decisions that they shouldn't have to make."

"There's too much focus on the short term," I said.

"Yes," he said, "and it comes at the expense of long-term benefit."

KEEPING IT SIMPLE

In his own highly competitive retailing world, Sinegal has found success through simplicity. He bristles when noting some of the extraneous costs that accompany corporate success. "Today, you've got to worry about the fact that you're seen as 'deep pockets'— somebody's going to file a lawsuit against you," he said with a grimace. "Or some agency is going to come and interfere with what you're doing. We're easy to identify, and we wind up spending an awful lot of our time on administrative stuff that really is very, very far from what we do for a living."

I knew exactly what Sinegal was talking about. In so many industries, the peripheral issues have grown, consequently reducing the amount of time and resources spent on the business. Over thirty years ago, when I started my airline career, the commercial piloting profession was mostly about flying airplanes. Now it's incredible how many additional things we must concern ourselves with as captains. For me, it's almost hard to remember the simpler days when my profession was mostly about flying.

"We buy and sell merchandise and services for great prices to our customers," he told me. "Getting ensnarled in the rest of that stuff is part of what you have to accept in a company our size, but it's not the fun part of the business."

He clearly has little patience for corporate legalese, or for the attorneys who wield it.

"I was joking with somebody the other day. At one time, back in our bakery, we were experimenting with these large sheet cakes," Sinegal said. "People used to like to bring them in and have a picture on the cake of the Little League team, or for a birthday party or something. And all of a sudden our attorneys are telling us, 'Well, you can't do that unless you get their signatures, until I get a release from everybody.'

"'This is a cake,' I told them. 'They're not going to sue us. I'll eat the evidence!'"

THE IMPORTANCE OF PASSION

Throughout our conversation, dozens upon dozens of weekday shoppers, all Costco members, recognized Jim Sinegal in the food court, smiling and waving to him and, as in the case of the older couple, sometimes stopping to talk. The fact that this multimillion-aire business leader was so approachable and also so intensely engaged and knowledgeable about the day-to-day details and pricing in his stores seemed remarkable. When I mentioned this, Sinegal shrugged it off.

"Let me tell you something, and this is the truth," he said. "When I walk around the building today, I will have somebody come up to me and say, 'This is a great operation. And these people in this place, *this* is the best Costco around.' But I get the same answer if we go to Livermore. I'll get the same answer if I go to San

Leandro. I always get those same comments: 'These are the greatest people. This place is the greatest. Of all your Costcos, this one's the best.' It's a consistent refrain with the customers."

I'd noted that the lingering effects of the recent recession did not seem to be affecting his business all that much. I shared my observance that ever since the doors opened promptly at 9 A.M., steady streams of shoppers had lined up at every cash register to buy every conceivable sort of product, from fresh produce to girls' soccer cleats to forty-inch LCD televisions.

"Wow," he said. "That's enough to bring a tear to the eye."

"And it's still not midday," I said.

"Let me tell you something," Sinegal said, "you've gotta love the business."

He shares that message with the many student groups he speaks to each year—the only sort of group he'll generally agree to meet with. He tells them that "if you're going to have to work for a living, you'd better *damn* well like it.

"I always tell them if you get into something that you dislike, get the hell out of there. You're not doing yourself any good, you're not doing your company any good, and you're going to wind up harming your family eventually as a result because you're going to be so dissatisfied."

"It has to be a passion," I said.

"Yeah, if you want to do it," he said. "You've really gotta love the business."

LESSONS IN LEADERSHIP

In the introduction, I said that the interviews in the book would provide insights into some key questions, including:

What is the essential nature of leadership?
What core qualities and characteristics shape our best
leaders?
And perhaps most important, how can each of us learn
something we can apply to our own lives?

These questions have all been of interest to me for many years, but they became far more relevant to my own life after the successful landing of U.S. Airways Flight 1549 on the Hudson River. A few days after that life-changing event, my first officer, Jeff Skiles, and I had a private meeting. We had been overwhelmed by the worldwide media attention we had received. Our discussion that day was about how we could best move forward as two private individuals who suddenly had unsought public notoriety on an enormous scale.

We decided that for as long as we remained in the public spotlight, we would use our new platform for the greater good. We weren't looking for personal rewards. We wanted to do what we could to advance the cause of safety in aviation and serve as advocates and champions for the piloting profession.

Whether we liked it or not, Jeff and I had larger roles to fill because of this one dramatic event. We both may have been leaders on a small scale before the emergency landing of our damaged passenger plane, but now we were viewed as leaders in our field, and we felt a responsibility and an obligation to become advocates for positive change.

We had long been concerned about cost cutting in the airline industry that, we felt, compromised safety. We were also among the many pilots who had experienced pay cuts and the loss of our pensions as our airline forced concessions from our union while threatening to declare bankruptcy. Now we felt it was our duty to bring those issues into the public forum since we'd been given this platform.

As an avid student of history, I'd read many biographies and autobiographies of great leaders. I'd studied what worked and didn't work through those books and in leaders I'd met and served under during my military and airline careers. Flight 1549 tested all my years of preparation as a pilot, and it was also the event that provided me with the opportunity to step up as a leader on a much bigger scale than I'd ever anticipated. I've had to grow and become a better communicator and public speaker, among other things, to fulfill my obligation to my peers by making the most of that opportunity.

I learned a great deal from the men and women, great leaders all, whom I interviewed for this book. I hope you have, too. I think their stories demonstrate that leadership can be learned. You don't have to have the highest IQ or the most charismatic personality. You just have to be willing to work incredibly hard, and you have to care about the welfare of everyone around you.

Competency, courage, integrity, empathy, determination, trustworthiness, respect for others, and concern for the greater good are all values that can be taught and learned. The ability to apply those values can be honed by those striving for continuous improvement and those with a driving desire to be the best and most authentic people they can be.

STRONG VALUES STAND OUT

I'm sure you've known people who immediately stood out because of their strong value systems. I certainly have, and they always leave a lasting impression. I can always tell when there is a strong moral compass guiding a person. It's almost like a magnetic force of some sort. Maybe you've had the same feeling. People with strong values simply make me want to be better. A couple of my classmates at the Air Force Academy have inspired me in that way since our college years.

Like me, Chris Nicholas was a fighter pilot who went on to become an airline pilot. Tragically, Chris lost a battle with cancer just a few years ago. His widow asked me to speak at his memorial service. I said that he was one of those extraordinary people who lived in such a way that his values were apparent to everyone he encountered. Chris didn't have to tell you what he believed, or have a poster hanging on his wall, or wear a T-shirt emblazoned with a slogan. If you spent enough time around him and paid attention, you knew everything about him you needed to know. And he made you want to elevate your game and rise to his level.

Another U.S. Air Force Academy classmate who has inspired me over the years is Sidney Gutierrez, who became a test pilot before being selected by NASA for astronaut training. On his first trip to space in 1991, he served as the pilot for the space shuttle *Columbia,* and in 1994 he was the commander of the space shuttle *Endeavour.*

There are many things to admire about Sid, who is now a safety director at a U.S. National Laboratory, but the leadership quality that really stands out is his moral courage. You see, he might have had a much longer career at NASA if he hadn't spoken up very early and quite publicly, beginning in 2001, about his concerns over the safety of the space shuttle and the need for some kind of crew escape system for the astronauts aboard it. In 2001 Sid participated in a report to both houses of Congress, warning that unless NASA changed the way it was doing business, "you're going to lose the vehicle."

Tragically, those safety concerns were proved valid when the damaged space shuttle *Columbia* disintegrated during reentry, killing all seven crew members, on February 1, 2003. This engineer and Master Parachutist had pushed NASA to develop escape systems for astronauts faced with shuttle problems like those experienced by *Columbia,* but NASA officials said that such systems were too complicated or too expensive. His response was to tell NASA officials, "Nothing is more expensive than an accident."

My classmate's moral courage is similar to that demonstrated by another great military leader, General Eric K. Shinseki, who also put his career on the line while testifying before Congress. In February 2003, just one month before the United States invaded Iraq to bring down Saddam Hussein's regime, General Shinseki warned that the country would need to send "something on the order of several hundred thousand soldiers" to stabilize Iraq after an invasion. He knew that defense secretary Donald H. Rumsfeld's plan called for fewer troops, but he gave his testimony anyway because he believed that Rumsfeld, his boss, was wrong.

General Shinseki was vindicated when insurgents battled U.S. forces after Saddam was overthrown, and President Bush agreed to send more troops in 2007 as part of a "surge" strategy. Although many military leaders, politicians, and activists praised General Shinseki for his moral courage, his military career was stalled as a result of his stand; and he retired from the army.

CARING LEADERSHIP

Courage is a quality that appears time and again in great leaders, but I think what surprised me most about the reflections on leadership in these interviews was that so many of these standout leaders demonstrated the importance of "human skills," which include empathy, humility, compassion, and making genuine connections with those who work under them.

It's the human part of the equation, the personalization of a mission or challenge, that makes a difference. For more extroverted people, flowing conversation and personal engagement come naturally, while for those who are more introverted, such interactions require more effort, *but everyone can learn to master these important human skills.* I am more reserved and more analytical by nature, but I certainly always knew that empathy—the ability to understand how others are feeling—was important. After these conversations I have an even greater appreciation for the importance of empathy in a leader.

Think of Lieutenant Colonel Tammy Duckworth, who served hot cocoa to her helicopter pilots and won the support of her fellow veterans across the nation; Sue Sheridan, who inspired an entire army of advocates and a huge systemic shift in hospital care; the engineer Gene Kranz, who challenged his NASA bosses over his concern for the astronauts; the retail pioneer Jim Sinegal, who insists on high wages and good benefits for his people; and the economist Jack Bogle, who requires that his employees be called "crew members."

Many of those I spoke with talked about the respect they have for those who work for them. I think that is critical for anyone leading for the long term. Another leader who believes in the importance of mutual respect is Dave Duffield, who has founded several successful companies including PeopleSoft, which was sold to Oracle in 2005 for $10.3 billion. More recently, this avid entrepreneur cofounded Workday, which provides software to help companies manage things like human resources and finances. He is co-CEO and "chief customer advocate" at Workday, where he emphasizes innovation, integrity, and fun, as well as a deep commitment to both employees and customers.

Duffield's approach to business leadership is based on his early training at IBM in the 1960s, when he was fresh out of college. He first worked there as a systems engineer and later as a salesman trained to put the interests and needs of the customer first. IBM's then-CEO Tom Watson Jr. insisted that all employees be respected as individuals, Duffield said. And along with that, he demanded that his company provide "the highest-level service organization on the planet. Respecting your fellow employee, yourself, your management, and also delivering outstanding service to the customer were critical," Duffield told me. "And that pervaded the company."

Duffield thrived at IBM and later as an entrepreneur because he learned to first see the needs of his customers and then to build businesses around serving those needs. IBM instilled in him great values and trained him in how to act upon them.

The Nature of Leadership

The stories from proven leaders have added depth to my understanding of the nature of leadership. They helped me to see that ultimately, those who become true leaders inspire tremendous loyalty because they care, because they feel responsible for others, because they want others to succeed, and because they want to contribute to the common good, a cause beyond their own basic human needs. While many who look only to the bottom line may regard these as "soft" skills, they are not soft skills; they are human skills. The value of empowering your workforce has been supported by many studies, including those done on the importance of recruiting top talent and investing in human capital. Warren Bennis, the leadership expert, cites a study of 3,200 U.S. companies, conducted by Robert Zemsky and Susan Shaman of the University of Pennsylvania, which showed that a 10 percent increase in spending for workforce training and development led to an 8.5 percent increase in productivity. A similar increase in capital expenditures led to just a 3.8 percent increase in productivity.

This reminds me of Bennis's statement that, traditionally, "American organizations have been overmanaged and underled."

Bennis has written also that there is no difference between becoming an effective leader and becoming a fully integrated human being, and that each individual's character "develops throughout life, including work life." Other studies have established the importance of trust and fairness in organizations and businesses, showing that they lead to more effective transactions and work teams as well as increased creativity.

Many leaders do not think it matters if their followers are happy. But they and their organizations pay a huge price for this misconception. They often don't realize it, because they don't account for it. It's a hidden cost, but it's real. There is a cost associated with having a culture lacking in cooperation and trust. There is a cost associated with having workers who are not engaged and motivated. Frustrated workers do not perform at their best. They are not as productive. They are not as innovative.

It's also true that quality suffers when a workforce is not fully engaged. Whether it's automobile manufacturing or aviation safety, quality must be designed into the process; it can't be "inspected in" after the fact. There is a strong business case for quality. Quality not only improves the outcome, it also improves the bottom line. Doing it right the first time is always cheaper than getting it wrong. When workers are engaged, when they feel that they are doing their best work, and when they have a sense of accomplishing something that matters, they are more productive and more innovative.

Most people who reach their retirement years look back and acknowledge that the most memorable and enjoyable aspects of their experience were the bonds they formed with others, the relationships that added to the richness of their lives. It's also true, as the conversations in this book have demonstrated, that the quality of the personal connections we make have a huge impact on the quality and size of our achievements.

Robert Reich demonstrated this at the Labor Department in just one meeting that he said significantly changed the culture of that bureaucracy. An employee raised his hand and said time cards weren't necessary. Reich took a quick poll of his managers and they confirmed the employee's statement. No more time cards. Done. He listened. He demonstrated that he cared. A culture shifted.

Retired Coast Guard admiral Thad Allen climbed atop a desk and spoke a few inspired words that transformed a beaten-down and chaotic rescue and recovery force into an inspired and reenergized group—simply because he spoke from his heart to theirs. He knew how to reach them because he had empathy. They needed a clear vision of their mission, and they needed someone to stand up and take responsibility. His words were eloquent in their simplicity. His speech was a classic example of real leadership.

If you ever doubt the power of a caring leader, look at Thad Allen's record of achievements and effectiveness during some of the most unmanageable crises of our time: Hurricane Katrina, the earthquake in Haiti, the Deepwater Horizon oil spill. Allen was instrumental in bringing order out of chaos in all three of those disasters, proving that there is strength in a humanistic approach to leadership.

THE COMMON THREAD

I always knew it was important for leaders to care about those serving under and alongside them, but the big surprise to me is that caring deeply seems to be the common thread that runs through all the stories in this book. Passion is part of it but not the essence of it. Your desire and how hard you are willing to work and how much you like what you do are important. But *why* you do what you do is really the underlying motivation. *Why does this work matter?* Because we care about each other. Because having that connection makes us better than the competition.

We can have the same training and the same equipment as the competition, but if our workforce takes ownership of the goal and derives something personal and meaningful while achieving it, we will be better and more efficient and perform at a higher level consistently and more safely.

Tough-minded Michelle Rhee acknowledges that she is not the best at bonding with others, and she may pride herself on having no qualms about firing people, but there is no doubt that she cares deeply about all children and their right to an education. She also sets high expectations, and measures and incentivizes them by setting the bar high and holding everyone accountable.

The same can be said of William Bratton, who is driven by ambition but spoke with great passion about encouraging his police officers to feel a sense of pride when they donned their uniforms. He sees himself as an agent of change, but he also talked about building esprit de corps and a professional sense of pride and responsibility.

Bratton found his life's calling at an early age, and his passion for law enforcement and public service has driven him throughout his career. He is a change agent and he has made a significant difference. Bratton also set high expectations for himself and everyone else by demanding accountability. His efforts to treat his police officers as professionals with strong values and pride in their work reminded me of my own profession as an airline pilot, because commercial pilots hold themselves to high standards and we take our obligations and responsibilities seriously. We must never forget that our profession is important and why, because how well we do our jobs matters. I had always hoped that at the end of my life, I would have done enough small things that they would add up to having made a difference, and that is what most people do—not one great deed, but many small deeds over many years that in aggregate add up to a life well lived.

CORE QUALITIES OF LEADERSHIP

The organizations and teams that do the best are those that behave consistently according to their core values. I see that as a common thread through all the leaders in this book. They all have a *why* as well as a *what* and a *how,* and it matters to them not only *what* and *how* they do what they do but *why* they do it. I believe that is what sets successful organizations, groups, and teams apart. They may not be able to identify those values exactly, but they know them when they see them, and they know when they are not acting in accordance with them.

When leaders are asked what traits are most important for those at the helm, most emphasize integrity, humility, courage, and compassion over intelligence, knowledge, or management skills. Empathy encompasses humility, courage, integrity, and compassion. So if empathy is the essence of effective and positive leadership, what are the other qualities consistently demonstrated by the men and women in this book? You may have picked out your own already. I identified the following:

Well-defined core values
Willingness to lead by example
Courage to make decisions and act upon them

Continuous self-improvement and learning

Respect for others

Realistic optimism

Congruency of words and actions

Mentoring rather than disciplining

Maintaining a long-term perspective

Nurturing other leaders

Working for the greater good

Having clear priorities and focusing on what is important

Ability to learn from failures and move on

Trust in their own judgment but willingness to listen to others

Setting high expectations and striving to meet them

Creating an environment in which everyone can do their best work

Creating a culture of trust and cooperation

Creating a shared sense of responsibility for the outcome

Ensuring everyone in the organization experiences their own successes and knows that their work matters

The other quality that is shared by all the people in this book is realistic optimism. I've long held that one of the greatest qualities a leader can have is a positive outlook grounded in reality and rooted in competence. Realistic optimism is a sense of self-confidence based on experience, knowledge, and proven skills. It is not cockiness. It is the secure belief that there is always a way out, always an opportunity to move ahead, even in the worst crisis.

Tony La Russa offered his own recipe for creating realistic optimism in our discussion when he described his three-step program for training his players. I called it his PEP program because the elements are preparation, exposure, and process. You may recall that his program requires a disciplined approach and builds realistic optimism based on hard work and mastery.

Step one is *preparation,* because if you know you are prepared you'll be more confident and feel less fear of failure. Step two is *exposure,* because the more you practice and do a task the less intimidating it becomes. Step three is *process,* which is about focusing not on the outcome—like winning a game—but on the process of doing something the right way—like hitting a ball.

I have long known that realistic optimism is important to leadership, and I think it is one reason that the story of Flight 1549 has resonated with so many people. It inspired and gave them hope that such a dramatic and potentially disastrous situation could be managed with good results. I certainly didn't think about it at the time, but later, upon reflection, I realized I had used my realistic optimism effectively during the flight. So when Katie Couric asked me during a *60 Minutes* interview if I really believed I could land on the river, my answer to her was "I knew I could do it."

My response to her wasn't bravado based on hindsight; it was a reflection of the fact that I remained realistically optimistic based on my education, my training, and my experience. I knew which options were possible. And equally important, I knew which ones were not.

LEADERSHIP LESSONS APPLIED

Robert Reich said in our talk, "You know, I love teaching. When I teach my students—I teach seven hundred and fifty undergraduates this term—I constantly play the devil's advocate. I mean, I never, never teach them what I necessarily believe. I always teach against what *they* believe. Because what I really want them to do is learn to think harder. . . . I don't want them to accept anything that I have to say. I don't want them to in any way take my values. I want them to be shaken up intellectually. And so, at a place like Berkeley, I spend most of my time telling them what they don't want to hear and forcing them to confront some realities that they'd rather not think about."

Reich is eloquent on the subject of teaching new leaders. I share his goal of nurturing independent, critical thought. My hope in writing this book is that after you've read these interviews with diverse leaders you will ponder them, weigh what works and doesn't work for you, and then form your own vision of leadership and of what sort of legacy you want to leave as a leader.

In conclusion, I am giving you a daily guide to help you hone and build your own leadership skills. Use it in whatever way works best for you, whether on a daily, weekly, or monthly basis, adding your own elements or customizing mine to suit your situation.

ESSENTIAL QUESTIONS

1. Have you identified your guiding values so that you have a strong moral compass to help you select your goals and make decisions that are in alignment with your values?
2. Are you investing in yourself through lifelong learning, including learning from failure, so that you feel prepared for both the best and the worst?
3. Do you exhibit integrity, humility, courage, and compassion?
4. Do your actions match your words?
5. Is your goal the greater good, or only your own needs?
6. Are you striving for a level of mastery that will allow you to practice realistic optimism and long-term thinking even when dealing with short-term crises?
7. For each mission or task, do you set priorities, clearly articulate a direction to head in, explain to your team how to proceed, and clarify each member's role, thus creating a shared sense of responsibility for the outcome?

8. Do you have the ability to focus on what matters and filter out distractions?
9. Do you have the confidence and courage to seize the opportunity when it arises or to rise to the occasion when it comes?

My hope is that this quest to be a better leader or follower will be a lifelong journey of discovery. All that is required for you to begin is to find at least one thing on this list that you can use tomorrow to be a better leader or team member while you learn to use the rest.

ACKNOWLEDGMENTS

As with everything I do, this book would not have been possible without my family. To my daughters, Kate and Kelly: Thank you for all your patience and support over the past three years. You have both grown into poised and mature young women, and I am infinitely proud to be your father. To my wife, Lorrie: There are no words to convey my gratitude for everything you have done for our family over the years. You are truly my partner in everything I do, and your guidance and counsel about all aspects of this book have been invaluable. I also want to thank my parents, who were my first role models and who laid the foundation for my understanding of leadership. The lessons that I learned from their actions still influence me today. Thanks also to my sister, Mary, for her enduring friendship and love.

I want to acknowledge Wes Smith for his hard work and critical role in shaping this book. Although he joined our team after the project was already under way, his flexibility, efficiency, and professionalism were instrumental to its completion. Wes, I cannot thank you enough. Thank you also to Douglas Century, who joined me for nearly every interview and whose initial pages laid the groundwork for this book.

Thank you to each and every person who took the time to sit down with me and share your story. Throughout these interviews, I have been inspired, impressed, and humbled by your remarkable accomplishments. I appreciate the honesty and frankness with which you approached our conversations; I hope that I have done them justice, and that my readers will learn as much from them as I did. My deepest appreciation and thanks to Admiral Thad Allen, Jack Bogle, Bill Bratton, Lieutenant Colonel Tammy Duckworth, David Duffield, Jennifer Granholm, Sidney Gutierrez, Gene Kranz, Tony La Russa, Robert Reich, Michelle Rhee, Susan Sheridan, and Jim Sinegal. I also want to acknowledge and recognize all of the people who helped orchestrate these interviews. It was a formidable task, and I thank you for your efforts.

As with any project, there were a number of people working behind the scenes to help guide me through the process. Thanks to the team at HarperCollins, whose advice and direction cannot be overestimated. David Highfill, Seale Ballinger, Liate Stehlik, Lynn Grady, and Andy Dodds, your help was critical to completing this book. I also want to thank everyone at Dupree Miller & Associates for their hard work on my behalf. My literary agent, Jan Miller, and her associate Shannon Marven, as well as their support team, Nicki Miser and Ivonne Ortega, worked tirelessly to make sure my vision was realized. It was not always an easy road to walk, and I thank you for everything you have done for me.

Thanks also to the team at Barbary Coast Consulting. Libby Smiley, Allie Herson, and Alex Clemens have all worked tremendously hard on our family's behalf since the days immediately following the Hudson River landing. I especially want to recognize Libby's contributions to this book; her guidance and advice have helped shape its direction from its inception. Lastly, thank you to Janet Lawson, whose help transcribing my interviews and conversations was instrumental in creating the final product.

Jon Liebman from Brillstein Entertainment Partners and Cece York from True Public Relations have always provided me with excellent advice. They are joined in this regard by Barbara Daniel and her team at Washington Speakers Bureau. Their collective efforts have helped ensure that I continue to be able to advocate for causes I believe in and make a difference on the public stage.

While the events of January 15, 2009, provided me with a new lens for examining leadership, the concepts discussed in this book are ones that I have been thinking about my entire life. I owe a special thank-you to Professor Warren Bennis, whose extensive work in the field of leadership has greatly influenced me over the years. I also want to thank Dr. Charles Denham for his thoughts on the subject, particularly as they relate to the field of medicine and patient safety. His introduction to patient advocate Susan Sheridan became a critical part of this book. Thank you, Chuck.

My experiences over the past three years, including the conversations for this book, would not have been possible if the events of January 15, 2009, had not occurred. I thank the entire crew of Flight 1549—First Officer Jeffrey Skiles and Flight Attendants Donna Dent, Doreen Welsh, and Sheila Dail—for their brave actions that day and their professionalism in the years that have followed. In particular, Jeff, my admiration and gratitude know no bounds. You were a great colleague that day and have been an even better friend since then.

Finally, thank you to everyone who has reached out to me, my family, and my crew to express your support. Your letters, packages, phone calls, and e-mails have made us laugh, tugged at our heartstrings, and given us hope. I feel incredibly fortunate to be able to share this book with you and hope that you will find inspiration in its pages.